Turning back the clock

TURNING BACK
THE CLOCK

The life and times of a motor trader

Geoff Owen

THE FITZJAMES PRESS an imprint of Motor Racing Publications Ltd
Unit 6, The Pilton Estate, 46 Pitlake, Croydon CR0 3RY, England

First published 2000

British Library Cataloguing in Publication Data

Owen, Geoffrey
    Turning back the clock: the life and times of a motor trader
    1. Owen, Geoffrey 2. Automobile dealers – Great Britain –
      Biography
    I. Title
    380.1'45629'222'092

ISBN 0948358 06 8

Typesetting and origination by Jack Andrews Design,
Croydon, Surrey

Printed and bound in Great Britain by MPG Books Ltd,
Bodmin, Cornwall

CONTENTS

THE MARKET

New cars being offered on the UK home market in January 1962 (source *Autocar* magazine):

THE BRITISH MOTOR CORPORATION:
AUSTIN – AUSTIN-HEALEY – MG – MORRIS – RILEY – VANDEN PLAS – WOLSELEY

THE ROOTES GROUP:
HILLMAN – HUMBER – SINGER – SUNBEAM-TALBOT

PLUS:
AC – ALVIS – ASTON MARTIN-LAGONDA – ROLLS-ROYCE-BENTLEY – BRISTOL – DAIMLER – FAIRTHORPE – FORD – FRAZER NASH – GILBERN – JAGUAR – JENSEN – LOTUS – MORGAN – OGLE – RELIANT – ROVER – STANDARD-TRIUMPH – TURNER – TVR – VAUXHALL – WARWICK

IMPORTS (EUROPE):
ABARTH – ALFA ROMEO – AUTOBIANCHI – BMW – CITROEN – DAF – DKW – FIAT – FACEL VEGA – FERRARI – FORD GERMANY – ISETTA – GOGGOMOBIL – LANCIA – MASERATI – MERCEDES-BENZ – MOSKVITCH – NSU – NECKAR – PANHARD – PEUGEOT – PORSCHE – RENAULT – SAAB – SIMCA – SKODA – VOLKSWAGEN – VOLVO

IMPORTS (NORTH AMERICA):
BUICK – CADILLAC – CHEVROLET – DODGE – FORD – LINCOLN – MERCURY – OLDSMOBILE – PLYMOUTH – PONTIAC – RAMBLER – STUDEBAKER

Notes:
When records of registrations by manufacturer began in 1958, the British Motor Corporation's share of the home market was a massive 42.9%.
In 1961 I was forced into resignation as director of sales with a Morris, Wolseley and MG dealership by executives of BMC for no other reason than I had dared to criticize the poor quality and total lack of availability of these cars in selected colours or specified options *(see Chapter 6)*.
In July 1962, photographs and first details emerged of the first new car shortly to be imported from Japan – a Honda (source Classic Cars magazine).
By the end of 1962 the British Motor Corporation's share of the home market had fallen to 39.1% due to the continuing disenchantment of the buying public, from which position it went into freefall, Ford taking over market leadership and imports, particularly those from the Far East, becoming stronger by the month. BMC never fully recovered, despite its many reincarnations as BMH, BLMC, BL and Austin-Rover. Today, known as Rover, it is a German-owned company which in some months is able to claim less than 10% of the UK market. – QED

PROLOGUE

It has long been my practice when compiling advertisements to describe my wares in considerable detail. Experience has proved time and again that the buying public are hungry for information, and that accurate and well written copy can 'sell' the vehicle in question even before the person who responds to it has actually visited the showroom to inspect it. Furthermore, and perhaps surprisingly, I have found that well written adverts tend to be read by potential customers on a regular basis over quite a long period before a visit is made to the showrooms, be it to purchase a specific car, or even simply to "have a look round".

One afternoon I was busy typing copy for my weekly newspaper ad when I found myself searching for the appropriate words and phrases to describe a particularly low-mileage and very attractive Vauxhall Cavalier which had arrived that week. It was an SRi top-of-the-range model, and part of my presentation was to use the manufacturer's proper name for the exceptionally beautiful two-tone colour scheme: Helios Blue over Anthracite Metallic.

At this point my mind wandered. My word, the motor industry had travelled a very long road indeed since Henry Ford's famous dictum for the Model T: "the customer can have any colour he likes, so long as it's black". Also, what a contrast between this Vauxhall and those of the Fifties, when the current pride of the Vauxhall range, the PA Cresta, was available in a somewhat garish duotone pink, colloquially known throughout the used car trade as 'Nipple and Monkeys' (the first being self-evident, I leave it to the reader to fathom which part of the monkey's anatomy the second shade referred to!).

It then occurred to me that this train of thought was really what my proposed book was all about, namely the incredible postwar growth of an oft maligned sales, service and distribution industry, together with its many changes of fashion and style, and above all its folklore, with its wry and sometimes black humour; certainly the motor trade has never been short on humour. In my experience the Ford Motor Company have usually managed to provide the most notable speakers on motor trade matters. For instance, back in the early Sixties I attended a Ford sales management conference at a large hotel in Blackpool. It was the final afternoon session and we had all eaten well, if not wisely, at Ford's expense. Heads, particularly at the back of the auditorium, were beginning to nod when Ken Scarle, at that time the sales director of Ford (UK), mounted the rostrum to speak.

Before beginning the afternoon's business he announced: "I feel that congratulations should be expressed to your colleague here today who this very morning has received confirmation that his win on last week's football pool runs to six figures." After a suitable pause, during which the atmosphere became electric and everyone suddenly became wide awake, Ken produced a piece of paper and continued: "He has sent the following telegram to his managing director: 'STICK THE JOB UP YOUR ARSE – RUDE LETTER FOLLOWS'."

What follows is a true story, for that is the only story worth telling. As such it represents the writer's personal experiences over a period of 55 years. My hope is that the reader will enjoy the content as much as I have enjoyed putting it all together.

Geoff Owen

To my late father, Stanley Nelson Owen
and to Christine, my wife

THE BACKGROUND

The changing face of the motor trade and its relations with the buying public over my half-century of involvement in it.

This is a fast-moving, high-tech world. New products such as home videos, computers and compact discs appear on the market, achieve dizzy marketing heights, and all but burn themselves out within a period of perhaps five to 10 years. It was not always so. The bicycle, the camera and the motor car, to name but three, took somewhat longer to achieve their present high-tech, mass-market status, probably for no other reason than that they were conceived in a less affluent age. My personal knowledge of bikes and cameras is limited to occasional use, my knowledge of the motor industry pre-Second World War is equally limited. Historically, however, the motor trade can be assumed to have started with the appearance of the first motor car around 1885, and the very first bolt-on motor accessory was probably the red flag. Growth was painfully slow by today's standards and general progress was further limited due to enforced closure for the duration of the two world wars. Nonetheless, the manufacturing side of the industry was given something of a boost in both instances.

During those initial 60 years until 1945, when I became directly involved, some kind of a worldwide manufacturing and distribution organization had been established, although this was but a pale shadow of the huge international organizations which exist today. The small percentage of relatively cheap family saloons being sold to the lower middle classes prior to the outbreak of war in 1939 were produced almost entirely by Austin, Morris and Ford, each of them striving to offer a four-seater at or very close to £100. Of particular significance, in the light of subsequent events, is that no cars whatsoever were being imported from the Far East, and precious few from elsewhere.

A further 25 years were to pass before mass ownership of motor transport became a reality, and the resultant phenomenal growth of the motor industry during the second half of this quarter-century was to present severe problems to an industry totally unprepared for such a rate of expansion. A significant consequence of this upheaval was that importers, particularly of products from the Far East, were able to encroach with ease on what by then had become a highly vulnerable home market.

In 1980, to my great delight, I was invited to join the Rotary Club of Sandy, where my wife and I had by then established our own business. In no time at all I was referred to good naturedly as 'the Arthur Daley of Sandy' (the 'image', but this I could live with in such august company). Part of the Rotary commitment is that you are expected to talk for 15 minutes on your commercial life and history, an initiation process which throughout Rotary is known – and often dreaded – as the 'Job Talk'. In my case I felt that this would give me an opportunity to clear the air a little, and consequently I prepared my talk with a great deal of care.

When I presented it to my wife for an opinion, she read it twice, then handed it back and said: "You ought to write a book". I took this as a sign of approval, and when in due course the talk was delivered, it was sufficiently well received to convince me that I really did have an interesting story to tell, and yes, I would try to put it into a book. The same job talk has since been presented to my present Rotary Club, with similar results, and at another, by invitation, following a radio interview on the *John Dunn Show*. Mind you, writing a short talk is one thing; assembling the manuscript for a full-length book, as I have discovered, is something else altogether.

When I entered the profession straight out of school in 1945 I was taking part in the rejuvenation of the same prewar cottage industry which had served the middle, professional and upper classes then representing the fortunate few able to own and run their personal transport. At the time my family lived in a North London avenue just below the Alexandra Palace, a road where, until I was called for National Service in 1948, you could find just one parked car, and that one was being used for private hire. Today I would be hard put to find room to park any car within sight of my old front door, a situation which will be all too familiar to those of you with long memories. As late as 1959, when I lived in Northampton, we had friends who lived on a large council estate in the village of Bugbrooke, and there were no more than three or four cars on the whole estate. These simple facts will at least convey some idea of the tremendous growth in the use of the car as personal transport over the past four decades.

The motor trade had all but ceased to function at the start of the war. Many of the larger garages were hastily converted to war work, often being used to repair military transport and even parts of aircraft. A great many motor trade personnel were dispersed, some, inevitably, never to return. Even before the war ended the trade had started to prepare itself for an uncertain future, hamstrung by austerity and a depressing shortage of everything from petrol and spare parts to complete vehicles. It was at this precise moment, in January 1945, four months prior to VE Day (celebrating Victory in Europe) that I came on the scene. I would be just 15 years old the following April, was disliking school intensely and looking forward to earning my living and collecting my first week's wages.

A few new cars had started to come off the assembly lines by 1946, although for the most part they were of prewar design, and after

10

a six-year trading gap there were precious few secondhand cars available for sale. The vast majority of war production vehicles were totally unsuited to civilian use, so a great many prewar vehicles which had been commandeered and converted into auxiliary fire engines or ambulances, together with an odd selection of former military pick-up trucks and staff cars, were purchased at government auctions by enterprising dealers and converted back to private use as timber-bodied 'luxury' estate cars!

During the following 10 years, while new-car production increased to at least a reasonable level (although most of the output had to be exported in order to earn desperately needed foreign currency), there was a gradual build-up in the availability of secondhand cars. Tragically, all too many of them came from families who were left to dispose of vehicles belonging to loved ones who would never sit behind the wheel again.

Within these limitations, sales departments in the big dealerships managed to keep the wolf from the door, and used-car dealers began to emerge from enforced retirement. Service departments, meanwhile, were kept busy reconditioning old cars and keeping them on the road, while parts managers cajoled manufacturers for much needed spare parts, and were reduced to searching scrapyards for vital parts which were no longer available from their original source. Against this background, the motor trade worked hard, if not particularly profitably, recruiting and where necessary replacing key staff, in an effort to restore its prewar cottage industry professionalism.

During the decade to 1955 not a great deal had changed from prewar days in the manner in which the motor trade conducted its day-to-day affairs. The service manager was a good friend to his regular clients, rather in the manner of the family practitioner; you could discuss your car's ailments at length with him and be confident that it was in safe hands while in for service or repair. The parts manager was invariably polite and knowledgeable, and from memory could quote the part number of virtually any item in the vast stock at the drop of a hat. But sales managers could do no more than compile waiting lists of their new car customers and arrange the occasional delivery to the lucky few as and when their car became available. Of course, not everyone engaged in the motor trade was a paragon of rectitude, hence the widely held view that anybody who was engaged in the sale of used cars was a dodgy descendant of a horse trader!

By the middle of 1953 there were clear indications that British business generally was emerging from those austere early postwar years and returning to normality, and soon there were to be some positive changes in the motor business. Cars that had been widely quoted as "four to five years delivery" suddenly became available as supplies of raw materials improved and production increased. Dealers had discovered that their valued clients had been placing orders for new cars all over the place on the off-chance of obtaining what hitherto had been identified as not just transport, but a valuable investment. Once the duplication of orders had been revealed, long waiting lists were to vanish almost overnight. When the dust had settled, however, and the backlog had been sorted out there was still just sufficient demand to keep ahead of supply. It was judged to be reasonably certain that this happy situation would continue for some time. In the event it was to continue beyond anyone's wildest dreams, almost without a break, for the next 15 years!

Inevitably, businessmen began to move in with an eye to the fast buck. There were the inevitable mergers and absorption of many of the smaller companies and groups. New names appeared on the scene and, with abundant new venture capital available, many of the old-established distributors and main dealers were to abandon their original town premises and move out to purpose-built showrooms and service areas on the outskirts of towns, often being attached to or close by new shopping complexes. A rash of brand new dealerships appeared, firstly for British cars, but later spearheading the rapid build-up of foreign competition This phenomenal growth over a relatively short span of time was to be the cause of major problems, the long-term effects of which were to be horrendous, including the almost total demise of the long-established wholly British-owned motor manufacturing industry.

In the beginning it had seemed that no matter how many cars were produced in Britain, and regardless of how many imported cars became available, there was an all but insatiable market just for the taking. Unfortunately for some, this happy state of affairs proved to be not quite true. The mighty British Motor Corporation, which for years had become accustomed to its clients forming an orderly queue and waiting patiently for the model of their choice until such time as BMC (and the dealer) were able to provide it, had its corporate head in the clouds as usual. It totally failed to appreciate, until it was far too late, that the queues were rapidly diminishing as customers discovered the attractive alternatives that were rapidly becoming available from Europe and, more significantly, the Far East.

By the end of the 1950s it was possible to purchase most makes and models of family car off the shelf if you were prepared to accept the model and colour available in the showroom or in the immediate pipeline. If you were to insist on a particular colour scheme, or a listed option such as a sunroof, for instance, you might have to wait for perhaps a month or two. This, of course, was providing the new car of your choice didn't carry an Austin, Morris, Wolseley, Riley or MG badge – the five British Motor Corporation marques. In that case, should you have the brass nerve to insist on a particular colour, or maybe the overdrive, duotone paint or a sunroof – all listed options on most cars in the range at the time – then you placed your order and you simply waited . . . and waited . . . and waited!

In 1958, the British Motor Corporation, then comprising only the five marques listed above, boasted a nett slice of *43 per cent* of the total home market. By January 1962 the share had dropped to 39 per cent as uncertain delivery times, third-rate quality and dated designs all began to have their effect on the buying public. The long slide had begun. As will be seen later, the blame was not entirely due to the trades unions, as was the popular theory at the time; management, at all levels, had a very great deal to answer for. The preface to this book carries a large list of alternative marques available on the British home market in January 1962, when BMC's market share was already in decline, but by the end of the decade an equivalent list would also have included many hitherto unknown marques and models from the Far East. By this time, even the tradition-bound British professional classes, many of whom were former service officers who a few years earlier would not have countenanced buying anything other than an 'Awstin' or a Morris, were happily accepting delivery of Citroens, Renaults, Volkswagens and – incredibly – even Datsuns and Toyotas! Yet while business overall was brisk, the British Motor Corporation, once so dominant a player on the home market, was already paying a heavy price for its sheer bloody-minded complacency.

The retail motor industry by now was growing fast, but the new investment was to be followed by rationalization. The major car manufacturers, notably Ford and BMC, had been aware for some time that they had too many retail outlets for all to be economically viable. Ford had tended to adopt a predominantly main-dealer network from the start, placing smaller retail outlets only in strategic areas where huge capital investment was unjustified. BMC, however, with a huge proliferation of large, medium and small dealers throughout the country, opted for a wholesale clearout. This resulted in many medium and in some cases large dealers of good repute losing their franchise almost overnight. They were promptly signed up by the Japanese or other foreign car manufacturers.

All, ironically, were to find this enforced change of direction a blessing: the shiny new vehicles they were now offering to their valued clients were not only better equipped and finished than the tired old BMC badge-engineered models, they were available! And delivery forecasts were to prove reliable on the special-equipment models. Sadly, the British Motor Corporation continued its decline while the car market as a whole continued its seemingly uninterrupted growth.

But growth in any industry is only fine so long as the industry is able to keep pace with it, particularly in regard to management, staff levels and matters of training. Hitherto all training in the industry had been like mine – 'on the job' and a process of gradually acquired experience and relatively slow promotion. As existing companies expanded and new ones were formed, there simply were not enough fully or even partly trained personnel available for the multitude of new situations created. Worse, the proprietors and managing directors of these new concerns were, for the most part, entrepreneurs pure and simple, who viewed the motor trade as a licence to print money. Most had little experience of what the motor trade was all about, and in consequence they were in no position to assimilate such staff as they took over or were able to recruit, let alone provide adequate training.

At this point, perhaps understandably in retrospect, it all started to go wrong. As the trade sought in vain to fill the situations being created, standards dropped alarmingly throughout the industry. Half-decent young car salesmen found themselves almost overnight in management situations for which they had neither sufficient training nor preparation, and without proper direction from the top. Actually selling the new cars presented few problems, so former television, carpet, fancy goods – you name it – salesmen found themselves welcomed with open arms at main dealerships where they were given a salary-plus-commission package, a brand new demonstration car, the current month's copy of *Glass's Guide*, and virtually left to get on with it. Consequently, through sheer ignorance, a great many of the used cars which were taken in part-exchange were by no means as good as they should have been relative to the price allowed for them. These would later be resold to a public who, at that time, were often totally uneducated in the workings of motor cars, and not surprisingly many of these cars were to cause problems for their eventual purchasers. With the problems came bad public relations.

To make matters worse, many of these cars were of prewar design and had no comparison whatever with the high-tech products produced over the past 20 years or so. Most of the mass-produced family car engines were in need of regular decarbonizing at around 15,000 miles, failing which they lost performance. By 30-40,000 miles they would use steadily increasing amounts of oil and the bearings would rattle. Any attempt to cure oil consumption on the cheap by fitting 'oil control rings' would provide an increase in compression which would promptly knock out the bearings. Clutches were known to fail at regular intervals on certain models, and on others, through a fault in the original design, the replacement of some relatively inexpensive part would often require the complete removal of an engine or other major components, which would be time-consuming and therefore expensive. One very experienced motor dealer I knew would not make an offer on any car until he had road-tested it for rear axle failure; an expensive fault at the time, but virtually unheard of today. Compare that, if you will, with your modern car with its long service intervals; even the cheapest family saloons can be expected to exceed 100,000 miles with nothing more traumatic than a couple of new clutches and a few sets of brakes.

With such ready-made built-in problems, plus the fact that many cars at the time were of dubious history and uncertain mileage, professional car dealers had been obliged to develop considerable expertise and a sixth sense in regard to used cars, a skill acquired by a combination of past experience and a methodical examination of the goods on offer prior to purchase. These professionals, of course, were the existing main and retail dealers referred to earlier, who had been established for years and had the advantage of properly trained staff.

Few of these basic skills being available to many a young and inexperienced sales manager, and even less to his team of carpet and fancy goods salesmen, things began to deteriorate markedly as time passed and growth continued. The awful moment of truth would usually arrive when dealer principals found the need to quickly reduce a bank overdraft to finance continued new stock arriving from the factory. Trade cash buyers would be called in and it would soon become apparent that offers for individual used cars were appreciably less than the prices allowed by over-eager commission-hungry sales staff, with the result that the perceived retained profits had in fact become unacceptable losses at a stroke. Often there was no choice but to bite the bullet on some of the worst examples, and in an effort to minimize losses to press on and sell the remainder at reduced prices to a public who, at the time, could be relied upon to be considerably less discriminating than the trade buyer, at least until after purchase. Then, inevitably, the faults would come to light, and with the faults came the problems, and with the problems came the bad relationships.

Even though the vast majority of dealers would endeavour to rectify the rogue cars under generous warranty terms, the public relations damage was already done. It is a fact of life that if a car is to fail at all, it will chose to do so at the most inconvenient time. Furthermore, when used cars of this period broke down so soon after purchase, they invariably continued to do so on a fairly regular basis. Small wonder, then, that hand in hand with growth, the motor trade in general was to develop a bad reputation, with which it was to be tarnished for a very long time.

Fortunately, these days the public are better educated, as indeed are sales staffs, and because of the inbuilt reliability of modern vehicles, high-quality used cars massively outnumber those of poor quality which are on sale by *bona fide* car dealers at any given time. One worthwhile offshoot of this modern reliability is that the public now has the opportunity of negotiating long-term warranties on almost any used car, in almost any price range, regardless of mileage, and in consequence public relations have improved considerably.

This, then, is the broad picture of events and changes over more than half a century of selling cars. What follows is the 'nitty gritty' as viewed by one who considers himself fortunate to have been involved throughout. It is the prerogative of experience (age) to pontificate that 'the old days were the best', or that 'they don't make them like that any more'. In many cases it is perhaps a jolly good job that they don't! Nevertheless, there were some delightful cars around in the Forties, Fifties and Sixties, as the ever-escalating interest in what are now referred to as classic cars now shows. I count it an undeniable privilege that I am able to say that I sold them – and I drove them – on roads that were picturesque, generally free of heavy traffic and a sheer delight to drive on. In those days, when we went for a drive, we went for just that – the simple pleasure of driving.

The motor trade and motor cars have been my life. As I have already indicated, the love affair began for me in January 1945, during the last months of the war . . .

CHAPTER ONE

IT ALL BEGAN IN 1945

Suffice to say that I did not like school. My father was in the Army for the 'duration', and during a short leave he decided that with what little schooling I was getting due to the constant disruption caused by air raids, I might just as well get myself some sort of a job. This suited me fine. The air raid alerts in 1944 were instigated by the V1 flying bombs, the 'doodle-bugs' which would arrive several times a day and send everyone in their path scurrying towards whatever shelter they could find.

The instructions from Dr Draper, the forbidding headmaster of Tollington School for Boys in North London, were specific: "If the warning sounds on the way to or from school, boys are to proceed at once to the nearest air raid shelter." At lunch break my immediate friends and I would delay returning to school until the last possible moment, anxiously awaiting the first wail of the siren, which usually went off around midday. Sometimes it would start just as we were entering the school building, in which case we would about-turn and hare off across the playing fields at high speed, hoping that in the general confusion we had not been noticed. Our aim was to get to the Muswell Hill *Odeon*, where there was a large deep shelter below the car park. However, that particular haven was not our true destination for we had long since discovered that, armed with a Boy Scout knife, free entry could be obtained into the cinema via the ladies' toilet at the rear exit. This way I clearly remember seeing Bernard Miles in *Tawny Pipit* (latterly shown several times on TV) some three or four times in one week.

By this time it was becoming quite clear that the war would not last for much longer. No doubt the 'old man' thought it would be a good idea to get me settled into something or other before it was all over, otherwise he might well end up having to give me a job in his company. I had no idea what I wanted to do, or how I hoped to finish up, so it was with something of an open mind that I visited the Youth Employment Office in the courtyard of the Hornsey Town Hall, as a result of which I was dispatched to an interview for a situation as trainee to a motor car company in Regent Street, London W1. The interview was entirely unsolicited on my part, for I had no special interest in cars other than those on the cigarette cards which I had collected.

However, on countless occasions I had been taken by my mother on shopping expeditions to the West End, during which we would usually visit my father at his office in Wigmore Street. The bus we took was the very same that was now transporting me, in my best suit, to meet my future employer, its route following the length of Great Portland Street, which then was largely boarded up through war damage. Before the war this had been the very centre of the London used car trade, and I could still recall very clearly sitting in my seat on the top deck and gazing down on all the expensive and powerful machinery that had been on display, with immaculate salesmen leaning nonchalantly on the gleaming Lagondas and Speed Six Bentleys. There was no doubt that this kind of life could hold a certain appeal to an impressionable young man!

The reality, of course, was somewhat different, as I was soon to discover. I must have given the right impression, for after being interviewed kindly enough by a Mr L G Shiel, an elderly and somewhat forbidding gentleman who had sold Model T Fords to the War Office during the First World War, I was taken on, though not as a showroom decoration in a smart suit. Instead I was told to report to the parts department in Chenies Street, off the Tottenham Court Road, at 8.30am – "Sharp, mind you" – on Monday next. At least I had a job.

There must be few people who are unable to recall clearly their first day at school or at work. Messrs Arthur E Gould Ltd, Ford main dealer, had substantial premises on both sides of Chenies Street. On one side in a small crescent stood Minerva House. This huge property, which backed onto Alfred Mews and Heals Ltd, the well-known furnishers, contained a commercial vehicle showroom at the front, with the company's general offices above on the first floor, which was reached by an elegant central staircase. At the rear was a large private car service area, with a body shop and central canteen above at first-floor level. The whole of the top floor was devoted to a paint spray shop, an engine shop and a tool room, all being accessible by a huge car lift and a rear staircase.

My immediate domain was opposite, on the corner of Chenies Street and Alfred Place, where there was another huge building, occupied mainly by the Kolynos toothpaste company, but with the whole of the ground floor area and basement used by Arthur Gould Ltd as a commercial vehicle workshop and parts department, respectively. The main building was set back from the pavement, forming a kind of moat surrounded by iron railings into which had been inserted a gate at the top of a small flight of stairs, with a notice and an arrow pointing down to: PARTS COUNTER – TRADE AND RETAIL.

On descending the staircase I had a good view of my future workplace through the front windows. Across the whole of the front area was a counter with a staff access door on the left and an office on the right. Behind the counter area were four or five corridors fashioned from rows of bins, each entrance neatly formed by panelled arches carrying displays of accessories. I took a deep breath, opened the main door and went inside. Behind the counter stood a tall lean gentleman with a neat moustache, wearing a smart blue overall coat adorned with the distinctive 'FORD' badge. I introduced myself. It seemed that I was expected, the staff door was opened and I found myself shaking hands with Stan Fowler, assistant parts manager. He was a kindly, most friendly person. In no time I was put at ease and allocated a clean towel, a tin of gritty but effective hand cleanser and, most important of all, as I was to discover throughout my shop floor working life, a tea mug!

Having dealt with the essentials I was taken to the far end office to be formally introduced to Mr 'Kim' Kimbell, who reigned supreme as the parts manager. Kim was a dynamic young man with a prodigious memory, able without effort to recite verbatim part numbers and bin locations of virtually any of the thousands of current Ford items held in stock. I was told, not unkindly, that my duties consisted of sweeping up, keeping the place tidy and doing what I was told. With that the interview terminated and I was taken on a short tour by Mr Fowler, during which I met the remainder of the staff.

The stores consisted of a large rectangle. At the front the trade and retail counter was run by Stan with a lady assistant. At the rear a smaller counter to the basement area served both the car and commercial workshops. On wet days the car mechanics from the rear of Minerva House had a long haul for replacement parts. This area was run by Paul, an incredibly handsome young man with dark wavy hair and a fine aquiline Roman nose, who also had a lady assistant. Outside, in part of the huge basement area, were wire cages which contained items far too large to be binned such as engines, gearboxes and body panels. This, then, was the place where I would begin a learning curve and start a career for life, although at that moment I am sure I didn't see the situation in those terms. The trainee sales bit, together with the comfort and luxury of the showroom, seemed a million miles away, and I suppose to an extent I had the feeling that I had been conned. One thing, though, it was infinitely better than school. Also, I had acquired a liking for tea, and at the end of the week I would be paid!

My first lesson in business life was that extraordinarily handsome young men with film star profiles were not necessarily all that they seemed to be. Paul was as bent as nine-bob note, with a penchant, initially, for trying to touch me up during the lunch hour. I simply avoided him and took to helping out at the front counter, which didn't close for lunch, or borrowing Kim's office while he was out and swatting up on the parts books. These, with their complicated drawings, were to give me my first insight into the workings of motor cars and the wonders of mechanical engineering. I began to seek out these strange items such as pistons, rings and conrods in the various bins, and after a while, when things got busy, I was to assist, under supervision, at the front counter; I would not dare to try my luck at the back, where the mechanics to a man were scornful of snotty-nosed 15-year-old trainees. In this manner, albeit unwittingly, I was doing exactly what I was supposed to be doing: learning and gaining experience. I bought a book called *The Modern Diesel* , which turned out to be a fortunate purchase for it was one of those rare books that explain things in basic and simple terms. From this I was to learn how an engine worked, and the elementary principle of the Otto cycle representing the four workings cycles of a four-stroke engine – induction, compression, ignition, exhaust. Another source of my early learnings were the prewar Ford car handbooks that Stan allowed me to borrow so that I might read them on the way home on the Underground and in my spare time. It was from these that I was to acquire a working knowledge of the mysteries of the clutch and the gearbox.

At this point some explanation is due, for it occurs to me that today a great many people are unlikely to appreciate that in those days only apprentice motor mechanics, or young men directly involved with machinery, were likely to acquire this kind of knowledge which, of course, is so commonplace today. Whereas your typical 18-year-old now drives his, or her, personal motor and is probably scornful of any of their peers unable to comprehend the workings of a 16-valve, twin-overhead-cam, turbocharged common or garden wonder of today's motoring scene, in the Forties and Fifties almost all teenagers, together with the greater part of the adult population, were unable even to drive a car. The majority of the male population who held a driving licence at that time had passed their test in the forces during the war, or later during their National Service, as indeed I did. Similarly, such of the fair sex who held a driving licence had learned in the women's services or civil defence. In 1951, when I went to an annual camp with the Middlesex Regiment as a 21-year-old territorial soldier, there was a call for someone at Shorncliffe Barracks to drive the 3-tonner. I got the job as I was the only person available from the 50 or so young men attending who had a driving licence!

To return to my mis-spent youth, I would not wish to convey the impression that I was studious and hard-working. I had simply found an interest, which was later to serve me well. But in the meantime, given the opportunity, I could skive with the best of them. After a while, when Paul had come to realize that I was not 'available', we became reasonably good friends. I saw very little of Mr Shiel and assumed that I had been forgotten, but then on one memorable day Paul and I came close to finishing the old boy off while playing silly sods with a parts trolley. At the far end of the basement was a ramp up to road level in Alfred Place, where parts were delivered in bulk by trucks from Ford's Dagenham works. The considerable space available between the foot of this ramp and our stores area had been utilized for the storage of hundreds of two-tier metal bunks removed from London air raid shelters. How we came to have them I never found out, but they were stored one on top of another, leaving passages for access to lift, stairs and the goods ramp at the far end. Paul and I would often have to return empty cases to the ramp, or collect fresh boxes on a trolley which had the front wheels hinged to the towing bar for ease of manoeuvrability. Inevitably, given an empty trolley, we would take it in turns to push or steer up and down the passageways between the bunks at high speed. With practice we had both become adept at cornering at maximum possible speed, just clipping the edge of the piles of metal bunks at each corner.

On this fateful day I was driving and Paul was pushing, and on rounding a particularly nasty double corner, for which I had developed a perfect technique, we came face to face with the great man quietly making his way to the lift. There was no time to think, and there were just two options: to go slap into the old boy, which at his time of life would probably have finished him off, or try and squeeze into one of the very narrow gaps between two rows of bunks. There was really no choice at all, and I judged it perfectly, but there was simply insufficient room. With an almighty crash the trolley caught the bunks on either side, toppling those on top, which effectively closed the gap behind me. Paul had already taken off just before impact, recognizing that discretion was the better part of getting the bullet, so I was on my own. Without so much as a pause for breath I scrambled across rows of bunks until I emerged at the far side, where I legged it up the staircase to the workshops above and the relative safety of the mechanics' lavatory. I stayed for some time.

In overalls and in the gloom of the basement I hoped we would look much the same as any of the many other staff employed in the building, and to my considerable relief nothing more was heard of the matter apart from written instructions on the staff noticeboard that in future anyone found riding the trolleys in the basement would be fired on the spot. Soon after this little episode I was transferred to Minerva House to work in the engine shop on the top floor. This was another world for me for it brought the parts book drawings to life and I was able to see, and to assist, while all of the bits were stripped down and eventually rebuilt during the process of reconditioning. Due to the insatiable demands of war, new engines were unobtainable, so old units when worn out had to be reconditioned with the result that the engine shop had become a very busy part of the Gould organization and was destined to be even busier in the years immediately after the war

Because of the acute shortage of manpower most of the stripping and assembly work was completed by a team of women, this long before women's lib! To work as a 15-year-old in that company was an education in itself. Being 'staff', which afforded a certain dignity, I was spared the initiation procedure carried out on the young apprentices, where trousers were pulled off in the lift by a bunch of sex-starved females and liberal portions of jam from the canteen spread wholesale over private parts. As far as I was aware, nobody ever complained.

The engines being rebuilt at the time were from the Ford Eight and Ten, and the legendary Ford V8 in both 22 and 30-horsepower guise, all with the simple side-valve mechanism. They would arrive at the shop less carburettor, fuel pump and distributor, ready to be stripped to the bare block. Cylinder heads would be removed for refacing in the machine shop, together with the crankshaft and connecting-rods. Main, big-end and small-end bearings might be salvaged for refacing, but pistons were scrapped for, as the blocks were rebored new, oversized pistons were to be fitted. All valves and valve gear were sent to the machine shop for refacing or scrapping if beyond repair. Should an engine get any of the original parts back it would be by pure chance. Once parts were refurbished they were boxed in sets, ready for delivery to the newly bored and grey-painted engine block now ready for rebuild on a special stand, so constructed that the engine could be turned or up-ended for ease of handling.

My initial tasks were the usual menial ones of sweeping the floor, fetching and carrying and assisting in the stripping operation, which got me involved in the handling and care of tools. As I was genuinely interested I enjoyed the work and the days passed quickly enough, though like countless innocent youngsters in any machine tool environment I was to be made the butt of the usual practical jokes. I can well remember being sent to the stores for a bottle of 'blue sparks' or a 'left-handed spanner', together with some unmentionable items of equipment.

The top man in that machine shop was George, the foreman. He was a rough, tough, giant of a man, of a very few words. He was also a strict disciplinarian who could destroy you with one look if the occasion arose. George was nonetheless a very competent engineer from whom a keen young man could learn a very great deal. One afternoon I had been assisting him as he carefully rebuilt a Ford V8 engine. He must have been in a good mood that day, not that he said much, but there may have been the merest suspicion of a twinkle in his eye as he meticulously set up and tightened the large crankshaft at the base of the block of cylinders The next task, I knew, would be to clamp up each set of piston rings and, one by one, ease the eight pistons, together with their connecting-rods, into the top end of each of the eight cylinders. The rods could then be married to the crankshaft. For a while all went well while I went on with my assigned tasks, at the same time watching George tighten up the crankshaft bolts in a predetermined order. I must have lost my concentration, for suddenly George barked an order: "Get to the stores, lad, and fetch the rubber mallet." By this time, of course, I had heard it all before. Failing to comprehend that whatever else George most certainly was not a man with a keen sense of humour, I made what I thought to be an appropriate remark! The silence was deafening. For a very long moment he just stood looking at me, cigar jutting from his mouth, his face going from red to purple, then back to red again. George pointed an outraged finger in the direction of the stores. "Bloody mallet, boy, and no bloody back answers, either!" I had learned the hard way that a rubber mallet was used to tap in tight pistons, and as such was a fact of engine shop life. Later that day George handed me a flat iron block, several sheets of coarse emery cloth and a cylinder block awaiting machining. I was told to "rub those bloody pits out, boy" and then left for two whole days. It was a deserved and salutary punishment which I never forgot. Come to that I never forgot old George, either. He was a good old boy for all his bark. He taught me to respect authority, to revere machinery – and to care for tools.

I saw nothing of Mr Shiel during the time I was in the engine shop. Again I assumed that I had been forgotten. VE day came, signalling the end of the war in Europe, and the country went mad. During the early part of the celebrations I managed to break my leg, and later, on a cot in the Royal Northern Hospital, I heard Winston Churchill on the radio saying that this was my day! By the time I got back to work the atom bomb had arrived, Japan had given up and world peace had returned. So indeed had my father, along with thousands of others, and slowly life started to return to some semblance of normality. I was enjoying my work, the ladies were a good laugh, and George, realizing no doubt that I was to be of no long-term use to him, allowed me to wander more or less as I pleased, finding fresh interests in the body and paint shops on the same floor. All good things come to an end, however.

One pay day George, with no sign of regret, told me that on the following Monday I was to report to Meard Street. All I knew of Meard Street was that it contained a garage which was part of the Gould organization. I had learned this from Maurice, who was a mechanic there and a regular visitor to us during tea breaks, being particularly friendly with one of the young ladies in the engine shop. With his help I tracked down Meard Street on the A to Z street atlas as a minor thoroughfare running from Dean Street to Wardour Street, in the heart of Soho. Not yet having enjoyed my mis-spent youth, this did not strike me at the time as being particularly significant.

On arrival that Monday morning I found that it was not so much a street as an alleyway. The only negotiable part for a motor vehicle led halfway down and straight into our garage. Next door was a seedy looking drinking club, complete with touts always on hand to attract the American servicemen who were still very much in evidence in Central London. On the corner of Dean Street was the somewhat more reputable *Gargoyle Club*, probably being used during this very time by one of its more notorious members, the infamous Guy Burgess. On entering my new place of work I found that the garage was on two floors – one at street level and a basement reached by an antiquated lift. The main function of the premises seemed to be overnight and daytime parking. There were a number of large and small vans which were left overnight and at weekends on both floors, together with some cars of regulars who arrived early each day. In the basement were several vehicles belonging to long-term parkers, whose owners were rarely to be seen. The place was managed by a decrepit and wheezy old character by the name of Mr Packman, who took no interest in me whatsoever and was therefore no problem. The only other inhabitants were a cheerful elderly cockney named Tom, who made the tea and kept the place tidy, a somewhat taciturn foreman, also called Tom, and the spry young mechanic Maurice, whom I later found was living with the lady from Minerva House, keeping her company while her husband was serving with the Royal Navy. Old Tom the cleaner was a great scrounger of fags. As he made the frequent cups of tea you could hardly refuse when, on taking out a packet, he would appear from nowhere like some pantomime genie with a "How's the old fag trade, then?".

Nobody took a great deal of interest in what I did during the day. Foreman Tom would give me a car to polish from time to time, and it was my job to operate the lift as cars and vans came and went, apart from which I didn't seem to have anything specific to do. With hindsight, foreman Tom and Packman must have been on a good personal fiddle at the time. Most of the daytime clients paid cash, many on a casual basis, nobody from head office ever came to Meard Street apart from the odd salesman wanting his car tuned or serviced, and those two jokers were certainly never short of money! Nor for that matter was I. I came to know many of the regular clients, and in my spare time, of which I had a great deal, I would supplement my income by washing or polishing a few cars. One particular client was the owner of a well-known Chinese restaurant in Wardour Street. He also owned a racehorse called Ki Ming, which was to run in one of the big races, and he tipped me off to put my shirt on it. I did, to the tune of my whole week's wages, which I had only received that morning. Of course, once done – in the heat of the moment – it was regretted, and for the rest of the day I sweated and worried, wondering what on earth I was going to tell my father if I were to arrive home broke.

That afternoon I had been sent out on some errand, and on my return I didn't risk asking Tom or Maurice, both of whom were betting men, for the result of the big race. Neither of them knew that I had had a bet on, for I had not dared to tell a soul. There was nothing for it but to await the arrival of the *London Evening Standard*. We had just settled down for the inevitable cup of tea when old Mr Packman wheezed his way over. "Guess what? Old chop suey has gone and won the big race, I'll have to put his rent up". I went to the lavatory; that horse had been a rank outsider and temporarily I was rich beyond my wildest dreams. I bought my mother a small gift and quietly blew the rest on God knows what. But I never bet again apart from a modest few quid on Ascot Gold Cup day, just once a year in later life, and I never, ever, won again.

With all the inactivity I had begun to wonder as to the reason for this posting to the Soho backwater, although interesting it most certainly was. The club next door was a constant source of amusement as Yanks seeking a good time were either enticed in, or frequently thrown out, having presumably complained about the prices. I was on speaking terms with most of the ladies who appeared from around 11 o'clock each morning from the numerous flats above the shops on each side of Meard Street, not a few of whom indicated that they were quite willing to provide a service during a slack period to an impressionable youth on a grace and favour basis. I was later told by a girlfriend, with whom I had confided in a weak moment, that I must have appealed to a mothering instinct! I have never quite been sure what was implied by that remark.

Anyway, I didn't have long to wait for the action. There were still no new vehicles being produced and very few used cars were available for sale. However, all over the country were dumps of ex-War Department vehicles being sold by auction. In common with other dealers Arthur Gould Ltd had been sending representatives to purchase almost anything on four wheels which might be recoverable for civilian use. A large proportion of their purchases had consisted of prewar Ford cars which had been converted into fire tenders for the Auxiliary Fire Service, or ambulances for the ARP. Most had been cut through the roof behind the front door pillars, leaving both doors, front seat, dashboard and the whole front end intact. All else had been removed and scrapped apart from the floor. A basic plywood box van had then been built, on which would be fitted a bell plus four bunk beds and a red cross or, alternatively, ladders and firefighting equipment, as the case may be. Simple – but invaluable during the blitz.

It was Arthur Gould's intention to satisfy a rapidly growing market for personal transport by stripping these vehicles to the bare chassis and carrying out a thorough rebuild from a chassis/front end format. On completion the bonnet and wings were resprayed, new front bumpers, lights and brightwork were fitted, and the relatively simple instrument panels refurbished as needed. Finally a pair of colour-matched rear mudguards were tied to the back. Once completed the vehicles were driven to selected coachbuilders in various parts of London to be fitted with timber-built estate car bodies fitted out with brand new upholstery, trim and headlining. This, though, was for the immediate future, and in the meantime the first batch of around 50 vehicles had been mustered in a huge field on the northern outskirts of Biggleswade, Bedfordshire. Inevitably, few were expected to be in running order, so it was decided that suitable rebuilt engines would be taken up three times a week to be fitted on site, and this is where Meard Street, in the shape of Tom, Maurice and yours truly, came in. Once removed, the old engines were to be returned by us to George and his ladies at Minerva House for the full treatment, and so the circle went on. On site meant just that – outside in the field, wet or dry, with only the most basic equipment. Mr Shiel doubtless considered this to be valuable experience for his young protege as I found myself consistently involved for some months, but as these were mostly summer months it was quite a happy period in my life. For starters it was a whole day out, inclusive of expenses and overtime fiddled, for the most part, by Tom and Maurice. Of course they were obliged to include me in these bogus calculations in order to preserve the *status quo!*

It all started one Saturday morning when I was taken by Maurice to Minerva House in the works runabout, an ex-Royal Air Force 10-horsepower Ford Prefect fitted with a pick-up body and a canvas hood. After tea in the canteen with Mo's ladyfriend and my lady acquaintances from the engine shop we took the truck in the lift to the top floor, where we loaded a rebuilt Ford V8 gleaming in its fresh grey paint, this one having been works-tested and complete with carburettor, distributor, petrol pump and everything else required to make it run given electrics and fuel. Nothing more being said at this stage, we arrived back at the garage where I had to help load some tools and lifting equipment. An old bench-type seat had already been fixed behind the cab. "That's for you", said Tom. "We want you in sharp on Monday as we are off for the day", and that was that. Tom was not one for prolonged conversation.

Full of curiosity, I arrived very early on the Monday. Maurice was already checking the truck and while doing so he gave me the details over a welcome brew. For all I knew of Biggleswade it could have been on the other side of the moon. This day out was to set a pattern, repeated three times a week for the next month or so, and I never tired of them, though the work was often arduous and sometimes uncomfortable. The routine was always the same: Tom or Maurice drove the old pick-up out of the garage, with me sitting on my cushion at the back, then we would head up Wardour Street and on through North London to Barnet and Hatfield on the Great North Road. This was on the old three-lane A1, the centre lane of which became the 'overtaking' lane for both northbound and southbound traffic. Inevitably, accidents, when they occurred, were spectacular and usually fatal. Traffic however, by today's standards, was almost non-existent.

Just north of Hatfield was the transport cafe where we always stopped for a leisurely breakfast, on expenses. Anyone who has not had the good fortune to eat in a truck drivers' cafe in the days before plastic food and motorway service centres quite simply has never known the good life: fried free-range eggs, bacon, real sausages, plus endless mugs of hot steaming tea, with the *Daily Mirror* and a fag to follow. Man, that was living! Cholesterol and lung cancer had not been invented, and what was more, in those days it really was cheap living. A good break, then off through the open countryside at a steady 40 miles per hour, up the A1 through villages – now mini-towns and by-passed – to the old market town of Biggleswade, our destination being a country garage on the far side of town with a large field at the rear, where Arthur Gould's purchases were parked. Most were in a sorry state, showing distinct signs of the rigours of the blitz, and they looked very drab in their wartime flat grey paint, with blackout masks still covering the headlamps.

Still, ours was not to reason why, for we had a full day's work to do. Tom started the proceedings by giving us a registration number to locate while he went to the garage with the paperwork to obtain the appropriate keys. We soon found the vehicle we wanted and on Tom's return we opened the engine cover and started work. As the young sprog I got the worst of the nuts and bolts to undo – those underneath, on the engine mountings and radiator hoses – while Tom and Maurice occupied themselves removing the ancillaries above. On the whole the vehicles were in quite good mechanical condition, having been fairly well maintained. The original blitz had been over for some years, and it is reasonable to assume that the regular fire and ambulance service with their purpose-built vehicles would have been able to cope with the V1 flying bomb and the V2 rocket incidents in the latter part of the war as they were spread over a wider area. No doubt these auxiliary vehicles had been kept mainly in reserve, just in case. Tom even managed to start one or two with the help of a slave battery, which was useful as we were then able to tow others into some semblance of order, and more importantly, onto higher ground; none of us wanted to work on those parked over bloody great puddles. I recall one particular day when Tom, displaying a rare sense of humour, crept into the back of a truck with a canvas top carrying a broom. The canvas had collected a fair bit of rain water, and our Maurice, spry and cheerful as ever, was pumping up one of the rear tyres with a foot pump. Tom gave one almighty heave with the broom on the canopy and a ton of water fell onto poor Maurice below!

The first engine change genuinely took a considerable time, and it established the overtime rate for the rest. Getting the old unit out was not too much of a problem, but fitting the new engine and lining-up the splines on the gearbox driveshaft in the open air on uneven ground was quite a challenge. By the time we had achieved this minor miracle, connected everything up, fitted a new battery and started up, it was quite late, and Tom still had to free off and adjust the brakes before carrying out a short road test. As the weeks passed we established a routine and the engine change was brought down to such a respectable time that on some days we had to kill time in the transport cafe on the way back in order to go into overtime! The first, however, seemed to take forever and I have no idea what time Tom and Maurice dropped me off in North London; my poor mother must have been worried to death. Once we had done our part, drivers were sent to bring the vehicles back to Minerva House, where the old bodies were removed and scrapped and work would commence on the chassis and running gear.

For me, however, this side of the business was for the future, and I had little idea what was to become of the vehicles on which I had split and broken my nails and ruined my hands. I was not all that bothered, though, because what with the expenses and the overtime I was doing fine. I was out three full days a week, which still left me with time to look after the cars of my regulars at Meard Street. By my own standards I was very well off and at 15, after all, this was what work was all about. I had a regular girlfriend, and I belonged to the local youth club where, with pockets full of money, I was regarded as 'a bit of a card' by my contemporaries, particularly as I was able to talk authoritatively, and with a good deal of fictional embellishment, of my 'relationships' with the ladies of Soho. My spare time at the garage was spent in the basement, where I was able to teach myself the basics of driving by moving various clients' cars backwards and forwards on the clutch and practising moving the gear-lever.

These illicit exercises, however, were to lead to my undoing. One of my regular customers had a 1936 Ford Ten. Now this was a very handsome car for its day, boasting wire wheels as standard equipment and known by and large as the 'barrel-type' Ford due to its rather bulbous shape. It was finished in immaculate pale blue and was the owner's pride and joy. Part of my agreement with him was that I should wash the car each week and polish it every fortnight, for which service, in Arthur Gould's time, I was very well paid. One afternoon, while everyone chanced to be out, the car had to be moved for some reason. Old Tom asked for a hand to push. "No need for that", I said airily, "I'll drive it". Old Tom was inclined to argue, but a fag settled the matter in no time at all. The car only had to be moved a yard or so towards the rear of the garage and with all the practice that I had in the basement it should have been a simple matter. My downfall was that I had an audience, and there is a basic need in human nature to show off. At first all went well as I climbed into the car, pulled out the choke, switched on and pulled the starter. After a nonchalant rev or two I eased in the choke a touch and carefully engaged first gear. Gently letting out the clutch, as I had done countless times in the basement, the little car moved slowly forward like a dream. There was nothing at all in front, so left hand hard down, followed by hard right brought the car over the required distance in a dozen yards or so. Now, with confidence, I was able to engage reverse, slip the car gently back towards the wall and stop. A little rev-up for good measure and then I released the clutch, unfortunately with the car still in gear! The Ford reversed smartly into the garage wall with an expensive crunch.

Foreman Tom, of course, had to report to head office on his return, so the following day I was summoned to the Regent Street showroom, which I had not visited since my original interview, and which I had hoped one day to decorate in my smart suit. Once again I stood before Mr Shiel, but in a somewhat different atmosphere. There was not a great deal to be said and I was solemnly handed my cards, together with wages due, and sacked. I left the showroom in tears, and in a state of considerable shock, to reflect on how life can change as a result of one foolish action. How, I wondered, could I face my father, who had held down his job in the Wigmore Street office since the end of the First World War? I decided first to face my mother, who had kept her wartime job as a saleslady at the C&A stores near Marble Arch, just a few stops on the Underground. I went round to the staff entrance and in due course she appeared, worried that I may have had an accident, which of course I had, but not the kind that she had in mind.

I was so obviously distraught that the kindly commissionaire had sat me in his office with a cup of tea, and when my mother appeared he tactfully left us alone while I poured out my sorry story. She said nothing while I recounted what I had done and the awful result. At the finish she simply told me what, alas, I already knew, namely that I had been careless and stupid. "Well", she said, "we shall just have to see what can be done." With that she somehow begged time off and took me back to Regent Street where, on arrival, she asked the duty salesman if Mr Shiel would be kind enough to spare her a moment. After a very short time she was invited upstairs while I was left below in apprehension. I never did find out what was said during her lengthy visit, but at last, when she came down the stairs, she told me that I was to wait and that she thought that it would be alright. With a final: "Now I have to get back to work, so for God's sake behave yourself", she was gone. Mr Shiel came down the stairs shortly after with his coat on, *en route* to Minerva House. I was gruffly told to get back to Meard Street and that a very close eye would be kept on me in future. Thanks entirely to my mother, I had got my job back, but I had given up all hope of working in that showroom for a very long time to come.

In the event I was quite wrong; I stayed at Meard Street until the end of that year, making several more trips to Biggleswade, then out of the blue, in January 1946, I was told to report to Regent Street on the following Monday at 9am. Staff hours, no less, and the start of my sales career. April was to herald my 16th birthday.

CHAPTER TWO

FORMATIVE YEARS – 1946–48

The Regent Street showrooms of Arthur E Gould Ltd were at Walmar House, north of Oxford Circus, on the right-hand side as you walk up to the BBC building between Castle Street and Margaret Street. These thoroughfares were the province of the fashion industry and in due course were to provide Goulds with a healthy turnover in new and used gown vans as well as cars. When I arrived the showrooms were still in their wartime garb, the four plate-glass windows being boarded up save for a very small area, perhaps 2ft by the width of each window at eye-level. The double doors in the centre of these, however, were of metal-framed glass. Either through reasons of economy or shortage of material, photographs in my possession show that the frontage was to remain like this until at least 1948, when I was called up for National Service!

To clarify the narrative, a brief description of the layout of the premises will be useful at this point. The showrooms were L-shaped, the base comprising two 20ft frontages divided by the double entrance doors. Both frontages were further subdivided into two window areas, those to the left (from the pavement) being part of sliding doors for vehicle access, while the two windows to the right were fixed, forming the base of the 'L'. This section of floor area contained a vehicle lift platform servicing the lower ground floor area. The wide stem of this L shape, being the main part of the showroom, was crossed, about two-thirds of its length down, by what may best be described as a bridge, exactly like that on a ship. This, in fact, was the second floor office area, which was reached by a staircase on the right-hand side. Situated below this, in a semi-private area, was an expensive looking desk and chairs together with matching settee, all for the exclusive use of the duty salesman and his clients. Further back was another staircase descending to the basement and the ladies' and gentlemens' washrooms.

On reaching the first floor you were confronted by a short corridor leading back to a somewhat narrow office with, on the left-hand side, two desks, both on little platforms and facing inwards. These, together with a secretary's desk straight ahead, made it all rather cramped for an 'executive suite', but that is exactly what it was. Within a few months, as the postwar action started, they were to cram into the same area yet another desk, complete with secretary. The first desk on the left as you entered was that of Mr Shiel. Fortunately, with regard to the demands on space and oxygen, he only stayed at Regent Street until 11.30am each day. Then he would don hat and coat and walk all the way to Tottenham Court Road, scorning a lift in a company car except in the most inclement weather. The second desk was that of the resident sales manager, Mr Arthur Thomas Barrow.

The remainder of the first floor area was divided into two equal parts. The front part of the 'bridge' overlooking the showrooms was the salesmens' general office complete with a purpose-built desk running the full width of the glazed area, into which was built a drawer for each of the salesmen. I was soon to discover there was a distinct pecking order in regard to each part of that chest-high desk. Every drawer, and corresponding place above, was the exclusive territory of its current inhabitant, as was the stool below. Not that it was intended that salesmen should be comfortable in this area, and clients were never invited in. It was simply a base for letter writing, telephone calls or follow-ups at the beginning and end of each working day. In between, all but the weekly duty salesman were expected to be out all day seeking new business. Behind was quite a large office occupied by a Mr Goodchild and his secretary, who were responsible at that time for the progress of the reconditioned vehicles during their various stages, and were shortly to take on a far greater responsibility allocating new vehicles through the waiting lists. So this was the building where I was to work for the next two and a half years before National Service caught up with me, and it was here that I met my particular mentor, whose dynamic influence I remain very conscious of to this day.

The general situation from the war's end in May to January 1946 had changed little. Few if any new cars were being produced, there were shortages of absolutely everything, and the only cars being offered for sale were prewar models and, of course, the first of the rebuilds with their timber estate car bodies. Considering the shortages and the parlous spare parts situation, those cars on sale were quite remarkable. During these early postwar years I was to see a great many reconditioned vehicles pass through Regent Street and both their construction and overall finish were surprisingly good, though, as regards their history, none could be offered with the claim of having had "one lady owner, very low mileage and only used for going to church on Sundays". The odometer, or mileage indicator at the time was universally recognized simply as a handy gadget which told the current owner how many miles *he* might have covered during ownership. Far from being regarded as an inducement to purchase or otherwise, it was totally ignored by prospective purchasers and sales staff alike as having no commercial value or interest whatsoever.

There were two Ford V8s available, the big 30-horsepower and its smaller sister, the 22hp. Both were four-door models and would accommodate three rows of bench seats, the centre row seating only two so as to allow access to the rear bench via the nearside rear door. There was seldom a back door on these models as there was little room for luggage. The smaller estate cars were based on the Ford Eight or the 10-horsepower models – either the Prefect, introduced just before the war, or its predecessor, the earlier 7W Fords. These were all in two-door form, usually in their original metal, with bucket seats at the front having folding backrests for access to a rear bench seat. The remainder was load space which was reached via two wooden doors at the rear. There were minor differences in appearance, depending on the whims of the bodybuilders, and in some cases individual customer requirements. A photograph album was available in the showroom from which clients could choose the body best suited to their particular purpose. There was nothing to differentiate the chassis as all were reconditioned to the same high standard, and all carried a 90-day warranty.

The motor trade in general, of course, was trying to rebuild itself to an established prewar pattern. Motor dealers with a new-car franchise, particularly West End dealers, were expected to run a gentleman's business, for gentlemen. Prewar, companies of the standard of Arthur Gould Ltd would rarely have soiled their hands with anything as common as a used car. Those which had to be accepted in part-exchange would have been discreetly hidden away in Meard Street prior to being sold to cloth-capped people from Warren Street or Great Portland Street, just round the corner. Although the new cars were as yet unavailable, the gentleman's image at the dealerships had to be preserved at all costs. Salesmen likewise were expected to behave and to appear like gentlemen at all times. This situation produced characters amongst the motor trade sales staff the likes of whom are seldom, if ever, to be found in the business today. A brief description of the sales staff employed by Arthur Gould in those immediate postwar years, and the manner in which they went about their business, is certainly worthy of record.

Staff were led, of course, by Arthur T Barrow, the resident sales manager. I have already indicated that he was a man whom I came to admire and respect to an almost extraordinary degree. Next to my father he was the only man I ever came to love, and it is a fact that the recollections of this period of my young life can still, after well over 50 years, bring a tear to the eyes of a cynical old motor dealer. ATB taught me the business. He was at all times the shining example of how commerce and the art of selling should be conducted. He had the florid complexion of the heart sufferer, with the quick temper to match. On average he would either fire me or threaten to return me to the anonymity of Meard Street at least once a week, but at heart he was, as will be seen, a kindly man with a great sense of compassion. He could have been the archetypal Rotarian.

Arthur was also a super salesman who had learned his trade in America with General Motors long before the war. I never did find out how he came to be with Arthur Gould Ltd, yet for me ATB was Arthur Goulds, and it was unthinkable that the company could possibly have existed without him. Each morning at 9am precisely he would stride through that front door, immaculate in striped dark suit, white shirt with thin red stripes, starched white collar and plain red tie. He always carried a carefully rolled umbrella, with a neatly folded newspaper under his right arm, together with a trilby hat, which he would only wear if it were particularly cold. I never once saw him dressed any other way apart from Saturday mornings, when he would arrive in an equally immaculate tweed suit, or in well cut sports coat and flannels with a knife-edge crease. Saturday mornings were something of a social occasion, when Arthur Barrow would appear with his lovely wife Wendy and their two Pekinese dogs. Likewise, most of the sales staff were expected to bring their wives so that the ladies might go on shopping expeditions during the morning. The ladies would all return in small groups between 12 and 12.15pm for a little chat, and at 12.30pm promptly the showrooms would close for the weekend, when the gentlemen and their ladies, led by Arthur and Wendy Barrow, would repair to *The Castle* pub in Great Portland Street for a midday drink. Being far too young, I was not invited.

Arthur Barrow was a stocky, well-built man, I would guess in his early-fifties, dynamic, with a clear and sharp but not unpleasant manner of speaking which could be heard all over the building. With customers, his old world charm was a magnet, which was why he could sell things. I may have been wrong about his heart, for he was certainly full of energy, although he did collapse on one occasion, giving us all a fright, but he was soon back at work as fit and decisive as ever. Nonetheless, he was a confirmed hypochondriac and it was no small part of my job to visit the local chemist for his boxes of pills and medications. He was certainly very much alive when I last saw him in the late-Fifties, albeit by then a broken man. This, however, was his heyday, and he was at the very peak of his career. During those early years and throughout the time I was in the Army he treated me like the son he never had and, I suspect now, had always wanted. While he was tough with me and would stand for no nonsense whatsoever, he saw to it that I had every opportunity to learn and to succeed in life. When one of the coachbuilders held a party somewhere to celebrate an anniversary, my father made it clear that I could not expect to go, "staying out till all hours indeed". It was Arthur Barrow who telephoned him, accepting full responsibility for my sobriety, welfare and safe return home at a reasonable hour in his personal car. When he discovered that I had an interest in photography with my cheap Kodak Brownie, he loaned me his expensive 35mm camera to take on holiday. Each month while I was in the Army I received a tin of 50 Players cigarettes with a brief note, even after he had left Arthur Goulds under some kind of a cloud and had problems of his own. A lovely man indeed, to whom I shall always owe a very great deal.

Next in line was the senior salesman, George R Grange, who was almost the complete opposite of Arthur Barrow. His suiting, while undoubtedly expensive, always managed to look as if it had been slept in. He was forever hitching up his trousers over his ample belly, while his poorly knotted tie would always be under one side or the other of his collar. For all that he was a man of tremendous style, with a distinguished, albeit loud voice and a great personality. You simply could not dislike George Grange; he was also a particularly generous man. His battered Ford Prefect reflected his appearance; it was the worst kept, the worst maintained and by far the most untidy vehicle on the company fleet. Nobody was unduly surprised when one day it caught fire in Castle Street and the blaze had to be extinguished with buckets of water from *Mario's* cafe. To this day I can still remember that its registration number was FGW 814!

George was not senior salesman by virtue of age, he had earned it. He had a way with people and was able to 'get in' where others failed. It was George who sold a whole fleet of reconditioned ex-Army trucks to the Manchester Co-op on a long-term contract basis. This one order was to keep us all busy for a couple of years. He had a unique style on the telephone, when he would invariably introduce himself as "Grange of London speaking", being in no doubt that he would be instantly recognized at the other end. Once, on returning from some errand or other, I was surprised to see three pairs of feet protruding from underneath a large American V12 Lincoln Zephyr saloon in the showroom. One pair were certainly those of Arthur Barrow, black and mirror-polished. Another pair were certainly those of George Grange, crumpled socks over brown shoes that had not seen brush or polish from date of purchase. The third set mystified me: professional striped trousers, like those of a barrister, well-polished black shoes together with pearl grey spats. Obviously a client, for George's distinguished voice could clearly be heard extolling some feature of the chassis, but equally someone of considerable importance to warrant the combined attentions of both sales manager and senior salesman. Who could it be, I wondered, royalty perhaps? In the event I was not that far wrong, for after some dignified scuffling they all emerged from underneath and a tall, portly gentleman was escorted to the door with some ceremony and waved goodbye. As soon as I was able I cornered George. "Who was that?", I asked. "Lord Dawson of Penn, old boy", said George casually, "King's physician."

Of the salesmen I particularly remember Harold Plaistow, a slim, dark and intense young man with very thick black-framed spectacles and close-cropped hair. He was a completely humourless man of whom I was to be vividly reminded years later when I saw his absolute 'ringer' on the television: 'Eagle', of the *Muppet Show*. Then there was Ted McKeefry, the mad Irishman, full of pure Blarney and a great charmer who would pull my leg without mercy given the chance. Both he and George had very attractive Irish wives. One of the more upmarket salesmen was Lionel Haylock who, it was said, played a mean saxophone in a dance band in his spare time. Be that as it may, he looked more like a Harley Street consultant than a car salesman. On the Saturday morning social occasions Lionel's posh wife was always accompanied by his equally posh mother-in-law who collectively added a touch of class to the proceedings. For a time we had Ron Johnson, a well-known New Cross speedway rider, who was said to have broken every bone in his body, and then we had Ray Gunther.

Now Ray was a character indeed with a unique personality. He looked a bit arty with his wavy grey hair and Van Dyke beard, but there was no doubt that he had a lovely speaking voice and impeccable manners. Lionel's posh mother-in-law would twitter like an adolescent schoolgirl each time Ray as much as looked at her, such was his devastating charm. Ray was always larger than life, and among other things he secured a huge order for new vehicles from a national newspaper. Now this was quite an achievement, shortages notwithstanding, for the Ford Motor Company allocated a number of extra vehicles for sizeable orders of this kind. To celebrate, Ray invited Arthur Barrow to lunch at some very exclusive gentlemen's club, which impressed Arthur no end until he discovered much later that Ray had not even been a member! Shortly after this event, though, Ray Gunther quietly vanished, never to be seen again. From time to time, though, and in great secrecy, Arthur Barrow would hand me 50 Players and a 10 shilling note to wrap up and post to a Mr Gunther at one of His Majesty's Prisons!

Those are a few of the sales personnel who made such a lasting impression on me, but there were others, of course, like Eric Holtham, who lived near me and could be relied upon for a lift to work each day. Later he took a job with a Rolls-Royce dealer and I would see him each year at Earls Court at the Motor Show, although by that time he was far too 'upmarket' to bother with the likes of me. As before, my duties were mundane, being those that nobody else wanted to be bothered with. But there was a lot to see and much to interest. Very quickly I learned how to file, for the attractive young secretary, Sylvia, pulled rank and unloaded that job onto me the day that I started. My first job each morning was to be taken to Minerva House by one of the sales staff to exchange mail and paperwork. The first thing that I noted was the difference in driving techniques. Harold Plaistow, Lionel Haylock and Eric Holtham were all steady, reliable drivers whereas a trip with the mad Irishman or Ron Johnson was an adventure; their little Fords were either flat-out or stationary. George Grange would provide an uneventful trip once he had cleared the car catalogues and piles of notes from the front seat so that one could get in. Mind you, getting out was often a problem for invariably a door handle would be missing or jammed. Other than that there were frequent trips to County Hall on the bus to obtain vehicle licences, plus the usual routine office and showroom jobs.

Each morning at 10.30 Messrs Shiel and Barrow would descend the staircase to the showroom area and proceed in a dignified manner to *Mario's* coffee shop just round the corner in Castle Street. Mr Barker, the elderly showroom cleaner, would unfailingly be on hand to respectfully open one of the glass doors. He did not actually touch a forelock, but the door was opened with a gesture and mannerism which came close enough! Protocol decreed that they of Arthur Gould's staff should go first. After a decent interval the duty salesman and any members of the sales staff who had particular business in the showrooms on the day would follow in pairs. Last of all, providing the premises were manned, I would go with Sylvia, the allowed time being 10 minutes. For some reason we both had a passion for plain cake and jam, that is on the days when we could afford it. If George was about we were home and dry, for he could always be relied upon to cover our bill. The strict protocol extended to the cafe, where Messrs Shiel and Barrow would always take a table alone at the bottom end, the sales staff sat somewhere in the middle, and Sylvia and I sat in the entrance, opposite the long counter.

After coffee, Mr Shiel would stride straight off to Minerva House, not to be seen again until the following morning, and Mr Barrow would return to the showroom, where another working day would progress. Sylvia and I were allowed one hour for lunch, usually at 'Joe Lyons' if we could afford it. But on most pay days we went a bit mad and lunched, reasonably enough in those days, at one of the big London stores. Each afternoon there would be a similar ritual at *Mario's*, when Mr Barrow would invite the duty salesman for tea, this time in the centre of the cafe. All salesmen had to be out seeking new business on a rota basis save the one who was duty salesman for the week. During this week he would occupy the expensive chair and the table below stairs and deal with any showroom traffic. All told things were pretty quiet in those early days, and the showroom was a huge gloomy emporium within due to those windows being all but boarded up, and of course the lights had to be on all day. Nonetheless customers came and went, and the used cars were certainly being sold on a regular basis. As business started to recover in its new peacetime role I was becoming more and more involved.

One afternoon there was a tremendous air of excitement and expectancy in the showrooms. Almost everybody was in on that day for at long last the very first postwar Ford car was due to arrive from the production lines at Dagenham: It was a Ford Anglia saloon, black of course, with the square radiator and wing-mounted headlamps, exactly as last produced in 1940. But this was brand spanking new, and as such was memorable as being the very first new car I had ever seen. I stood transfixed at the top of the stairs that afternoon as Harold Plaistow, showing off like crazy, backed it into the showroom past a few curious Regent Street shoppers. It gleamed from front to back and when switched off the hot engine ticked and exuded that unmistakable aroma of newness. It was like viewing something from another world as we all stood respectfully back so that Arthur Barrow be permitted to slowly walk round the car, followed by George Grange, and then each were to sit awhile in both the driver's and passenger seats passing suitable comments. By the time they had had their turn, followed by the rest of the sales staff in strict order of seniority, it was time to close the doors and it was the following day before I got my turn behind the wheel. But no matter, this was an historic occasion, and the price of that first new Ford I can remember to this very day: £293 7s 3d ex-works, purchase tax paid.

It was a very basic two-door saloon. There were two bucket seats for driver and front passenger, with a bench seat at the rear, all in an imitation leather material known as Rexine. The Bakelite dashboard contained a speedometer, petrol gauge and ammeter, together with a combined ignition key/light switch, plus two pull-out knobs marked 'C' and 'S', representing choke and starter. Apart from the rain there was certainly no windscreen wash, indeed there was only one windscreen wiper, the twin being extra, and there was no heater. This present day essential was then a bolt-on luxury goodie on all but the most expensive cars, available only from the accessory shops. Indeed, heaters were not available as factory units from the mass-market manufacturers until the all-new postwar designs were in production, and then in most cases only as an optional extra! The Ford Motor Company, for instance, certainly didn't provide a heater as standard equipment until the introduction of the Mk III Zephyrs and the Cortinas of the early-Sixties.

After a suitable time on show, the little Ford Anglia was fitted out for Mr Barrow as a demonstration car, with frills and extras as appropriate to his senior executive position in the company. On its return from the Minerva House service department the car had a heater, with a two-speed motor. This circulated the air within the car and as such was universally known as a 'fug stirrer'. There were no demisting facilities, so two miniature electric elements were fitted to the windscreen by suction discs, but they were no match for the condensation generated by the recycled air and therefore of very limited use. The car also had a Phillips radio, the powerpack of which was so large that it occupied a considerable space under the dashboard – no microchips in those days! – and tuning of the very few stations available was by remote cable control. Within a few days this Anglia was followed by others, together with its bigger brother, the four-door, 10-horsepower Prefect. In no time at all the showroom seemed to be full of new cars. In retrospect it is astonishing that for all too short a time we were actually able to offer virtually immediate delivery on these, the only two Ford models available, yet within a few weeks delivery times were to be quoted in terms of years and the secondhand values of these same cars were to go through the roof.

There was, at the time, a phenomenon that many years later was to be aptly described as 'a wind of change'. Each day the salesmen were chased out to seek business and the showrooms would be deserted apart from the duty salesman hidden away under the staircase, reading his paper and reserving any burst of activity for when Mr Shiel and Mr Barrow were to descend the stairs *en route* to coffee. The only occasions when there was any real activity would be when George was on duty. During his week the phones would be red hot, and everybody was kept busy, including me, and as if by magic customers would appear in the showroom. The cracks in the sales organization were beginning to show, and the effect of this was to provide me with lessons for the future which I never forgot, not the least of these being that movement and activity always attract attention. At heart I was still very much the 16-year-old office boy, chatting up the two secretaries at every opportunity and avoiding any hard work or unpleasant task as much as possible. But I was interested, and I had all the pent-up enthusiasm of youth.

The truth of the matter was that with the exception of George the sales staff were lazy and, for all their personal charm, were all on the fiddle. This early postwar period was the heyday of the black market which had flourished throughout the war. Almost everything was still 'on the ration' – food, clothing, even sweets and confectionery and, most important for the motor trade, petrol. If you had the money you could buy anything, and if you were sharp money was easy enough to come by, as I was shortly to discover. A bright young salesman with time to spare, plus the use of a company car and petrol, could scratch a good living without difficulty, and I knew for a fact that they all had sidelines. They would make the very minimum of genuine calls, making up their fictitious daily reports in the cafe. Later, as delivery times lengthened, it required little effort to obtain orders for new vehicles with delivery expectations running to at least three years, with every hope of a quick profit when the time came. Meanwhile, the motor trade – and Arthur Gould Ltd – were going through a phoney period during which those who had their wits about them could get delivery of almost any new car with relative ease.

All of the new cars available at this time were prewar designs which had been produced right up to the moment in 1940 when conversion to war production had brought the lines to an abrupt halt. In a very short time, though, both Armstrong Siddeley and Riley were to announce to the world breathtaking, completely new postwar models, and in due course all the major British manufacturers followed. At Arthur Gould Ltd they were already starting to take orders, based solely on speculation, for an anticipated new 'Big Ford', which eventually appeared in 1947 as the legendary V8 Ford Pilot (although still displaying quite clearly its prewar ancestry with its V8 30hp engine installed under the former V8 22-style body).

As the motor trade began slowly to recover from its enforced wartime break, I was fortunate indeed to be an enthusiastic young man growing up hand-in-glove with an industry which was to expand beyond recognition in less than half a lifetime. Had I but realized it at the time, this was the stuff of which dreams are made. Now, with the benefit of hindsight, it is all too clear that the 20th century was indeed destined to be the century of the common man, certainly as far as the ownership of personal transport was concerned. In America, long before the war, thanks to Henry Ford, the motor car had become almost a necessity of life, but in the British Isles we still had a few years to go before that happy situation would come about.

I had three positive advantages at this time. As I have already said, apart from George Grange the sales staff were lazy to a man and prone to extend to the maximum their lunch, tea and coffee breaks. I was enthusiastic and willing to talk to anybody, whereas the salesmen would only dally with customers who walked in virtually asking to buy a car: Most important of all, I had the ear of the sales manager, and as such I was the embryo of what would be referred to today as a whizzkid. Arthur Barrow was out a fair bit, leading, as it were, from the front, so during most working days that showroom was about as lively as a morgue on early closing. The two front doors were kept tightly shut save on the hottest days, when a concession was made and one of the doors might be kept open. From time to time the general public would peer through what there was of the showroom windows, hands over eyes to foil reflection. On rare occasions the bolder ones would walk in for a look round, with a hasty "just looking" if the duty salesman even bothered to get up from his comfortable chair. I had noted that people were reluctant to venture into what must have appeared as imposing premises. When one of the doors was open they would stand with toes on the brass threshold between showroom floor and pavement and lean their bodies forward to get a better view. What a contrast to those used-car showrooms in Great Portland Street, just round the corner, which I would visit in my spare time. Here nothing was closed, and cars for sale were even nosed forward just over the pavement area, where passers-by could not fail to see them. Certainly these were predominantly used-car premises, but then, we were also selling used cars!

I learned from them, and as soon as the salesman of the day popped out for his extended lunch break with a casual "Keep an eye on things, Geoffrey" I seized my opportunity. In no time at all both of the entrance doors would be wedged open, and in the summer for good measure I would also open one of the sliding windows. Initially this brought forth the wrath of old Mr Barker, whose job it was to keep the cars clean and free of dust. I managed to keep him quiet by helping to leather off the cars each day and by threatening him with the displeasure of Mr Barrow, of whom he was terrified. This done I would station myself with a duster by the car nearest the door and gladly talk to anyone who looked in for any reason. And it worked – *my God* it worked! – people who were on shopping trips or lunch breaks realized that we were in business. It would be nice to be able to say that I sold lots of cars. I certainly *talked* to lots of people and, yes, I did sell a car or two, if it may be termed selling, to people who were usually only too willing to buy during a period when it became increasingly obvious that the shortages were here to stay. In any case I was limited to little over an hour a day, for as soon as the salesman returned with a gruff "Shut those bloody doors, you can't hear yourself speak with all that traffic", the place would die again.

It was not long before I was to sell my first car to my very first customer. His name was Tommy Stern, and inevitably he was in the clothing business, just around the corner in Margaret Street. I shall always remember him: a small, round, immaculate Jewish gentleman with pale watery eyes in a friendly face and a courteous, almost apologetic manner. I had studied the paperwork and knew exactly what to do. The car required was a Ford Prefect in the first available colour, and I had obtained a deposit and completed the paperwork before the duty man returned. I had the good sense not to tell him, but later I handed the order to Mr Barrow to receive a "Well done, Geoffrey", and when the car was delivered a week or so later I received the appropriate commission.

By the time I had taken my next order the delivery time had extended, and it was to be some months before I received the financial reward for that one. However, there was another deal on a new car in which I was involved, with a more or less instant commission, for the client was a doctor. He came in the showrooms one day armed with a priority certificate from the British Medical Association arranged in conjunction with the Society of Motor Manufacturers and Traders (SMMT). Anyone in the motor business at that time could confirm that in those days some members of the medical profession earned nearly as much from their motor car dealings as they did from treating their patients, that is before the SMMT managed to put a stop to most black market transactions. My medical gentleman was a Dr J H Taylor, then practising at the Whitechapel Hospital in the Mile End Road. The order, which I was pleased to accept, again during a salesman's lunch break, was a formality. With an SMMT priority certificate I was able to hand the new car over within a week or so. There was, however, a shortage of some kind, and the following day I was sent to the hospital on the Underground to deliver this item and to collect a signature. I was too late; without a trace of embarrassment the good doctor told me that he had already sold the car for a substantial profit and that, whatever it was, the item was no longer required, thank you very much!

He was not on his own, for the medical profession had become notorious black market leaders until the SMMT and the BMTA (the British Motor Trades Association – now known as the Retail Motor Industry Federation), alarmed by the implications and the possibilities both from within and outside their substantial memberships, decided that something had to be done to eliminate all forms of illicit trading in new motor vehicles. To its eternal credit, the BMTA instituted a legal and binding covenant precluding all purchasers of new cars from reselling, other than at an agreed price, within six months of purchase, later extended to one, and then to two years. It must be emphasized that these rules also applied unequivocally to *all* new-car agents and dealers who were running new cars of their own. Not all motor dealers were necessarily members of the BMTA, so with the aid of the SMMT an application was won through the Law Courts for the means to control everybody connected within the industry. The method used was simplicity itself and became notorious at the time as the 'Stop List'.

Any person or company caught offering for sale a new vehicle still under covenant at a premium would run the risk of having their name and/or their company's trading name and address published on the Stop List, which was circulated monthly throughout the motor trade. Once a name appeared it automatically became an offence for anyone to supply that person or company with goods or services of any kind on a trade basis. Effectively this ensured that the offending company was instantly out of business, for the penalty for continuing to supply goods to persons or companies appearing on the Stop List was equally harsh: the supplying company would also be placed on the Stop List. As all suppliers are totally reliant on their respective manufacturers and distributors for their stock in trade, the effect was salutary and instantaneous. On receipt of the monthly Stop List it would be checked very carefully for known customers, and daily for strangers applying for trade services. Anyone, be they doctors, private individuals or company traders, who sold or purchased used vehicles which were still the subject of the covenant without the specific agreement of the BMTA could be, and in many instances were, successfully prosecuted and when proved guilty faced punitive fines which made the exercise highly unprofitable. Car dealers could also lose their new-vehicle franchise agreements.

Those motor dealers who wished to replace their own 'demonstration' vehicles were obliged to apply to their manufacturer, who would calculate a price based on initial cost and an agreed reasonable margin of profit. Perhaps the most widely publicized case was against a well-known racing driver and car dealer who, after a prosecution dragging on for over two years, was eventually fined £2,500 with £4,000 costs for illicit dealing, which was a very great deal of money in those early postwar days

Trendy editors of so-called consumer magazines and media commentators who are all too ready to snipe at the motor trade on every possible occasion will probably not have realized or ever bothered to find out that the trade, through its own elected representatives, were very quick indeed to put their house in order in those days, when huge profits could have been made. As I recall, it used to be called 'orderly marketing'. Now, of course, any attempt by a trade organization to ensure that a business earned not one penny more or less than their rightful profit would be deemed to be acting against the public interest! When one views the present quite ludicrous situation, where in many instances some national companies advertise nothing whatsoever other than in a 'Sale' situation at 'up to' umpteen per cent off a completely bogus, so-called maker's recommended price, I very much doubt that the public interest is quite as well protected as it might appear to be. Of course, the efforts of the BMTA and the SMMT could not entirely eliminate black market trading – someone somewhere will always find a way round the most stringent regulations – but they certainly came very close to doing so. Within a year or so the Stop List ran to several pages and the commercial activities of those on it were so restricted that most were obliged to discover ways of black market dealing other than in the motor business.

Meanwhile, life at Arthur Gould Ltd went on, but soon there was little hope of my being able to sell and deliver any more new cars in the foreseeable future. Delivery quotations had evened out at "four years for these models, sir, but we may get down to three". Nonetheless I was still talking to people as often as possible whenever I was able to open the showroom doors, for I desperately wanted to sell a used car. I was soon to do just that, although in somewhat odd circumstances. Harold Plaistow was duty salesman that week, which restricted me somewhat, for Harold was a mite conscientious in regard to both tea and lunch breaks; he would hardly be through the door before I was sliding the big glass window open to make the most of it. On the day in question I had not noticed that as I was pushing the door a person had walked into the showroom behind me. Sitting on the lift top in the 'L' was one of our reconditioned Ford Prefects in a pale beige colour, complete with varnished wood estate car bodywork. Now the lift was always surrounded by a length of plush red cord, draped from hefty brass posts so that should the lift descend for any reason we would not run the risk of losing valuable clients down a black hole.

Standing just outside the plush cord was a scruffy little man in a filthy brown raincoat. I had yet to learn the old motor trade maxim that you never, ever, judge someone by appearance. The standard "Can I help you – sir?" (the mildly contemptuous pause being quite deliberate) produced the instant reply: "I like that." Yes, and don't we all, I thought, but said nothing. There was a pregnant pause, I looked at him, he looked at the car. Suddenly the old boy brought both hands from his raincoat pockets and produced handfuls of large, dirty, lovely white fivers. "I'll have it." In an instant Geoffrey was all charm and courtesy. Order forms were produced and completed and I dashed upstairs clutching bundles of money which I was too nervous to trust myself to count, so I dropped the lot on Sylvia. After it had been checked and the client departed I reported to Mr Barrow that I had sold(?) a used car. He was delighted, and said so. I did not, however, tell him the full story.

But on his return from lunch Harold Plaistow was far from impressed. The odd new car that he would probably not have been even aware of was one thing, but a used car in a prominent position with a bloody great 'SOLD' label on it was something quite different. Jealousy reared its ugly head and there were discussions later with others on the sales staff with the inevitable result that lunch breaks were drastically curtailed, and some even brought sandwiches. My conversations with potential customers were to be severely restricted and there was general agreement that Geoffrey Owen was getting to be far too big for his boots. There were still to be times when I managed to get hold of somebody, and I even found a contact or two of my own, including a neighbour, but in the meantime I was to learn another practical, albeit hard lesson which hurt at the time, not least through my pocket, although it was a valuable, if painful experience which was to stand me in good stead for all that.

The gentleman, for very obviously he was just that, was the complete opposite of my client who had bought the Prefect estate car. For a start he could only be described as 'posh' – very distinguished, very well dressed, and he spoke with a plum in his mouth. When I first approached he had been viewing the most expensive used car in the showroom, and as the most costly carried the best rate of commission he was accorded the full treatment with a great deal of "Yes sir, no sir, three bags full and kiss your bum, sir". After a suitable interval he expressed a desire to purchase. However, there was it would seem a slight problem, or rather two to be exact. Naturally it was company policy that no order could be accepted without a cash deposit. Now gentlemen of his situation would hardly be expected to walk the streets with their Burberry top coats stuffed with fivers. But not to worry, the gentleman wished to pay the full price in cash that very day, so perhaps a taxi might be hailed so that we could proceed forthwith to his pad to obtain the required loot. Oh, and by the way, it would seem he had just run out of his favourite Rothmans No 5 hand-rolled Turkish fags. Pausing only to slap a 'SOLD' label on the car, I dispatched Mr Barker to Rothmans, which was just up the road, with my money for a box of 50, the smallest box available. With that I hailed a cab after calling importantly to Sylvia upstairs that if needed I would be back within the hour.

The gentleman gave the cabbie a prestigious South London address and off we went, chatting on the way of this and that. On arrival I was asked to wait in the cab for half a tick, old boy, and with that he was gone, never to be seen again! It was the cabbie, to whom I had outlined my story while waiting, who was the first to realize that I had been conned for 50 expensive fags and a free taxi ride to South London. Even then I could not accept that a gentleman would behave in this despicable manner, and after the cabbie had gone, sympathetically refusing my proffered tip, I waited for some time, sure that he would reappear. Of course he never did, and I returned disconsolately to Regent Street by bus and Underground. There was worse to follow on arrival, when I had to remove the 'SOLD' label from that expensive car before an amused sales staff, understandably delighted that Geoffrey had fallen flat on his face. After a while I wrote it off to experience. You need to be sharp in my business, and oddly enough, some 20 years later someone was to try exactly the same ruse with one of my salesmen, seeking a free ride home in a demonstration car. That time I was ready!

What with all the restrictions on my sales activities and the hopeless situation with new-car availability, I was getting bored. Mr Barrow was out a great deal of the time and the showrooms were just dead, with the doors tightly shut, particularly in winter. Almost every day, though, I had to go to County Hall at Westminster to obtain motor licences for new and used vehicles, which at least relieved the monotony. Motor vehicle registration was a complicated process in those days and nobody could put a journey time on my excursions. To licence a collection of used cars would involve visits to a series of different rooms where vehicle records were kept depending on the letters in the registration numbers. New cars were dealt with in another department entirely, following which you went to a large circular hall in the basement to queue, first for the licences, then again for the petrol coupons.

To avoid going back to the monotony of the showroom I had several choices, depending on the weather and the state of finances. If funds were good and the weather bad I would pop into 'Joe Lyons' for tea and cakes and read a good book or, if time permitted, I would visit one of the many News Theatres in town where one could enjoy two or three newsreels, a selection of cartoons and a feature film, perhaps of one of the big-name American bands of the time. Another favourite movie quickie would be the travelogue, which unfailingly would end with those immortal words: "And so we say farewell to the sun-kissed sands of Iwojima", or whatever exotic place was featured at the time.

For a shilling or two this would kill at least an hour in a most comfortable seat, and if need be you could always stay a while longer as the programme was continuous. Even if cash were short it didn't matter too much as long as the weather was fine. There was always something to see in London. For free entertainment on a bad day the best value in town for a teenager was the HMV record shop in Oxford Street where, given the ingeniousness of youth, I would request a bundle of the very latest 78rpm records at the counter, make my way to a private booth with electric gramophone and comfortable chairs, light up a fag, relax and play the lot at leisure. When ready I simply made my way back to the counter, reserved one or two for payday and walked out without paying a penny!

In the midst of these little skives I was to stumble across my very own private black market fiddle. With hindsight, of course, it was dishonest, and most certainly would have cost me my job if I had been discovered. At the time, though, it all seemed harmless enough, and as an offshoot, it sold a few used cars. It all started one fine day when, in a bit of a dream, I had walked halfway over Westminster Bridge from County Hall, *en route* for 'Joe Lyons', when it occurred to me that I had completely forgotten to draw the petrol coupons for the cars licensed that day. This was not a problem for I knew that petrol coupons could be obtained at any post office, indeed it might well turn out to be an advantage to do so for the inevitable queue would probably be shorter than at County Hall; the GPO in Whitehall was all but next door to 'Joe Lyons', anyway. On arrival I handed over the old-style registration logbooks and the lady clerk entered the serial number from the book of coupons into each logbook, stamped the entry, then handed back the documentation for each car together with full books of coupons for the current year. Now this was most unusual. At County Hall they always handed over petrol coupon books with all coupons prior to the current month torn out, even though, being valid for two months, the previous month's coupons were still legal tender.

There were perhaps four or five coupons for each calendar month, and each had a specific value in gallons. Books were also in three colours, red, green and black, respectively, representing cars in the small, medium and high-horsepower ranges, where the coupon values, of course, were progressively higher. I literally had one month's petrol ration for each car going spare! While enjoying my tea I thoughtfully removed the old coupons from each book, placing the still valid previous month's in my wallet on the basis that they would no doubt come in useful. By the end of that week, thanks to the post office, I had more petrol available than the Sultan of Oman and it was becoming something of an embarrassment. I had slipped a few coupons to George Grange without telling him where they came from, and passed a few to friends for nothing, but what on earth was I to do with the rest? Of course I realized that they had a black market value, but I could hardly offer them to the sales staff or to Arthur Barrow! By pure chance I sold a used car on my own doorstep and in so doing I acquired an agent, who would not only buy petrol coupons on his own account, but had a ready-made market where he could shift all the petrol that I could lay my hands on profitably for us both. That market was also to provide some useful used-car business.

In my spare time I would go roller-skating at Alexandra Palace, or alternatively I had a racing bicycle on which I used to travel miles into the country at evenings and weekends. I also had Kepel. Now Kepel was an unusual name for an unusual person. He was ugly, undersized, and in this day and age would generally be considered to be short on his marbles. But Kepel was my neighbour and the proud owner of a prewar Rudge Ulster Grand Prix motorcycle. In return for a regular supply of petrol coupons he would often take me for fast trips round the Hertfordshire countryside. On that Rudge, a superbike of its time, Kepel was an ace. He rode it with confidence, he rode it with competence, and he rode it fast, very fast. The roads were clear, we were not required to wear crash helmets, and with the wind rushing through my hair I experienced many times the sheer exhilaration of 80 miles per hour on two wheels up the A5 and down the old A1, which in 1946 was pretty damn quick. Now Kepel lived with his slovenly married sister, his brother-in-law being one John Harold Burden, a noted virtuoso of the French horn and a protege of Dennis Brain, famous for his excellent recordings of the Mozart horn concertos, but later tragically to be killed on the A1 at Hatfield while returning by car from the Edinburgh Festival. John was a leading soloist in the London Symphony Orchestra, and because of his profession and the sheer bulk of his chosen instrument, he needed a car. Kepel introduced us, with the result that John purchased a prewar reconditioned Ford Eight, and was delighted when I was able to provide coupons for all the petrol he could use. Better still, most of his colleagues in the LSO were car owners, so we had a ready-made market for the rest. A price per unit was agreed, below the usual black market rate, and we were in business. The situation was perfect; not only was I able to market my petrol coupons, but several members of the orchestra were introduced by John on a commission basis, from which useful used-car sales were achieved. Just before I was called up for National Service John Burden bought from me a large and luxurious 1939 Ford V8 30hp saloon, and why not, he had plenty of petrol to run it!

I was to sell and deliver just one more new car in that early postwar period. A South London garage proprietor by the name of Sydney Allard had started to reproduce his Allard sports cars based on the Ford V8 engine. These were marketed by selected Ford dealers, and while expensive, were as hard to obtain as any other new car.

However, some were marketed in a chassis/front end form so that clients could have their own bespoke bodies constructed, and as they were to appear on an *ad hoc* basis, as and when raw materials were available, we had no waiting list as such, so when a chassis arrived it was invariably available for instant delivery. As luck would have it a client called in just as one was available, and I just happened to be in the right spot at the right time. When my customer came to take delivery I begged a lift on the temporary wooden passenger seat to Great Portland Street station and he was delighted to oblige. On arrival I reached across the chassis to shake his hand and bid him farewell, when he promptly drove off and ran over my foot!

In August 1948 I finally received my summons to report to the Royal Armoured Corps at Catterick, in Yorkshire. I bade my farewells to Arthur Barrow and the remainder of the staff at Regent Street and at Minerva House, where I had made many good friends. With a whole extra month's wages in my pocket I set out on August 19 for the unknown. It was to be April 1950 before I returned.

CHAPTER THREE

THE WARRIOR RETURNS – 1950

I spent my short service life in the Life Guards, and this being an armoured cavalry regiment I came out with a full driving licence having learned my trade in Daimler armoured cars! As I was not qualified to drive on joining the Army, it was almost inevitable that having passed my test in a small Scout car after just two and a half weeks' tuition I should be selected as a potential driving instructor! After a further two and a half weeks' training I was handed my very own Daimler armoured car complete with 2-pounder gun and a selection of trainees, some of whom may well have had considerably more driving experience than me. Nonetheless it was a great way to learn, and by then I had the indisputable advantage, in the forces, of rank.

I also met some interesting people. Of the many officer-class pupils who were to pass through my hands in this exclusive regiment, one was a full-blooded Earl, another was to become a High Court judge, while a third carried the household name of a world-renowned preservative company. To aspire to a commission in that regiment required a very great deal of personal wealth: on most of our days spent out in the lovely Buckinghamshire and Berkshire countryside we were provided with a packed lunch, usually comprising 2-inch thick doorsteps of bread filled with cheese or spam. Of course, this had no appeal whatsoever for these young blades, who clearly were used to better fare, and without exception they all insisted that I enjoyed a proper lunch in some of the most exclusive restaurants in the area at their entire expense. The lads, for the most part, were well-known to the head waiters and very well received. This was just as well, for establishments like *The Compleat Angler* at Marlow and *The Bel and The Dragon* at Cookham do not usually favour guests who arrive in army tank suits and clutter up the car park with Armoured Fighting Vehicles, Daimlers notwithstanding. In this manner I managed to survive my National Service quite well, my initial basic training providing a bearing and a sense of personal pride which has never left me. I returned to civvy street in fine fettle.

The motor trade as a whole was very different from that which I had left in August 1948. Alas, I had missed the unique Motor Show which was held at Earls Court in October of that year and introduced many of the new cars which later became the early postwar classics. The sensation that year was the all-new Morris Minor, retailing in two-door saloon or tourer form at £359 and sharing stand space with the equally new Morris Oxford and Morris Six. Other innovations were the Standard Vanguard, at £544, and the ill-fated but nonetheless very attractive Austin A90 Sports, at that time in drophead-coupe form only, at £953 complete with power hood. But the star of the show without any doubt had been the striking Jaguar XK120 which, at £988 plus purchase tax, was generally acknowledged to be the most beautiful car ever made in that price range. There were many other all-new models at that show, and it could be said that 1948 was when manufacturers at last went truly 'postwar' in innovative design and construction. None of these cars, however, were yet available, so at least in that respect little had changed, although closer to home there had indeed been some drastic changes.

At Arthur E Gould the unthinkable had happened. Mr Barrow had departed under a cloud and Mr Shiel had at last retired. The new management were delighted to give me back my old job, but only in the anonymity of Meard Street, the first floor of which had been converted into a used-car showroom. The circumstances of Arthur Barrow's demise were vague; Sylvia thought that he had accepted some kind of Christmas gift from one of the bodybuilders, and while this was never properly substantiated it was certainly entirely possible. Discipline was very tight in commerce at this time, and while a gift could have provided no commercial advantage at a time when there was far more work available than firms were able to keep up with, there can be little doubt that such a gesture would have been frowned upon. One of the new Regent Street salesmen of this period with whom I became particularly friendly was a gallant ex-bomber pilot with a DFC to his credit. He was later sacked for no other reason than that he had placed his personal car for sale on a sale-or-return basis with a used-car dealership in Great Portland Street!

On my return to Meard Street I found that all the old faces had gone. Mr Packman and old Tom had retired, foreman Tom had been promoted to Minerva House, and only Maurice remained, having married his lady love when her husband decided not to return to the matrimonial home. Another wheezy old boy had taken over the garage, and a young salesman named Terry was in charge of car sales. Part of my job, with my new driving licence, was to ferry cars to and fro and generally make myself useful. I came to an arrangement with most of the sales staff whereby I washed and polished their cars each week for nothing, providing only that I was allowed to complete the final handover of all new cars to clients. A customer who had waited perhaps three years for his new car was inclined to be generous, and I collected a great deal in tips simply by being helpful and polite. This was handy as someone else was now doing the County Hall run, and not surprisingly, John Burden from next door had run off with an attractive lady French horn player without leaving a forwarding address.

Later that year the first of the Mk I Consul and Zephyr cars arrived. These days all of the new cars were arriving at Meard Street for showroom preparation and I had the joy of driving the very first Ford Consul to Regent Street. The lights were red at the junction of Wardour Street and Oxford Street and I had to stop. That was as far as I went, for I was quite literally swamped by people wanting to see and touch the car. At length a friendly policeman managed to get me on my way to Regent Street, where the same thing happened all over again before we were able to back the car into the showrooms. After a while a way was cleared and I managed to back through the showroom doors, showing off just like Harold Plaistow had those four years ago. Imagine if you can one of today's carbon-copy, computer-designed clones holding up the traffic in London! The sales staff certainly took some orders that day.

I was not very happy during those first months because not a great deal seemed to happen at Meard Street, and most of my time was spent ferrying cars round from place to place. The driving bit was OK, but I had expected to be where the action was. By chance I heard that Arthur Barrow was now the sales manager at an upmarket dealership in St James Street. I gave him a ring and was invited round on the spot. I was shown into ATB's huge office, where he rose from his desk to greet me. I was directed to a comfortable chair and given tea, during which we engaged in the usual polite formal small talk; nothing was said in regard to his leaving Arthur Gould, and in any event I was not interested. All I wanted was a job, and I was not disappointed. The group now employing ATB were always seeking new trainee sales staff to man their many branches, and at least I had some experience. I was offered a situation at Mr Barrow's own branch, Hoffmans, to start as soon as possible.

Hoffmans of London was part of the recently formed Swain garage group based in Halifax. It was run by a character called Percy Fritz Swain, who had been a conscientious objector during the war, but this had not precluded him from making a pile manufacturing munitions in a converted mill in Halifax! He now owned or leased showrooms in Halifax and London, and part of his empire at this time was H R Owen Ltd, of Berkeley Street, latterly part of the Heron Group. The Swain Group's stock in trade were expensive prewar and early-postwar exotica, Bentleys and Rolls-Royces predominating, all fitted with high-class British or French bespoke coachwork. He also stocked used Mk VI Bentleys with the standard-steel bodies and a selection of continental rarities such as Delage, Delahaye and Alfa Romeo, with the odd Cord thrown in for good measure. Percy Swain also dealt in 'bread and butter' cars, but in a novel and unusual way. In essence he was a bullshitter with an inbuilt ability to charm the birds from the trees – but he was certainly no mug.

Arthur had briefed me to turn up early for the daily sales meeting so that I might be formally introduced to the great man. He was immaculate, tall and charming, and I was immediately drawn to his uncanny likeness to James Mason, the well-known film actor. He shook my hand in a firm and friendly enough manner, but there was something else. My mother would have said that he had a 'BUT' about him. There was an indefinable feeling of something being not quite right! By now the various sales staff had gathered and we all sat down round a huge oblong table. At the top sat Arthur Barrow and Percy Swain, with Percy's poofy male secretary on his right. At the far end were two immaculate gentlemen who were very well-known indeed in the London motor trade at that time: Messrs Jim Twilly and Phil 'Pony' White, who collectively constituted the buying department. Scattered down each side were the sales staff of the London-area showrooms. Most were of a type: faceless ex-Army, Navy and Air Force officers who liked to maintain and be addressed by their grand wartime titles. As Arthur went round the table it was Lieutenant Commander this, Captain that and Major someone else. By the time it got round to me it was 22058699 Corporal Owen – Sir! I remember the elegant George de Moore, who was to grace the showrooms of H R Owen for many years to come, and the late Frank Lazenby, who started with me on the same day and later was to found and run a very successful motor business in Leicestershire. Of the rest I have no recollection at all.

The function of the meeting was to record the daily achievements of individual sales staff and to review the progress in respect of sales and buying departments. Someone was employed to tour the motor dealers of London seeking likely secondhand low-mileage cars. They were rarely purchased, for it was the function of the representative to record the most minute details of these cars on special forms, known as 'blue sheets'. These were handed in each day and meticulously filed. If, at the meeting, a salesman were to announce that he had a good inquiry for, say, an Austin A40 Somerset, under 10,000 miles, colour not important but not black, must have a sunroof with 'heat and music', the files would be searched for a suitable car or cars. Jim Twilly or Phil White would then phone round to try and borrow the car at an agreed price, when it would be collected by a uniformed chauffeur and beautifully prepared ready for presentation to the client at absolutely top price. Initially the trade were scornful of this novel method of trading with their money, but most came to realize that they could obtain over the odds for their cars if sold, with instant payment, and at worst, even if the Swain Group were unsuccessful and failed to make a sale, their cars were always returned in super-clean condition.

When the meeting was over we all retired to our respective posts, leaving Jim and Phil to their task of locating cars, and the daily routine began. My situation was to act as reserve salesman upstairs in the St James Street branch. Each salesman was given a loose-leaf book the size of a large photograph album, on each page of which was to be recorded, again in the most minute detail, every person spoken to in the showrooms or on the telephone during the working day – all on a one-to-a-page basis! Apart from the obvious name, address and telephone number, this record contained a wealth of detail such as hobbies and interests, or whether the client and his lady liked sugar or cream in their coffee. Every day the staff were expected to wade through this list, bringing it up to date by telephone call, or the sending of an elegant brochure of a stock vehicle which might be of interest. Every piece of exotic machinery was professionally photographed and the prints filed under its stock number. These could be inserted into a special folder, embossed with the company logo and containing a card on which would be typed full details of the car's history and specification, the whole being tied with blue cord and posted to the client in a special envelope. I must say it was all very impressive.

Being the new boy I had an empty folder and a pile of dud prospects that nobody else wanted, so I spent my first few days having a good look round. The very palatial showroom had ample room for seven or eight expensive cars and a few desks. Downstairs was a huge basement area containing an open-plan typing pool and Jim Twilly's buying department. Across the back were private offices for Arthur Barrow, Percy Swain and the administration. There was also a staff canteen and the meeting room. As there was a unique selection of talent in the typing pool I was prone to spending more time in this area than I should have done; I was destined not to remain for very long with the Swain Group.

The clientele were completely at variance with Arthur Gould's. During a period when only the comparatively well off might consider the purchase of a car, new or used, those clients who could afford to frequent St James Street and Berkeley Street showrooms were very well off indeed. As such they sought a more dignified and experienced approach. Several clients I met were to write to Mr Swain stating how well they had been received, but I simply didn't sell anything. One very regular client of the time was the late, great, George Formby, who collected cars like others collect suits of clothing. One morning Percy Swain was showing George over a particularly fine V12 Lagonda when he spotted a mark on the otherwise immaculate dark blue paintwork. Without pausing to think, I took out my breast pocket handkerchief, spat on a corner and removed the offending blemish. "Ee lad", said George, "me and thee should go into business. With thy spit and my cheek we'd make a bloody fortune!"

It was, on the whole, a rather depressing period for me. Arthur Barrow had such faith in me, but week after week the staff sales totals continued to show me with a nil return. On top of this I had been having a bad time with my father, which had led to me leave home. He had always been strict, particularly in regard to late nights, and as a teenager I had been expected to return home at reasonable hours and furthermore he had always wanted to know where I had been and with whom. This was by no means unusual, for my generation were not allowed to roam the streets aimlessly at night, committing acts of vandalism or glue-sniffing. Now all this was fine until I came out of the Army with a sense of self-discipline and my own set of standards. I certainly didn't expect to come and go as I pleased, but indoors and in bed by 11pm, or 12 o'clock on Saturdays, was a bit much for a 20-year-old ex-guardsman. The old man's point of view, though, was that as long as I lived in that home I was expected to abide by the rules. In later life, and with hindsight, I have to say that he was absolutely right.

The finality was a mixture of tragedy and comedy: getting home on the late side one night from someone's party, I had dialled for a early call which failed to wake me. It did, of course, wake the old man, who was not at his brightest and best at 6am and tripped over the family cat on the way down to answer the persistent ring. On finding that he had been dragged from his bed for my alarm call, he promptly lost his temper. By this time the general noise and bad language had roused me from a deep sleep and I had just about got out of bed when father burst in, followed by my anxious mother trying, in vain, to calm him down. Acrimonious words were exchanged and the old man threw a punch! That did it. I had just spent almost two years being trained to react to just this kind of situation, and without pausing for thought I ducked, stepped into the punch and threw a sharp one of my own, which found its target. That was the first and last time that I clobbered my old man. After that there was really nothing more to be said, so I moved out and into local digs.

It could not be said that my employment with the Swain Group was a total success, for in three months I had sold nothing, the simple truth being that I was completely out of my depth. Fortuitously a vacancy had come up in the buying department for a person to go round the trade finding used cars and completing 'blue sheets'. In some desperation Mr Barrow had put my name forward and Percy Swain had agreed, so I had a reprieve. While I did not like the job, which I considered a demotion and as such an end to my sales aspirations, it did undoubtedly have several advantages, not the least being the free use of virtually any company car within reason which had a bit of road tax and was waiting for showroom preparation in the company's storage garage below the *Park Lane Hotel*. It was there that I had been allocated a small office and a secretary, so the choice of machinery was quite extensive on a day-to-day basis. Company security being non-existent, I was able to enjoy the free and uninhibited use of some very classy cars in those days, to the unconcealed delight of my landlady, Mrs Wareham, who felt that I added a touch of class to the driveway. For several weeks I favoured a prewar 20/25hp Rolls-Royce with drophead-coupe body by Saoutchik of Paris – ideal for traversing London and the Home Counties on sunny days and impressing the young ladies at night.

In such opulence I would set off each day to visit sundry car dealers in the London suburbs, examining endless numbers of cars and completing hundreds of 'blue sheets' for Messrs White and Twilly. While many dealers, quite understandably, were downright rude and told me to **** off, I managed to make friends with most, and nearly all treated me with good humour. In any event I was doing far better than I realized at the time, for most previous occupants of my new-found situation had skived and submitted false reports. Because of the sheer volume of genuine reports that my secretary had to type out each day, many really good cars had been located for clients, and Jim Twilly himself had remarked to Mr Swain as to my reliability. The job was also a good way of getting to know London, and in later years, when I used all the short cuts, my father was often to remark that I would have made a good taxi driver. Driving to and from the London suburbs in those days was very pleasant indeed, with none of the present traffic jams and hold-ups.

I had managed to trace John Burden, who was living with his young lady in South London, and a good friendship was re-established. Poor old John was a bit hard up at the time, and in the process of his divorce, but he was still the top horn man with the London Symphony. One day he telephoned to offer two tickets for a concert at the BBC with a small party afterwards. I had just broken off an engagement, so not having anyone else to ask I invited my attractive secretary, who until then had just been a good reliable friend to be admired from a distance. I had been aware that Sheila was unmarried, with no particular boyfriend at the time, but she was 35 against my tender 20 years and had served in the Women's Royal Air Force during the war, where she had been both a fencing champion and a useful sportswoman, holding cups for swimming and running. By my standards Sheila was mature, to say the least, and while I was no virgin I had not as yet enjoyed anything like her varied experience of life.

To my surprise my tentative invitation was charmingly accepted. On the night we set off straight from work to Portman Place in the Rolls. The concert was magic, and the party afterwards for the guest conductor was quite short, so we all moved on to a local pub. Sheila got on with John and his attractive lady like a house on fire, so we all parted rather later than intended, after which we drove to Sheila's little ground floor flat at the top end of Ladbroke Grove. Inevitably I was invited in for coffee, after which it seemed natural that I should stay the night. Within the week I had moved in! It was a very small flat, but warm and comfortable, and certainly far superior to the restrictions of a guest house. Sheila was a superb cook and good company. We made no demands of each other and shared everything. Each day we would set off for Park Lane in some exotic car or other, where I would leave Sheila with the previous day's collection of 'blue sheets' for typing, and report to the sales meeting at St James St, then off on my travels round London. At the end of the day we would meet at Park Lane and drive home to our nest in Ladbroke Grove.

Of course it was far too good to last. First off Arthur Barrow had a flaming row with Percy Swain and left to join the old Car Mart company in South London. Soon afterwards I was posted to Brent Cross, in North London, as a salesman, which meant that I lost the use of a car. Travelling each night to Ladbroke Grove by public transport became less and less attractive as time went on. Meanwhile, my mother had been begging me to return home for some time, so Sheila and I regretfully parted company, still good friends. I did not like Brent Cross or Mr John Coombes, the manager in charge, while Peter Reynolds, the salesman, who was to rise to the very top of the company when the Heron Organisation took over, pinched all the best customers, so in due course I was summoned to head office in Berkeley Street and fired for the second time in my short commercial life. This time there was no reprieve.

There was, however, a sequel: some years later Percy Swain purchased the old-established Rolls-Royce and Bentley coachbuilding company Freestone & Webb Ltd. This enabled him to have a stand at the Earls Court Motor Show. While wandering around on preview day I chanced to pass the stand and caught his eye. "I think I know you", he said after a pause. "You should do, you once sacked me", I replied. "Did I really, now. Did it do you any good?" "Never looked back", I said with feeling. "Bloody marvellous", said Percy, full of charm as ever, "Come on the stand and have a drink".

Well, why not indeed?

CHAPTER FOUR

BACK TO SALES – 1952

To find gainful employment I had made use of the contacts made while touring London on behalf of Mr Swain. It seemed to be sensible to start on home ground, if only to save on bus fares. I was back at home on far better terms with my dad than I had ever been; the temporary parting of the ways had been good for both of us and formed the basis of a relationship that was to last 30 years through to his death. I still miss him and remember him with affection virtually every day of my life. Mother firmly believed that I had been respectably living throughout with Mrs Wareham, my landlady in North London, and I chose not to enlighten her; father thought otherwise, but never asked. I started in East Finchley for no other reason than I had a meeting with an old Army friend in Muswell Hill, and this was the most direct call by public transport. At Halls, a well-known used car dealer, I drew a blank, but opposite were Lindsey Brothers, at that time Rootes main dealers for the Humber, Hillman and Sunbeam-Talbot ranges, latterly Chrysler and now Peugeot. Here I had better luck. Mr Lindsey was pleased to see me, as always, and while he had no use for extra staff he was quite certain that there was a vacancy at the Rootes dealer in Tottenham, where a salesman had just left. With this encouraging news I immediately made my way to Robert Chidley Ltd, in Tottenham High Road, hard by the Spurs football ground.

Chidleys were a long-established family business. The original Robert had sold out to his brother Albert, who was now running the business with the help of his two sons – Cyril, acting as sales manager, and Reg, who was in charge of parts and accessories. I had called many times and was well aware that the company had an enviable local reputation. On my previous visits it had been Cyril who usually found time to have a friendly chat, but on this occasion I was greeted by the supremely imposing presence of Mr Albert, Cyril being out somewhere on business. Now if Percy Swain was a dead ringer for the actor James Mason, Albert Chidley was the spitting image of the late Billy Cotton, the well-known dance band leader and racing driver. In this case the likeness was incredible, the same build, the same features, and the same immaculate appearance, even down to the thick-rimmed black glasses that were Cotton's frequently parodied trademark. Together, Albert and Billy would have passed anywhere as twins.

I was greeted affably enough by this imposing gentleman in his well-cut suit and his expensive looking grey trilby perched four-square on his balding head. I was soon to discover that the hat was an infallible guide to Albert's mood and temper; the further it was tilted to the back of the head, the more you kept out of his way if you were wise. Had I but known at the time, this was a good day. I introduced myself: "Good afternoon, Mr Chidley, I am an experienced car salesman looking for a job." Albert was not impressed. "You are far too young to be experienced, but never mind, I need a keen young man", and coming straight to the point, "you can start Monday, five pounds per week plus commission, and you can travel on the bus till I think you're worth a company car." I started Monday!

This was to prove an extremely fortunate employment. The year 1952 marked the beginning of a new era in the motor business, for the postwar tide was on the turn and within a few months the availability of most new cars was to almost equate with the demand. The previously quoted four to five years delivery on most new models was to change almost overnight to a matter of days, or at worst weeks. Fortunately for the manufacturers and their dealers, the continuing steady increase in demand would equate sufficiently with the rate of production to maintain the *status quo* over the next decade. However, the constant series of strikes throughout the industry contributed to this by creating sufficient shortages of product to maintain a demand that was never in truth quite what it seemed. Some manufacturers were by no means as firm with their employees as they should have been, taking the short-term view that production had to be kept going at all costs. In later years, when fresh and in many cases far superior product lines appeared from the Far East, the real cost of this head-in-the-sand attitude was to prove tragically high in terms of markets lost, in some cases forever.

But this was all for the future, and in the meantime I found myself working for a small family business with an impeccable reputation in the northern suburbs of London. The clients were down-to-earth and approachable, and by the end of my first day I had sold two used cars and was feeling very much at home in my new environment. The day-to-day running of the business, as stated, was in the hands of Albert's eldest son Cyril, who was a touch older than my 22 years. His younger brother Reg didn't seem to have a great deal of interest in the business, and all in all we didn't have a lot in common. Reg Chidley's main interest in life seemed to be the speed at which he could drive round the back streets and how long it took to get from point A to point B in a company car. Cyril, by contrast, was a super bloke, and good with the customers, of which the firm had a great many 'regulars'. Perhaps inevitably, he lived a little in the shadow of Albert, but on the whole the atmosphere was good and it was a pleasure to go to work each day. My predecessor, a Cecil Redfern, had only recently left to take up a management situation with Godfrey Davis, the huge North London Ford dealership, where in later years he was to become group chairman! Indeed, at time of writing he still was.

I had started at Robert Chidley Ltd just after the introduction of the Mk V Hillman Minx, when other cars in the Rootes range included the Humber Hawk, the soon to be replaced Super Snipe, together with the stretched limousine versions, and the highly sporting and very pretty Sunbeam-Talbot 80 and 90 models. Like all motor dealers at this time, Robert Chidley had a huge backlog of outstanding orders for the complete range of cars due to hopeful clients placing orders all over the place, particularly since the ever vigilant Motor Agents Association had advised dealers that cash deposits should no longer be taken against orders due to the protracted delivery situation. Albert had sensed that the time had come to evaluate the strength of these orders, so one of my first jobs was to go out three evenings a week with batches of outstanding orders to discover if the cars were still required. One advantage of this arrangement was that on those evenings I had the use of a company car once again, so I was able to meet my young lady at the bus stop on the way home to dinner and give her a lift home. After a hasty meal it would be off to the streets of Tottenham, Edmonton, Wood Green and Enfield, seeking out customer addresses and drinking endless cups of tea while hearing why a particular car placed on order for several months might not be required now that it could very soon be available. I met some interesting people and their reasons were certainly diverse; at least one hopeful prospective Rootes Group car owner had actually died waiting! There were just a few, however, who welcomed me with open arms when hearing that the vehicle they had waited so long for was at last in sight. This, of course, meant money in my pocket.

At the end of the day very few of these orders were to be converted into actual sales, which was hardly surprising as some had been outstanding for up to three years. But at least we knew how we stood and, thanks to Albert's perception, we were able to offer future customers sensible and accurate delivery forecasts long before our competitors. The more expensive Sunbeam-Talbots and Humbers were almost 'off the shelf' in no time at all, although the sales psychology was not to advertise this fact of life, and for a time all new cars in the showroom displayed a 'SOLD' label as a matter of course, regardless; it is astonishing how quickly human desire for something can diminish relative to availability. I remember one irate client who called in one morning to inquire about the Sunbeam-Talbot he had had on order for some two years. For some reason his order had been mislaid and as he had not been contacted to discover if the car was in fact still required, he was not aware of the true position. I managed to calm him down and suggested that he took a seat for a moment while I spoke to Mr Chidley to see what could be done. I had no need to consult anyone, for I guessed what had happened. We had a new and unallocated Sunbeam-Talbot 90 in the workshop, so, I thought to myself, this, Geoffrey, is where you earn yourself a few bob!

I returned to the showroom: "Well now, sir, I have spoken to Mr Chidley, but you do realize how difficult things are at the present time, and that we have to try and keep good faith with all of our clients." Pause for effect, and to see how we are doing. "That's all very well", said the client, "but I have had to wait two years, the price has gone up twice", and so on. When he had had his say and run himself down, I played my trump card. "Well, sir", I said brightly, "we have had a brand new Sunbeam-Talbot arrive this very morning and Mr Chidley has asked me to tell you that as your need is so great you can have it with pleasure." I beam encouragingly, but the client's face drops. "Ah, well now", bluster bluster, cough cough. I wait politely. "Well, what colour is it?", he asked at length. I told him. "Well now, I'll just have a word with the wife and let you know this afternoon." With that he almost ran out of the showroom, never to be seen again.

Robert Chidley Ltd stood on a corner of Tottenham High Road and a minor side road. The frontage was all showroom, with large windows and sliding doors on to the High Road. At the rear there were offices on one side with a parts counter on the other, leading to the stores area behind. Above were the accounts offices and that of Albert Chidley. Behind this block a small courtyard divided the showroom and parts area from the newly constructed L-shaped workshop. As the showroom was invariably for the display of new cars, there was not a great deal of room to store the used cars, apart from the courtyard. Therefore, up to the time that I joined, most of the used cars were sold in the trade, not a few of these to Albert's brother, Bob Chidley, who had premises in East Ham. Because I needed the money I was to change this policy to some extent.

It is astonishing to reflect today that each Saturday Robert Chidley Ltd would close their doors at 12.30pm and everybody would go home for the weekend. This was common to all motor dealers in London at that time, and I have no hesitation in claiming original thinking when, at my suggestion, I elected to remain open on Saturday afternoons. If space permitted, the occasional expensive or better-class used cars were given places in the showroom, while others could be displayed in the courtyard, and no-one seemed to mind if one or two were on display in the side road next to the showroom window. And it worked; it would be a poor do if I failed to sell at least one used car on a Saturday afternoon and I certainly sold a few new ones. It didn't take long for the idea to spread to some of the other dealers in the area, but we were most certainly the first. And I was still going home each day on the bus. These days there is nothing as common as a 'car salesman'; they like to be referred to as car sales executives (a grand title indeed) and as such they regard a company car as a divine right. I had to earn mine.

During the week there was not a great deal going on on the sales side. In any case it was never intended that I should handle all of the car sales as this was primarily Cyril's function in life. My situation was to pay my way by providing extra business. It was Albert, ahead of his time as always, who suggested that we should canvas the business houses on the very large industrial estates in the immediate area. I must say that this idea did nothing for me at all, but as the old man's hat was hovering around the 60-degree angle that morning I didn't care to argue the point. So off I went in Cyril's brand new Mk V Hillman Minx to make a few desultory calls with, it has to be said, not a great deal of enthusiasm. In those days I had a bit of a complex and was a little on the shy side. People who know me now find this hard to understand, but from the outset I had to work very hard to overcome this feeling. Customers coming to me on my own ground was one thing, but meeting people uninvited on theirs was something quite different. I was to spend the next six years of my life selling cars and vans in this manner, with demonstrable success, yet almost to the end I had to make a conscious effort every day to make that first call, after which I would be perfectly OK.

To my astonishment, on the whole I was well-received, although in retrospect this was not really surprising. Company directors and senior managers had become acclimatized to grovelling for the privilege of buying a new car, and all of a sudden here was a young man trying to sell them one. While I was perhaps unable to supply the precise model they were interested in, at least they were prepared to invite me in for a chat. In this manner I was to make several contacts that were to prove invaluable in later years, though I do not recall any instant orders. At any event Albert Chidley was delighted with my verbal reports, and when I offered to provide written ones his gruff reply was typical of the man. "Written reports can be completed in the transport cafe. All I want from you is results. In any case I'll know soon enough if you're doing your job or not."

As I became more interested in what I was doing and found that I could still earn my corn on Saturday afternoons and the late weekday afternoons when I returned from my rounds, I decided to get organized. Accordingly I adopted a simple policy that henceforth I was to use to good effect. I divided the area into sections, into which I listed the name and address of every firm visited, large and small, together with my contact's name and a few relevant notes. By this method I was able to arrange my calls in a systematic manner so that I visited on a regular basis without outstaying my welcome. My diary told me if a particular firm required a visit or I had to call out of sequence for some other reason. I had noted at an early stage in my career that most people have an interest of one sort or another on which they like to talk. I would make it my business to discover these interests and record them so that they be casually raised in the future.

I didn't go out specifically to sell cars. This is where a great many, so-called salesmen in the outside selling field go wrong. It is unrealistic to expect there to be a market for your product that very day. My aim was to make absolutely sure that when the question of a replacement car arose, the first person who came to mind was that nice young man from Chidley's. The rest would be up to me. Certainly it was long-term, but it worked.

It was not to be long before I became acquainted with Sod's or Murphy's Law: no matter how methodical, no matter how careful, no matter how many calls you make, you miss any one of them at your peril. Of all the many firms, both large and small, comprising the extensive trading estates around the Tottenham and Edmonton area, I was to miss just one. Tucked away at the back of one of these estates was a small engineering firm who were to buy a brand new Humber Super Snipe, one of the most expensive cars in the range, from a competitor in Chingford, less than 10 miles away. Worse, it was Albert who somehow found out and was to tell me the dreadful news! At first I refused to accept that I had missed anyone and frantically searched my book for a name that, deep down, I knew I was not going to find. Fortunately, Albert was too observant a man to believe that I had been skiving and that my book contained nothing but a worthless list of company names. Much later I was to find out that he was very well-known in that close commercial community and he had received plenty of evidence from his many friends and acquaintances that I had been out grafting. Nonetheless he gave me the works, trilby practically falling off the back of his head, and rightly so. I never missed another!

What with spending most of my weekdays canvassing and working every Saturday, I didn't have great deal of free time. However, all work and no play makes Jack a very dull boy indeed, and I had time at weekends to enjoy myself. In this business, though, even at play you develop an eye for a good contact. John Burden, for instance, who still gave me free tickets for concerts from time to time, not only provided many introductions to the orchestra members who purchased cars, but he was fond of changing his own cars on frequent occasions and became one of my best clients over the years. Albert Chidley had at last decreed that I had earned a company car, provided a log was kept of the mileage, for I was expected to pay for my own private petrol. For the benefit of present day sales executives, my long-awaited car was a seven-year-old Morris Eight Series E, which I was to wash and polish till it shone. Anything that is earned is cherished! Every Saturday would find me dressed in a smart suit, car polished like new, *en route* to the Hornsey Town Hall, which provided the best evening's ballroom dancing for miles around in those days. The magnificent ballroom, right behind the imposing entrance, was superb. It boasted a unique sprung maplewood floor, a huge stage, a balcony with a bar for relaxing or a quick cuddle between dances, and yet another large bar and lounge on the floor below for more formal drinking. The Town Hall had its own resident semi-pro big band, the Stan Davies Orchestra, and the dancing, of course, was all strict tempo. There must be many of my contemporaries who would agree wholeheartedly that those indeed were the days.

I was 22 years of age and a car owner at a time when it was doubtful if more than two or three of the bevy of eligible batchelors in that hall hadn't arrived on foot or by public transport. This provided a distinct advantage when selecting a young lady, perhaps for a Sunday date. Not for me the cautious "Live local, do you?", simply to find out if it was safe to offer to escort the lady home without running the risk of an impossible return journey on foot from God knows where. The invitation of an escort home, followed by a casual "It's no problem, I have a car", would guarantee to pull the best-looking bird in the house, no danger. No matter that the car might prove to be some old banger that required the lady's assistance with a push-start – and this happened more than once – the lady could go to work on Monday and legitimately let it drop casually that she had met a bloke on Saturday who had, "taken me home in his car".

This happy situation was to last for 12 months or so until I got married. Then we still used the Town Hall on Saturdays, but made more use of the formal basement bar, where my parents would often drink with Stan Davies and his manager Les Wingrove during the interval. Through them we joined a sports club called the *BRILEG*, which had the dual advantage of coming to life after the Town Hall closed for the night and providing me with some useful business contacts. *BRILEG* was a corruption of the two words British Legion, and as such it was a Legion club. Not only was it a *bona fide* cricket club with a very respectable team, it also boasted a substantial clubhouse containing a large bar and a snooker room with two full-size tables. On Saturdays and some Sunday nights, after the pubs were shut, it was to pre-empt the modern disco. Two of the members, both very close friends, were gramophone crazy and used the club to house their huge collection of 78rpm records together with an expensive electric turntable and amplifier. As the club was located on top of an old tip in an obscure corner of the Hornsey playing fields, with its own private drive at least 200 yards from a back road and the nearest house, licensing hours were not thought to be a consideration, and many an impromptu party was held until the small hours. On Sunday mornings, not having to work, I would help my father and the rest of the committee to clear up in the lounge, following which, in the summer, while the cricket team would begin the day's play, my father would enjoy a game of snooker. I would drive off to collect my wife, my mother and a picnic lunch, after which and a pint or three the old man and I would select deckchairs and sleep off the effects of the previous night's excesses while the cricket progressed.

One Sunday morning we had rather more to clear up than usual: Paddy Gallagher, one of our Irish members and a drinker of some repute, was a traveller, literally, in ladies' undies. Only a few weeks earlier I had sold him a white Ford van in which to transport his goods. The club, as I have said, was built on an old tip, and the car park was somewhat restricted. During the small hours of Sunday, Paddy had attempted a three-point turn, which he found difficult enough in broad daylight when sober. With an almighty crash the van had rolled down the tip, its rear doors flying open under the strain, and come to rest on its four wheels some 30ft below. The noise attracted the few of us who were still at the bar having our 'one for the road', so we went out into the night air to find Paddy clawing his way up the slope in a somewhat unsteady fashion. He was assisted to the bar, where suitable medication was produced, and he was found to be in perfectly sound condition although quite unaware of what had occurred. Someone took him home, and the next day father and I arrived with others to find the trees and shrubs liberally scattered with assorted knickers and bras, etc, and a rather forlorn looking Ford van at the foot of the slope. I went in search of the local tractor and driver while the committee started to collect the assorted undies. The tractor was not hard to find, but locating the driver involved visits to various club bars, where the story was told and retold to the accompaniment of several halves of best bitter. Eventually I found him in the Calthorpe Club and between us we managed to tow the van through the undergrowth to the lower track where I was able to start it without difficulty and drive it back to the club, dented and scratched, but generally sound and still roadworthy. Later that morning a dejected Irishman paid out for several rounds of drinks and was the butt of many an unkind joke for some weeks to come.

All good things, it is oft said, come to an end, and at any rate this situation was too good to last. It had been noted in the local rag that a new chief constable had been appointed for the area and that two of the cricket and tennis clubs on the playing fields had been raided. The committee felt that prudence was the order of the day, so it was arranged that the bar would close dead on time until further notice. All went well until the local police team arrived for the annual darts match several weeks later. Come closing time, when the bell was rung the fuzz made it perfectly clear that the night was still young and that policemen are as thirsty as the rest. The bar remained open. Once the rules were relaxed it would have taken a committee of saints to revert to normal hours, and in any case the initial scare had worn off. In no time at all the Saturday dances were back in full swing and the bar closed when everyone had gone home. Within weeks we were raided!

I have kept to this very day the *Hornsey Journal* of September 10, 1954, which related the bare facts as heard in court. The truth, however, was not quite as prosaic. The paper reported:

DRINKING AFTER HOURS AT SPORTS CLUB
MEMBERS TO SUFFER VOLUNTARY PENANCE, COURT TOLD

"Stanley Nelson Owen, of Park Avenue North, Hornsey, summoned for supplying drinks after hours on July 31 and before noon on August 1, was fined a total of £3 with two guineas costs.

"Les Wingrove and others on the committee were fined like sums for other dates in July and August and Stanley Bert Davies (our worthy band leader) as secretary was summoned to show why the club should not be struck off the register."

None of the dates related to the night of the police darts match, of course, but they showed that the police had been keeping watch for a week or so. Mr N Weston, the police prosecutor, was generous enough to make it clear to the court that "although there were a number of summonses before the magistrates, he could not put it before them as a bad case, although it was one which was properly brought."

He went on to state that: "On the night of July 31/August 1 it was a matter of midnight having been passed and another day entered upon. Drinks were on occasions supplied up to 12.17am. The club was entered 10 minutes later by Inspector Davies and 'other police'. There were seven people in the club, among them Owen, Addy and Burnett. These being committee members."

Two of those seven people were my mother and myself. This is what really happened on the fateful night:

By our standards it was a quiet evening, and as stated there were only seven in the club. Why it was quiet I don't know, but I do know that one of the others involved was one Duggie Figg, a likeable friend of my father's and a compulsive gambler. Like most of his kind, when Duggie lost, he lost a packet. Likewise, if he won, he won a bomb. That night, at Harringay dogs, Duggie had taken the bookies to the cleaners, so this was clearly a night for celebration. While having a jar and a few laughs there was an almighty crash as the front door was smashed in; as it happened, I know for a fact that it was unlocked. However, in came the worthy Inspector, and behind him, looking a bit sheepish, one of the darts team. Duggie, having consumed a fair amount of drink by this time, completely failed to weigh up the situation. Taking the poor bobby by the arm, he said: "This is a bloody fine time to come up for a drink, what are you going to have?" The copper had the good grace to blush. Behind came the 'other police', including a policewoman. She, doubtless seeking vital evidence, went to my mother and asked her what she was drinking? Now my mother on occasions could be deliciously naive, I suspect deliberately. "How very kind", she replied, "I'll have a Guinness". This not being at all well received, names and addresses were taken and cautions duly given. But it was a fair, albeit unreasonable cop. I am certainly not anti-police and simply record events as they happened. Anyone who has contact with the police off-duty will know all too well that they are as fallible as the rest of us.

Despite all these late drinking excursions I was never once late or absent from work, and I never let my private life interfere with my business. If I had a morning's canvassing and it was particularly hot I might take my sandwiches to a quiet spot on the marshes and maybe doze for an hour, but I would make no secret of this and would expect my employer to appreciate that I was always ready to graft in the evenings if need be, so what the hell. In any case I was not out calling every day of the week as there were often other things to do. For example, at that time, if we so wished, we were still able to collect our new Hillman cars from the factory at Ryton-on-Dunsmore, something that the trades union would never allow today. Many times Reg and I would be trundling down the A5 at a steady 35mph only to be passed by some mindless delivery driver pushing a brand new vehicle at 50-plus, this at a time when careful running-in was a vital part of a new car's life. We would always collect our own Humbers and Sunbeams to prevent such abuse, but these came from storage at Barlby Road, near Wormwood Scrubs in West London, to where they would have been delivered by transporter.

There were other interesting jobs that came up from time to time, like the day that Albert won the tender for the Mayor of Tottenham's new Humber Pullman Limousine and took their seven-year-old Humber in part-exchange. Now, I thought to myself, what the hell are we going to do with that? After all it was a mite specialized, with real leather, a fixed bench front seat, a glass division and West of England cloth rear seats together with the occasional centre folding seats. Albert, of course, had the answer, and as usual it was to involve me. "Weddings and funerals", he said. "Take it to all the hire firms, you are bound to sell it." Well, I certainly tried; I took it to every private hire firm I could find, but none were interested. At length Albert heard from a friend in Southend that someone down there would at least like to see the car in view of its history. So, one Friday morning I headed down the Southend arterial road, in those days the nearest thing we had to a motorway, with dual carriageways east and west, plus a cycle track and nothing as tiresome as a speed limit. I wonder, I thought, what will she do? It had 4.1 litres no less and a speedometer that would read up to an optimistic 100mph. I was doing perhaps 60 or 70 when the engine developed a strange noise. I stopped, opened the hood and had a look at the works. There was nothing untoward to be seen, but there was undoubtedly an ominous metallic clank, clank, clank, in synch with the engine tickover. I decided to return to base at a reduced speed. By the time I got to Walthamstow the engine was unquestionably poorly. A telephone call brought out Reg with the firm's Commer van and a towrope, and thence back to Tottenham, where Stan Goodsman, our service manager, and Albert were waiting. The car was pushed into the workshop for an examination.

I hadn't a care in the world, and when the red buzzer on the intercom signalled that Albert was on the other end and wished to communicate I was not in the least put out. "Come up, old son, will you?", the voice said. On entering his private office I must have noted that the hat was at an ominous angle, that is if I had time, for without preamble Albert told me that I had seized-up his bloody low-mileage Humber, that's bloody what. I was both incredulous and stupid all at the same time. "That's not possible, I was only doing 60." For a moment I thought he was going to have a heart attack. "*Sixty!*", he said, "*Bloody 60* – that car has never seen more than 30 in it's whole life! And that touring the streets of Tottenham." A modern engine would have survived treatment of this kind without harm, but this basically prewar-design side-valve unit had been used to better drivers and it rebelled. It had blown a bearing.

I had a very long weekend to review my transgressions as Monday was a Bank Holiday, and it was with a heavy heart that I returned to work on Tuesday. However, Albert kept out of my way, I certainly kept out of his, and nothing more was said. In due course the engine was repaired and the car returned to the showroom where I was able to redeem myself by selling it to a local family butcher not more than half a mile away. The father had a gammy leg and liked to be driven by his sons with his feet up on the occasional seats!

Another of Albert Chidley's part-exchange deals was to cause me a problem of a different nature. He had sold a fleet of Commer vans to an old-established bakery. Part of the deal was that we were to take in three Harbuilt electric delivery vans. These were in common use before and after the war in the milk and bread industry in towns where the rounds were confined to small areas. They were not so much a van as a large trolley, and the roundsman would walk in front controlling the vehicle with a long lever, rather like one on a vacuum cleaner, on which there were two controls – an on/off switch for the electric motor and a handle for the brake. They were about half the size of the horse-drawn milk float. Cyril and I fell about laughing when we found them in the courtyard one morning, so the old man quietly sold them to an engineering firm at Edmonton, who saw their value for the internal movement of goods and small machinery. As we had found it so funny Albert decreed that to save expense the batteries were to be charged and we could walk them up the Tottenham High Road to Edmonton. As they were unlicensed we had to deliver them on our licensed trade number-plates. With just the one set we could only deliver one vehicle at a time, and I drew the short straw for the first go.

That very day I was wearing my newest business suit in which, I must say, I was feeling a bit sharp. Both Cyril and I being very snappy dressers, a new 'whistle' was always something of an event. While admiring my reflection in one of the showroom mirrors I had a call from Stan in the workshop to tell me that my carriage was ready to roll. Fortunately it was a fine day. The vehicle had been placed in the side road, so I switched on, released the brake and away we went up the High Road. I had a distinct impression that everyone was watching me, which was really not so because there were plenty of these vans in daily use at the time and in reality I don't suppose I warranted a second glance. Nonetheless I felt a bit conspicuous trying to match my pace to the contraption behind. The first thing I had to learn was that there were two speeds only, and one of those was stop. It was fundamental on a warm day to appreciate that a thing of that weight could not be forced. But I tend to walk fast, so by the time I got to the traffic lights at White Hart Lane I was sweating. Waiting for the green light I had a welcome rest. When the lights changed I decided to relax and to let the thing push me, this being exactly what I should have done in the first place. I was just beginning to feel that I had got the hang of it when I was distracted by a lady shouting at the top of her voice: "Baker, baker, your number-plate has fallen off!" With as much dignity as I could muster I thanked her and retrieved my rear trade-plate just as one of my better clients drove past with a toot toot, and a huge grin on his face

The greater part of our part-exchanges were run-of-the-mill cars, identifiable in *Glass's Guide*, the bible of the motor trade. These we were able to sell without difficulty, whereas the scruffy and the 'odd ball' we traded out. Of the latter, one which particularly sticks in my mind, for I could have bought it for nothing at the time, was a 1933 Alvis Crested Eagle in very presentable condition, which I had accepted in part-exchange for a new Sunbeam-Talbot 90. We had the greatest difficulty in moving it on – oh that I had that priceless automobile today!

Another part-exchange I have cause to remember was a very pretty little Sunbeam-Talbot 80 saloon. A charming elderly couple had spotted it while out shopping and there was no doubt that they had fallen for this attractive green metallic sports saloon with its sunroof and rakish good looks. The only problem was that the gentleman was not at all sure that it would fit his garage. It was a simple matter to arrange a demonstration run during which I could give them a lift home and try the car in their garage for size. I was very confident, for the Sunbeam was only a small car anyway. On arrival at their home, by which time it was obvious that to all intents the car was already theirs, the question of the garage became all too apparent. It was not that the garage was small, indeed it was reasonably large, if a bit narrow. The problem was that it had been built far too close to the rear of the house, and offset, as it was wider than the driveway.

In our business you become accustomed to manoeuvring cars in very confined showroom spaces, so it was not too much of a problem to back the Sunbeam down the short driveway and into the garage, though I had to take two bites and climb out through the passenger door as the driver's was tight to the wall. The client was visibly relieved. "I reckon that I could do that with practice," he said, "perhaps you would be good enough to show me how to drive it out." That proved to be the problem. Try as I might I simply could not extricate it. On the one side were the house drains and on the other the fence posts, which made it quite impossible without the aid of a trolley jack. Eventually I got out of the car, the gentleman's wife having made tea and been watching the proceedings through the kitchen window. We lit cigarettes while I unwound and relaxed as we surveyed the car tucked neatly in the garage. His wife broke the silence: "Well now you'll just have to buy it, darling, so you had better give Mr Owen a cheque."

Another very early lesson was to come out of Chidley's in a particularly odd manner, for it was well ahead of its time. We only retailed the best of the used cars, which would be given a thorough service by Stan Goodsman's mechanics, followed by a wash. If we had time between other jobs we would clean the windows and perhaps give the paintwork a quick polish. This was about the norm throughout the trade at the time. As we were now selling more and more cars, both new and used, Cyril had advertised for an odd job man to clean cars and perhaps act as a driver as needed. The man we took on was called Bill. He looked exactly like a chauffeur as it happened in his white shirt and thin black tie, but he didn't have a great deal to say for himself, though he seemed a nice enough bloke.

On his first day he was handed the firm's leather, which looked like an oily rag, a grubby sponge and a black Austin 16hp saloon. A little later I noted that he had started to wash off the Austin with what seemed to be a brand new leather. "Where did that come from, Bill?", I asked. "You gave it to me, so I washed it", was the answer. "How?" "Cold water", he said and carried on with his work. Oh well, that's me put in my place, I thought, and wandered off to the showroom office. Some time later I went out to see how he was doing. At first sight he didn't seem to have done very much, yet somehow the car seemed to be in better condition than when I had last seen it. Then it struck me: the front of the Austin 16 had a rounded chrome grille made up of countless thin horizontal bars, close-meshed, with a chrome strip running down the centre from the chrome winged Austin badge on the front of the bonnet. Somehow the car had acquired a new radiator grille and Austin badge in the past two hours, which was not possible, and the visual improvement was quite astonishing. "Bloody hell, Bill, how on earth did you manage that?", I asked incredulously. "Just wire wool and a bit of chrome cleaner. Look, I'm just cleaning up the chrome window surrounds, I'll show you." And show me he did; there he was polishing away at this tarnished chrome and it was coming up like it was brand new.

Cyril being out for the day, I had to leave him to it as I had enough to occupy my mind, so I more or less forgot about our William until much later when he put his head round the door to wish me goodnight. "Hang on a tick, Bill", I said, "let's have a butcher's at the old Austin before you go." With that I got up from my desk and we made our way out to the yard. As we rounded the corner we passed Stan Goodsman on his way home after locking up the workshop. "Didn't know we were selling new Austins", he said with a grin as he got into his car. When we got to the Austin I saw what he meant: the car had been completely and utterly transformed. The black cellulose gleamed, the chrome was like new, but there was more, much more, Bill had polished inside the door shuts, the leather upholstery had been cleaned and even the Bakelite dashboard and interior window surrounds were polished and fresh-looking. Stan hadn't been so wide of the mark. Nowadays, of course, this would be just another five-year-old used car, perhaps rather better prepared than most by a trained car cleaner, but in 1953 it was a revelation. Only the Swain Group came close to these standards with their expensive Rolls-Royces and Bentleys, but even they were not in this class.

By chance we had a bit of space in the showroom that week so I gave the Austin a good position and increased the price sufficiently to cover Bill's wages for at least a month. The car was sold and delivered by the weekend! By the Sixties detailed car cleaning had become the accepted practice throughout the trade to one degree or another. The Ford Motor Company, for example, promoted cleaning and preparation as part of their A1 used car warranty scheme and employed teams of professionals to visit their dealers to provide training. They even marketed a range of Ford A1 cleaning and preparation materials exclusive to Ford dealers. Bill was considerably ahead of his time, but far too intelligent for that job and all too soon he left us to become manager of a local TV and radio shop. Nonetheless I saw to it that the standard was maintained, for our used cars continued to sell well, and profitably.

An unexpected result of this methodical cleaning, however, was Albert's reaction. I have since found that motor dealers on the whole are a conservative lot who tend not to take kindly to anything that may be considered unique or out of the ordinary – unless, of course, it is an idea or a promotion put forward by the car manufacturers, in which case they will swallow it hook, line and sinker, right or wrong, good or bad. One morning Cyril greeted me with a long face: "The old man's been on the warpath over the time spent cleaning cars." I was completely taken aback; we had been doing very nicely indeed with used-car business, particularly on Saturdays, so much so that Cyril had been in touch with Cecil Redfern at Godfrey Davis, where he had arranged to buy the best of his ex-fleet cars for resale. These were supplementing my income, which I needed as I was saving up to get married. This could be serious. "Would you mind if I had a word?", I asked. "Please yourself", he said, "but I don't think it will do any good". Two of my weekend sales had been confirmed that morning with the result that I had a fair bit of cash to be checked and paid in. Instead of giving it to Cyril I waited until he went out for a time and then buzzed the old man.

"Come up then, old son", was the cheery reply when I told him that I had handfuls of fivers to dispose of. These were the old postwar white fivers, about 7 by 4 inches and, depending on when printed, of widely differing thickness from flimsy up to the standard of good-quality notepaper. In consequence it could take as many as three recounts and a good deal of heavy breathing to agree a sum of perhaps £500 to £600. At last we got it sorted. Now, as I had surmised, with all businessmen the banking of a stack of readies generates a fair bit of goodwill. Albert signed my receipt book with a flourish, then with a smile and a "there you go, old son", handed it back. The trilby, I noted, was four-square on his head like a Grenadier Guardsman's cheese-cutter. There was never to be a better moment: "I would like", I ventured, "to have a word in regard to car cleaning." There was an instant reaction. "Well, it's taking too bloody long, that's for sure. Daft in my view to take hours cleaning up one bit of chrome." There was a lot more in like vein, ending with: "Half the motor dealers round here think that I've gone potty." So that's what it's all about, I thought. I knew, of course, that on most evenings the local motor traders met for a jar or two in one of the pubs up the High Road for I had seen Albert's and other distinctive cars lined up outside. Not a few of these had bought Albert's trade-ins in the past, which doubtless they had turned to profit. Now that we were retailing used cars on our own account, this would not be appreciated, the clear inference being that the exercise was not cost-effective.

Cyril and I knew differently and I was concerned that the situation should continue for the used cars sold for good money and generated the extra profit on which my commission was based. I therefore put our case in a concise and forceful manner, quoting examples, including the deals represented by the stack of fivers on his desk. When at last I realized that if I was not careful I would go too far, I abruptly shut up. The old man, who had listened without a word throughout, leaned back in his chair. "Right ho, old son, we'll give it a go then." And that was that, nothing more ever being said on the matter. But Albert was that kind of a person; given a sensible argument he would listen with care. If you failed to establish your case, the trilby would eventually be pushed back an inch or so, and when he could get a word in, were you so foolish as not to recognize the signs, he would simply say: "Well, old son, we shall have to disagree on that one." That would be the end of the matter. Like my father, however, he would not accept it from his own son!

New-car deliveries had by now improved a lot, and most were available on demand providing you were prepared to accept the colour and the spec of the model on the showroom floor or in the firm's compound. The exceptions were the brand new models, where availability would take perhaps a year to settle down, depending on export popularity. The country was still in dire need of overseas trade, discounts were unheard-of, apart from *bona fide* fleet operators, for whom there was a fixed percentage scale depending on the number of vehicles operated. Even these required a certificate from the Motor Agents Association. All motor dealers were required to sell their cars at the maker's list price – no more, no less. Any dealer who sold a new car other than at 'list' risked loss of franchise. Indeed, so tight were the rules that in those days of 'pounds, shillings and pence' we were not even allowed to round up or down to the nearest pound when we priced a new car on display! The prospective client might obtain fractionally more for his car in part-exchange for another make, or from another dealer, but the difference would be so small it would not really be worth the effort of touting around.

One very early sign of growth and change in the early-Fifties were the 'bomb-site' used car dealers, who were springing up all over London in places where the facilities had thoughtfully been provided by Adolf Hitler & Co during the blitz. The rubble having now been cleared, these sites were ideal for the display of used cars, requiring little more than an iron gate set into a wire fence for security, a prefab garage for minor repairs and cleaning, and a wooden office for the convenience of the punters. Many, indeed, still exist to this day, like your 'Arthur Daley' of TV fame. In the years following the war they were a completely new innovation, to be followed as time went on by slightly more upmarket dealers in converted double-fronted shops. One highly respected department store in Hornsey was later to find it profitable to close down its furniture department and convert it to a car showroom, eventually going over entirely to cars and obtaining an Austin franchise. One bomb site dealer was to open in Wood Green on the corner of Westbury Avenue and Lordship Lane. It was called after its owner, Horner's Car Sales, and for us it was a handy place to get rid of our 'bangers'. Mr Horner was only interested in the very cheap cars; he was a likeable rogue, well representative of the question: "Would you buy a used car from this man?", but many did, and he was around for many years.

Another industry just starting to grow at that time was the purpose-built specialist car auction. There was nothing new about car auctions as such, for these had been about for some time, but they had been held on auctioneers' premises in conjunction with other items such as furniture or even livestock. Without any shadow of doubt, the 'Henry Ford' of the motor auction business has to be David Wickins of the British Car Auctions Group. David, on demobilization from the Royal Navy after the war, advertised his Riley Lynx, not realizing its true potential value. On returning to his mother's home he found some 40 people on the lawn fighting over the car, so he held an impromptu auction on the spot and sold the car for £220 more than the advertised price. David Wickins, together with his brothers, then rented a field for a pound a week and set up a marquee where they held their first full-scale auction, selling 14 vehicles for a turnover of £8,250. I recently attended an auction of low-mileage used cars from the Ford Motor Company where £8,250 would have just about represented the average price realized per entry! For a graphic indication of the explosion of the car and commercial vehicle industry over just three and a half decades from 1946, when that original sale took place, it is recorded that during 1981 over 500,000 used vehicles passed through the 13 British Car Auctions centres in the UK, while the Group *nett profit* was £2,914,000! Whatever problems this extraordinary growth may have left in its wake for the new and used-car retailers, it most certainly didn't do David Wickins a great deal of harm!

The first motor car auction I ever attended with Cyril Chidley was at Measham, subsequently purchased by BCA, but at that time owned and run by a character named Charles Hill. The reason for our going was that we had somehow acquired in part-exchange a couple of 'lemons' in the guise of a tired Sunbeam-Talbot 80 and a clapped-out Morris Six that, given elbow grease and a rub-down with T-cut, would hold its maroon colour for a day or so then revert to a sort of dirty grey. Even Mr Horner couldn't get excited with these two, so off to the auction they went. Measham, being fairly close to Ashby de la Zouch, is not a million miles from Tottenham, but nonetheless, as we didn't know the ropes Cyril elected to drive up on the day prior to the sale, get the cars booked-in and stay the night. I had no argument with that idea whatsoever, and in due course we arrived in the late afternoon at a very large building like an aircraft hanger, surrounded by a great deal of space and more used cars available for sale than I had ever seen on one pitch. Inside we met Charles Hill, full of boom and personality, and we were assured that the cars were "as good as sold, old boy, just leave it all to us. Oh, and by the way, cash for the entry fee if you don't mind."

We had booked in at the local inn where, we were assured, the beds were clean and the food good. Having got rid of the cars we decided to have a look around, not that there was a great deal to see. A drive through for the cars, an auctioneer's rostrum with a microphone, each side of the mike prominent red and blue lights and, opposite, tiers of seats from end to end of the building. We noted rows of powerful spotlights above but the red and blue lights puzzled us a bit. No matter, we thought, all would be revealed on the morrow.

The meal must have been OK, but after we fell among some hard-drinking motor dealers from up North, the next day I was feeling decidedly fragile. One of the first people we ran into was Cecil Redfern, a regular visitor it seemed, who was selling off some of his self-drive hire cars, most of which had completed a high mileage. All, however, had one thing in common: like all Godfrey Davis fleet cars they were registered in the name of Leslie George Selway, of Eccleston Street, London SW1. Every ex-hire car sold to the trade one day would almost without fail be on sale somewhere else the next day as 'one careful owner from new'. These days, of course, consumer protection regulations outlaw this practice, so all such cars are eventually sold as registered in the company's name, which may or may not be that of a self-drive hire business. Redfern knew the form, and from our allotted lot numbers he was able to give us a good idea of what time our cars were likely to go through the saleroom, and as this was later in the afternoon we decided to study form. Once again we entered the huge saleroom, this time transformed by people and atmosphere, but surprisingly, perhaps, not a great deal of noise. The crowd were mostly motor dealers, instantly recognizable clutching well-worn copies of *Glass's Guide*. There were almost no private punters in those days, members of the general public in evidence being simply curious bystanders.

As we entered, a car was just being driven out from under the battery of spotlights; we found a couple of spare seats, made ourselves comfortable and took it all in. Behind the rostrum Charles Hill, gavel in hand, was ready for the next car just being driven in, which stopped under the lights. The driver alighted carrying a selection of labels and, incongruously, a pot of glue. She left the door open so that the assembled punters could 'view the goods', which had already been the subject of close examination in the car park; you certainly don't buy a car at auction on spec!

The procedure, which I will now describe, follows a consistent pattern which was adopted for all the British Car Auctions sites throughout the country. But most motor dealers will instantly recognize the unique style of 'Major – as seen on TV – Pip Bircher', who had provided endless entertainment in the course of his profession at Measham on behalf of the BCA Group, and would have made a worthwhile subject for *This Is Your Life*.

The auctioneer first reads a description of the car from the entry form, listing any faults or other non-visual items which might be recorded. Nowadays he will also state if the mileage is 'warranted genuine', but will seldom state that it is not. You need sharp eyes, ears and quick wits at a car auction. Neither vendor nor auctioneer accept any responsibility for visual faults. Almost before you realize it, battle has commenced, during which time the auctioneer will not only accept bids, or alternatively conjure them up out of thin air, but manage without apparent effort to keep up a continuous banter in respect of the car's desirability for certain mysterious regular clients who would always be referred to as 'Mr F' or 'Mr C', or whatever. Even on occasions when the car, which to the uninitiated gleams so enticingly under the lights, attracts virtually no interest at all, the casual observer would never realize this from the bids which seem to come from all directions, keeping up the furious pace and the illusion of perpetual interest, even though a sale may not actually be achieved, in which case it will be announced that the car has been 'provisionally sold'. This usually means that the highest bid is close enough to the reserve price for the owner to be contacted for further discussion.

Scenario - Enter Ford Consul left: Everybody there 'in the know' is able to place the car as an ex- Godfrey Davis hire car from the registration number; it is one of batch of consecutive numbers issued by the London County Council and there are at least 20 Ford and Morris cars outside with similar registration numbers.

"Now look at this, gentlemen, lovely little Consul, with heater, one owner from new". At this point there is an audible titter from the crowd. Pause, while the auctioneer surveys the assembled audience with a look of self-righteous indignation. "I know what you're thinking, but I am telling you, you're all wrong," Further pause for effect. "Is the owner about, could we have the Colonel to the rostrum please?"

After this little pantomime serious bidding would commence, for there would be no shortage of willing buyers for these very well-maintained cars, regardless of mileage or antecedents.

"One hundred pounds, thank you gentlemen, one hundred and ten, twenty at the back, can I have thirty, thirty bid", and so on with bewildering speed up to something like the car's true value of, perhaps, two hundred pounds, when bidding would slow down to increases of five pounds. "Right, gentlemen, now this is what you want, nice clean cars for the weekend, I'll take two hundred and five, two hundred and five anyone? Two hundred and five, thank you, Mr C, I thought you had nodded off." Then on would come the blue light: "Right now, on sale and with you"; translated this meant that reserve price had now been reached. From this moment things would move very quickly indeed, perhaps two or three more bids, then: "Two hundred and twenty, have you all done?" Down comes hammer with a crash, on goes the red light. "Sold to Mr D, next entry please. The driver selects the appropriate 'SOLD' label, slaps on some glue, pastes it to the inside of the windscreen, and drives off to the car park.

At that time, all of this drama, inclusive of banter, would be achieved in an average of 2 to 3 minutes unless there was something special being sold or television were visiting, which was by no means unusual, both channels having made short documentaries at one time or another. On these occasions the Major would be at his best. At one Measham sale he was due to auction a prewar Morris Cowley car that was reputed to have been owned by the late Lord Nuffield. The stately old car was driven in through bigger crowds than usual, the cameras were rolling, and the Major cast his eyes slowly over the multitude. "Look at the silly so and so's", he said with mock contempt to no-one in particular. "Not a *Glass's Guide* in sight!"

This, then, was the general scene in 1954, with subtle variations, as the cars went through the sale to be sold or withdrawn as the afternoon wore on, and at length our little Sunbeam appeared. As recommended, Cyril and I went to stand out of sight at the back of the rostrum below Charles Hill so that he could communicate with us if need be. The last car had been one of Redfern's, and as he had a huge grin on his face we surmized that his car had reached its reserve price. "Good luck, Cyril", he said as we passed by. Charles Hill read out the description of the car from the entry we had completed. Redfern had advised us that it was pointless not to declare faults; "the car will only be rejected subsequently by the buyer and you won't have a leg to stand on." Even small faults were listed by those regular vendors who knew all too well that buyers sometimes get carried away and regret a purchase on a second, more detailed examination. If they are able to find a single justifiable undeclared fault at the end of the sale they can reject the car and the sale will be lost. In any event the declaration of a minor fault would not affect the realizable value in any significant way.

As it happened the car, while well used, had very few faults which were not all too apparent and these, of course, had been declared. At first we both wondered if this really was our car, so glowing did the description sound. The few faults were smartly dismissed with a contemptuous sneer, but nonetheless recorded, then the bidding started, depressingly low, but fresh bids seemed to be following at a steady pace. We noted, however, that below the rostrum, out of sight of the masses, the Hill hand was moving rapidly from left to right in what clearly was a negative gesture. Suddenly it stopped. "Two ten, Mr C?", said Mr Hill incredulously, "Two ten?", your watch must have stopped, mine says it's four fifteen!" As the laughter died away a further two pounds ten shillings was added from somewhere, but nothing else seemed to be forthcoming. We were perhaps £50 off our reserve price, so what with Mr Hill's commission and the entry fee this would mean us losing some £65, which in 1954 was a great deal of money. He pressed the switch to cut the mike and leaned towards us. "Let me put it on sale, it will make all the difference." There was no time to think. "OK, put it on sale and do your best." On goes the blue light: "Right now, gentlemen, he's not at all pleased with that, but we are going to have a go." Another fifty bob anywhere? An ominous silence. "Are you all done then, for the first, second and third time." Crash – down came the hammer. We had, it would seem, 'done our money'. The Morris Six arrived shortly after and no genuine bids being offered it went straight out, 'sold provisionally'. But at least we had a lift home. An interesting exercise, but a financial disaster.

Another of our less salubrious used cars I had cause to remember was an old prewar Riley with a fabric body. This had been the proud property from new of a fishmonger somewhere down the lower end of the Kingsland High Road. Cyril had sold the gentleman a new Hillman Minx and had accepted this little gem in part-exchange. As Cyril had another car to collect in the area I was to drive him down in the Hillman to effect delivery on his behalf and return in the Riley. On arrival it became clear that I had been quietly conned. The Riley was a heap. In insurance parlance there was absolutely no doubt whatsoever that this car had been 'used in connection with the owner's business or profession'. It reeked of fish! A great deal of work with the starting handle was required to coax the engine into life, after which it generated clouds of blue smoke. The steering left a very great deal to be desired, while the brakes would eventually stop the car, given time. Of course it was raining, for the sunroof would not stay shut, this having no connection whatsoever with the available acceleration.

I was halfway to Tottenham when I had a distinct feeling that all was not well. The car was slowly filling with smoke and the fishy smell was assuming a kind of cooked aroma. When I stopped at the next set of traffic lights flames began to rise from the wooden floorboards. At that point I switched off and abandoned ship; 20-odd years' accumulation of wet fish and dry rot, plus a fabric body, caused a bonfire the like of which had not been seen in Hackney since 1940. The thick black smoke brought traffic to a halt and could be seen for miles around. The fire brigade were on hand with commendable efficiency, but too late, far too late; this car was never to see the blue light of Measham and was publicly cremated. Having sorted out the inevitable paperwork at the local nick, and arranged for the remains to be towed away, I returned to base on a trolleybus.

These various diversions made a nice change from the daily routine, but they were not profitable as far as I was concerned. I relied on calls to generate sales, so I aimed to be out as much as possible. One of the firms I had been calling on for some months without success was the old-established Thorn Electric Company on the Great Cambridge Road. I had never got further than a somewhat frosty receptionist, but you have to keep trying. That afternoon, therefore, I was more than a little surprised to be told that the transport manager would see me. I was even more surprised to find, on being shown into the spacious office, that the transport manager was, in fact, a manageress! In the mid-Fifties it was rare indeed to find a lady occupying an executive position of this kind, but she was a very precise lady and came straight to the point. "We have a Humber car that we wish to sell, it is just two years old; would your company be interested in the purchase?" After trying to meet the lady for some time I thought that I should at least investigate further, if only to prolong the interview. I therefore asked if I might view the car? I was taken through the back to a private garage wherein stood an immaculate black Humber, which at first sight I assumed to be a Pullman Limousine. Closer inspection proved it to be an Imperial saloon, which was much the same but, while it had the row of occasional fold-down seats, it didn't have the glass partition between the bench-type driving seat and the rear passenger compartment. The car had hardly been used. When I was again asked by the lady if we were interested I felt that I could hardly say we were not.

"How much?" At this point I began to realize that I was rapidly getting out of my depth for I really didn't have the authority, as far as I was aware, to purchase a car of this class, but at the same time I didn't wish to appear foolish in the presence of a mere woman. To gain time, and to give me a chance to think, I asked if I might try the car. I was told sharply not to be all day and to report to her office on return. I felt rather like a little boy asking to be excused; the lady certainly had presence. To this very day I can remember test-driving this huge car down the Cambridge Road, the smell of that luxurious West of England cloth upholstery and the power of the big six-cylinder engine. I turned into a side road, parked and had a long hard look at Glass's Guide. The cost of this car new would have been *circa* £1,783. The two-year-old valuation would have reflected a heavy depreciation in regard to the limited secondhand market, and the high cost of running relative to insurance and engine size. 'Book' price, therefore, would have been on the low side. Against this the car had completed only a very low mileage and had been chauffeur-kept to an impeccable standard. I had enough experience to know, however, that it was doubtful if the car was worth 'book'.

I returned the car to the garage and made my way to her office. She certainly had a formidable personality, and I felt all of 15. "Well?", she said. I felt the colour rising to my cheeks and blurted out what I thought was a low offer, but close enough to the car's value to be justifiable. "Another fifty and it's yours." To my horror I realized that the offer was not only acceptable, but without doubt the highest they had received to date. The room seemed suddenly to be considerably smaller and very hot, and she must have noticed my discomfort as I became aware that it was looking very much as if I had bought myself a car. Was there actually a ghost of a smile on her face as she sat looking at me over the rim of her glasses? Commonsense prevailed at last. After all, I reasoned, had this Humber been on offer in exchange for a new one, nobody would have questioned the transaction. We were in business to sell cars, and there had to be a buyer for this one somewhere, apart from me! With these thoughts came renewed confidence. "No, that is as far as I am prepared to go." "Right", she said, all brisk and businesslike, "we will accept your offer, but retain the radio and the road tax." With that I stood up and with a firmness that surprised me I looked straight into those formidable grey eyes. "Sorry, but that's not the way we do business." The lady knew how far to go, and simply asked if I could call back with a cheque that afternoon, for they needed the space.

I drove back to Tottenham wondering what on earth Albert was going to say. But the more I thought about that car the more I was able to convince myself that it could be sold for a worthwhile profit. By the time I reached the showroom I was quite enthusiastic, and with Albert enthusiasm went a very long way. Cyril was out so I was on my own; I pressed the buzzer and, having requested a moment of his time, was invited upstairs. I breezed into the office, took a reassuring glance at the trilby and a deep breath. I gave him a detailed account of what I had done, giving a full description of the car and the price that I had committed him to. When I had finished he simply said: "Well, that sounds alright to me, old son" and wrote out the cheque, just like that. I drove him to Thorn Electrics in my little Morris Eight, where I introduced him to the lady transport manager, to whom he handed the cheque in exchange for the car's documentation, almost without a word. Albert, like me, was clearly out of his element with this lady whizzkid. On completion of the formalities we went through to the garage where he got straight behind the wheel with scarcely a glance at the car and drove off. On the whole, I thought, a bit of an anti-climax.

With the available power and the clear roads of the time Albert was back well before me. On my return he had been examining the car with Stan Goodsman and as I parked the Morris he started up the back stairs to his office. He caught my eye, and to my delight gave me a broad grin and a wink, and so he should have. The crafty old devil had someone in mind for that car and within days it had gone for a handsome profit. At the end of the month I received a hefty commission cheque, and a salary increase.

December not being one of our busy months for selling cars, I was delighted when a gentleman walked in one cold morning just prior to Christmas and without any preamble placed an order for a new Sunbeam-Talbot 90 convertible standing just inside the showroom window. The car was to be delivered by us at a pre-arranged time to be hidden in his garage with a large bow across the seats; it was to be his wife's surprise Christmas present. It was a straightforward transaction with no part-exchange. At the client's request all financial arrangements were to be handled through the United Dominions Trust Ltd, where, he assured me, there would be no problems. He told me in the course of the dealings that he was a successful butcher with five shops. All of the expensive shop fittings for these premises, together with his own Jaguar car, had been financed by UDT and, naturally, he wished to maintain continuity. As this would require completed documentation I telephoned the London office, who confirmed that our mutual client was, indeed, a valued customer. To save time, and with due regard to Christmas post, it was arranged that I should collect the paperwork from their offices near Waterloo Bridge the very next day.

On arrival at these palatial premises I was met by a uniformed commissionaire, as big as a house, clutching an envelope and demanding sixpence! This paltry sum represented the value of the postage stamp then required on the document to legalize the hire-purchase agreement, this in respect of a valued client who was now placing extra business to the value of some £1,000. The late chairman of UDT, Mr H Gibson Jarvie, was of course a Scotsman . . . I declined to pay!

During my latter days at Arthur Gould's I had delivered a new Ford Consul to Chesterfield Motors Ltd, one of their sub-dealers in Chalk Farm. Since this visit I had become good friends with Jack Carpenter, the proprietor's brother-in-law, who was also a director of the company. Jack was a few years my senior and something of a playboy. He was quite well off by my standards and the proud owner of an MG Midget, which was every young man's dream at the time. Before I was married we had many a bachelor weekend up in Cromer in the MG, where Jack had relatives with whom we were able to stay, and a seemingly endless collection of upmarket girlfriends. Jack's brother-in-law, Sam Chesterfield, was in his sixties and appreciably older than either Jack or his sister. He was a prewar Warren Street motor trader of the old school, as different from Albert Chidley as chalk and cheese. Sam Chesterfield was a dealer, pure and simple, self-made, tough and uncompromising. Not for him the ethics of gentlemanly motor dealing. Sam was interested in one thing and one thing only – PROFIT!

Sam had been astute enough to realize that new cars would be in short supply when production resumed after the war. He had therefore purchased this somewhat tatty garage in Chalk Farm with its postage stamp showroom for one reason and one reason only. It held the collective franchise for Ford, Austin, Morris, Wolseley, MG, Standard and Triumph, together with Ford and Morris commercial vehicles. With a selection like this he was reasonably certain to have at least one vehicle in stock at a given time, and it had become common knowledge in the local business community that you could usually get delivery of a new car at Chesterfield Motors, cash down and no back answers. But, of course, at a price! At the time I first met Jack he was able to holiday in Majorca at any time in Sam Chesterfield's private villa, and this was in the Fifties!

While Sam Chesterfield was making his pile, Albert Chidley, in common with the vast majority of new car dealers, never once sold a new car over the proper price. To do so would have been contrary to all his principles. One of the firms he had dealings with in the early-Fifties was a huge local company manufacturing duplicating machines. Albert's allocation of new cars was strictly limited, like everyone else's, but nonetheless he saw to it that this particular company was well looked after throughout the shortage. As depreciation was non-existent they had been able to run their cars for nothing, even showing a profit in most instances. It is interesting now to reflect on that company's reactions in regard to this transparent honesty when, much later, marketing restrictions had been removed and the new cars became freely available. The company, which had once gladly been prepared to accept every Humber, Hillman and Sunbeam-Talbot they could get their hands on, switched to another make because they were offered a slightly better discount than Albert felt able to allow!

By 1954 the majority of the popular family saloons were more or less freely available and I knew that Jack Carpenter, in common with some other multi-franchise dealers with limited space, was having problems in finding homes for all the cars which by now were being allocated by the various distributors. It was not that there was a glut of cars, it was simply that by now Chesterfield Motors were enjoying a reasonably regular supply from too many sources. I was not unduly surprised, therefore, to be invited to the Chesterfield home, in an exclusive part of Highgate, for a drink and a discussion. Jack had hinted many times that I might care to join the company, for experienced outside representation was exactly what they were in need of. It was, by any standards, a beautiful home. I parked outside behind a rather sad-looking old car, which I found out later belonged to the Labour MP who lived next door and used it for visits to his constituency, the Jaguar not being considered appropriate! I had only met Mr Chesterfield once or twice and thought him a rather forbidding old gentlemen with shrewd tiny, almost black eyes. Jack had insisted that it would be in order to call him 'Ches' as everybody else did! He knew how to charm, and was an excellent host. I was certainly glad that I had some time to consider the situation.

The position being offered had a considerable advantage. I was married by then and the housing situation in London was impossible, so we were living in a flat consisting of three rooms near Holloway prison, with a shared WC, a sink on the half-landing and no running hot water. Above the showroom at Chesterfield Motors was a flat with hot water and a bath! On the other hand I would be breaking new ground, but with a larger selection of vehicles. Nonetheless, if I was unable to bring in the business in a reasonable time there would be no Saturday afternoon used-car sales to fall back on. For one thing there was no room, and in any case, Regent's Park Road was no high street; Saturday afternoon opening had not even been contemplated. On balance the pluses and minuses were about even, the biggest draw being the rent-free flat and that bath! All would depend on the salary, and I suspected that Ches would expect to pay rather more than I was getting at the time for a track record in successful outside selling. I was correct in my assumptions; he made me an offer which I would have been hard put to refuse and I managed to slightly better this on the commission terms, though neither Jack nor Ches could figure out why I wanted the flat as part of the deal. It was simply a question of the rich not realizing how the poor live!

But it was with real regret and a heavy heart that I gave the news to Albert Chidley. He made no comment one way or the other, his final handshake was firm and friendly, and with a "Good luck, old son", that was that.

CHAPTER FIVE

MORE VALUABLE EXPERIENCE – 1954

After working in Robert Chidley's magnificent showroom with its adjacent super-clean modern workshops and parts back-up, my first day with Chesterfield Motors was, to say the least, something of an anti-climax. There were moments when I had doubts about the wisdom of my move, and two or three visits to the flat were required to provide moral uplift. Even this was in dire straights, being in need of complete redecoration and some alterations before we would be able to move in. But the bath was there in all is glory, together with a large immersion tank for the sheer luxury of hot water. The showroom was clean and tidy enough, but it was so tiny. It was simply an oblong with just room to display four cars, two behind two, with enough space left at the rear for two desks and a small toilet area. There was barely enough room to open the offside doors of two cars, and both nearside and offside doors of the others in order that clients could at least try them for size. A small side door halfway down led onto the petrol forecourt, behind which was the workshop area which, with a floor area of perhaps 4,000sq ft, was reasonably large. At each end were large roller shutters and the area between them was recessed and intruded into the workshop to accommodate three petrol pumps and a small office for the pump attendant. The forecourt and workshop area were separated from the showroom by a steep ramp which led from the road down to the rear of the buildings, forming a split level in which there were some small engineering companies. There was also a yard area where we could park a few new cars during the day so as to keep the workshop clear.

If nothing else it was compact, and there was just room on the forecourt to park Jack's MG and Mr Chesterfield's car. I was expected to use whatever was in stock at the time, so often my car was parked in the road. The workshop was gloomy and none too clean. Most of the time the shutter near the showroom was kept open, and behind this was the office of the service manager, behind which in turn there was a wire pen which served as a stores. The stock being of doubtful age and quality, I never once saw any of the mechanics use it, and replacement parts were bought in as and when needed instead. Service management seemed to be in the hands of a Mr Hempson, who was introduced to me as a director, but he passed away shortly after I joined the company so I never really got to know him.

There was hardly enough space available for the new cars, so used-car sales were out of the question and most part-exchanges were moved on to the trade on arrival. As the Austin, Morris, Wolseley and MG cars produced by the British Motor Corporation were continually in artificially short supply because of the constant industrial action at the BMC factories, there was as yet little danger of our being swamped providing there was a reasonable flow of sales.

My first day was spent getting the feel of the place, but during the morning I had spoken to someone who required a price for his car in part-exchange and I asked Ches where the *Glass's Guide* was kept. He looked at me with those tiny, shrewd bird-like eyes: "We don't use it", he said at length. "If you need a book to value a used car you won't be of much use to me", and with that he went to the client's car, examined it methodically, noting a mark on the bodywork that I had missed and concluded by saying: "If it drives well give him £XXX for it". We didn't complete that particular deal, but subsequent investigation proved his off-the-cuff valuation to be spot-on. Clearly I had much to learn. Once I had got used to the very different atmosphere and accepted that come what may my bridges were well and truly burnt I soon settled down. Nobody interfered with me in any way and I was free to come and go almost as I pleased. Results, it would appear, were the name of the game. Being out for most of the time, I would see Ches on few occasions apart from Saturday mornings, but when we chanced to meet his habitual greeting would always be: "How many have you sold today, then?"

My immediate priorities were to get myself established in the area, thereby to sell some cars and provide some income so that I could get to grips with the flat at evenings and weekends. It was clear that the first would require some planning for this part of London had little in the way of factory estates. Small business houses, which experience was to establish could be in the most unlikely places, had to be searched for. After some thought, following an initial trip round the area I decided that the only possible way was to work square by square on the *London A to Z* map in the immediate vicinity, exploring each and every street in each grid square in a methodical order, calling and listing as I went. As the area became known I could further expand my coverage to suit a timescale. My first call was not encouraging; it was a large electrical contractor in a high street. The owner was delighted to see me for only last week he had replaced his two cars and a van from Chesterfield Motors. Well, as they say, you certainly can't win them all!

I cannot recall how long it took me to obtain my first sale or where it came from. It could well have resulted from one of the regular petrol clients, but the first is invariably the hardest to achieve, after which it should all be plain sailing. On the whole my calls were a great deal more interesting because for the most part they were to small businesses where the owner would be grafting with the employees on the shop floor, or shops that looked as if they would run a car or a small delivery van. By the end of my first year I was covering quite a sizeable area of North London and was to get to know my patch like a policeman. As at Robert Chidley's, I found that persistence and thoroughness worked and, of course, I had the added advantage of being able to offer a wide range of new cars, with all the model variants. At a time when most were not quite immediately available, I could usually offer something from stock. Also, within the area I was now covering there was a steady demand for the Ford and BMC light commercials, and even a few middle-range commercial vehicles. By year end my personal sales had built up in a most encouraging manner, and my initial doubts had long since been forgotten.

All of my spare time was spent working hard on the flat. My first problem had been to convert a very large front room into a bedroom and a small dining area. The back half, which was the same size, had already been divided in roughly the same manner but the other way around. In other words, on completion, the small dining area would back onto a fairly large lounge, while the fairly large bedroom would back onto part of the lounge and the kitchen. Within the kitchen was the bath, covered when not in use by a hinged worktop; a somewhat novel arrangement in that it was technically possible to bathe and prepare lunch at the same time! At least the loo was separate on the floor below. When you have lived for any length of time without bath or hot water, a kitchen/bathroom is luxury indeed. I had some DIY experience at Holloway and I was reasonably good with my hands, so I set to work building the partition to divide the front room, complete with door. I then called in specialist labour to deal with the electrics and plumbing, etc, after which my wife and I decorated the lot, room by room, and even constructed a special false ceiling in the kitchen complete with vents to get rid of the steam. One 'specialist' called in to assist was our cat. The electrician needed to run a cable under the floorboards, but as I had constructed my dividing wall it meant that he would have to saw through the boards to be able to run the cable through the joists. I had a better idea; we simply removed a floorboard from each end of the run and put the pussy cat down one end with a length of string round his tail. A saucer of fresh salmon at the other end provided the irresistible incentive and we were in business! It took us just over three months to complete the alterations, but by the time we had the carpets in, plus some new furniture on the 'never never', we had a real luxury pad not 10 minutes from the West End. Jack gave us permission to have an extension from the switchboard, when it was rare indeed to be on the phone, so on the whole we really had done very well for ourselves. I certainly didn't have far to travel to work so I could enjoy my morning bath in some comfort complete with a handy cup of tea.

Most days I would be out by 9.30am or so looking for new business or cultivating fresh calls. One of my initial calls had been to an expanding laundry owned by a charming Polish ex-Army officer. He was to buy several Morris 1-ton vans as his business expanded, together with some private cars, and he became one of my best clients and a valued friend. He would spend hours trying to teach me to play poker, a game at which he could easily have made a black fortune had he had the inclination. Another call that I had cause to remember, but for rather different reasons, was the one I made one morning to the head office of Dorothy Perkins, the national retailer of ladies' underwear. It was one of those calls when I seemed to have turned up at precisely the right time. The lady receptionist departed with a 'you'll be lucky' smirk after I had introduced myself and proffered my card, only to return moments later wearing a somewhat different expression: "Mr Barber, our managing director, will see you now."

Now managing directors of companies of this size are not prone to granting interviews to reps on spec, so it was with considerable astonishment and speculation that I followed her into the most luxurious office I had ever seen. We shook hands and the great man asked me to be seated. Years later I was to be reminded of this visit when, following the antics of the late Leonard Rossiter as 'Reginald Perrin', the only item missing being the whoopee cushion, Mr Barber likewise had not got where he was without coming straight to the point! So he came straight to the point: "Could I", he asked, "provide them with a Ford 3-ton chassis/cab?" I tried, and probably failed, to remember my poker lessons. "Yes, sir" – not half I couldn't, we had had one in stock from the day I started, taking up valuable space in the workshop. "Right, then, how about two?" Bloody hell, I thought, now I know that I'm dreaming. I had no idea what the delivery situation was, but that was Jack Carpenter's problem, not mine. Mine was to get the orders. "Seven to 14 days", I guessed, tongue in cheek. Mr Barber turned to his secretary and told her to give Mr Owen an order for both vehicles. While she was typing these out he became quite chatty.

It would seem that my one-time employers, Arthur Gould Ltd, had let him down, and these chassis were required urgently for national delivery vans. There was to be further business of perhaps four a year, which I could have provided that I arranged to deliver the chassis to the bodybuilders at Cambridge and the eventual collection and delivery to their premises of the completed vehicle. Oh, and by the way, of course they expected a 10 per cent discount. Knowing full well that Arthur Gould were not likely to offer any form of discount in those days we settled for five. I could hardly wait to get back to Primrose Hill with my order, but I had to stop twice to re-read it to make quite certain that I had what I thought I had. Sure enough it was all in order, and as it happened, when I arrived back Ches was standing at the showroom door. I waited with baited breath, but he didn't disappoint me and the inevitable standard greeting followed. "Two", I said smugly, and before he had a chance to inquire further, "the 3-tonner in the shop and another like it if you can provide it within two weeks". Ches managed to look astonished: "Bloody good, I'll get the other for you, you leave that to me. What's more I'll buy you a drink when they open!"

Ches got the second one sure enough, but in the event I never did get the promised four orders a year. Nonetheless they bought two more over the next 18 months, and orders for vehicles of that kind were well worth having. I continued to make regular calls on the company in the course of my rounds, but Mr Barber would never see me, that is unless he wanted something. One day I was again invited into the sanctum, so in I went full of optimism. It would seem they had a large van that had been on the fleet for some time which they wished to sell and nobody wished to buy. Mr Barber wondered if I might know someone. Now it is a poor salesman indeed who will not go out of his way to try and help a client, so I asked for more information. The vehicle in question was a Morris pantechnicon, the largest in their fleet, with a diesel engine and a Luton-type body. In simple terms this meant that there was storage space above the driver's cab. I told Mr Barber that I would see what I could do and left. I spent that afternoon telephoning contacts in the heavy-goods field and soon discovered the problem. Diesel engines shortly after the war were not generally available in the mass-production heavy-goods market, and none of the makers at this level were producing their own power units. Both Ford and Bedford were buying in diesel engines from the old-established firm of Perkins, at Peterborough, while BMC had been experimenting with a Swiss engine made by a company called Saurer. The unit had proved less than a success, in fact they had been trouble from day one. "A Morris Saurer, old boy, is not worth a light", I was repeatedly told by the experts.

I returned to Mr Barber with the sad news, but it was apparent that he knew the score well enough. He admitted that they had had no end of trouble in the first two years, but now that the problems had been ironed-out it had behaved very well on the whole. He even took me to their yard at the rear of the building to have a look. It was as big as a house, and no doubt a very useful vehicle. I thought to myself that there must be someone, somewhere, with a use for a vehicle of this size. "How much are you asking, Mr Barber?", I ventured. He named a price that, to me at any rate, seemed silly relative to the vehicle's probable original cost and replacement value. On an impulse I stuck my neck out: "Tell you what, let me see if I can advertise it for you, and we'll see what can be done, but I shall need it on our premises for a day or so." Mr Barber was delighted: "You can have it with pleasure if you think you can move it." The following week I placed a full description in the *Commercial Motor* magazine, collected the van on the Friday morning and drove it to the garage to await results. This was not to be the last time in my commercial life that I was to be told that a particular vehicle was 'unsaleable' by all the experts, only to prove them wrong. Everything has its price, no matter what, and it soon became obvious that this particular vehicle was on offer for rather less than its true commercial worth.

The telephone started to ring at midday and continued to ring during the afternoon and into the following week long after the van had been bought and paid for. The first prospect to arrive was a somewhat grubby little man who walked round it once, then climbed into the cab and started the engine. Above the roar of the engine I could just hear him muttering something on the lines of "Bloody foreign diesel – load of rollocks", which I assumed to be some obscure technical part of the engine. He offered a cash price, which I declined to accept, at which point another grubby gentleman arrived on the scene whom we both assumed to be the next prospective buyer. "OK", he said, handing me a roll of fivers to count, "I'll pay your price". Without further ado I directed him to the showroom and turned to my next gentleman. Could I, he asked, please direct him to Haverstock Hill? My next hard-earned commercial lesson in life was never, ever, do owt for nowt. Ches was in Majorca, which was just as well for he would have killed me had he found out. On the Monday I had presented myself at Mr Barber's office with the same roll of fivers intact. I was feeling mighty pleased with myself. Mr Barber was delighted, and said so. He did not, however, feel so delighted that he felt able to make the gesture of offering me a fiver for my trouble, even though this was most certainly not required. Indeed, he didn't even offer to pay for the advertisement, though I later sent an account which was met. My personal view was that I had done a service for a customer, for whose gratitude I might expect further and valuable business in the course of time. How naive can you get?

I heard no more of Mr Barber for some time because although I called at Dorothy Perkins on a regular basis, on every occasion he was "not available". One morning, though, he telephoned me to say that the time had come to change his personal car, that he had narrowed his choice to one of three. Could I, therefore, arrange for a demonstration drive in each model? Two of his choices were cars handled by us, so I was able to arrange for loan cars from our distributor without too much difficulty. The other, being a Rover, was not so easy, but as usual Ches was able to solicit help from one of his many old friends in the business. Having tried all three, and after much discussion in regard to pros and cons, Mr Barber elected to choose the Wolseley 6/90, which delighted me, it being one of ours, so to speak. I was invited to make an offer for his old car in part-exchange, for which I provided rather better than a fair price, and was told that I would hear further in a day or so. I was foolish enough to tell Ches that afternoon, in reply to the inevitable question, that I had sold a new Wolseley to Mr Barber.

I heard nothing, my frequent telephone calls resulting in the advice that Mr Barber was with a client . . . in a meeting . . . not in, etc, etc. After a week or so I managed to speak to his secretary, who told me that Mr Barber had indeed been very busy, but she was also able to tell me that he had purchased his new Wolseley from the local dealer near his home, where they had serviced his old car. They had been able, she advised me, to top my offer by £20! Quite apart from the fact that I had arranged all three demonstration runs and done all the donkey work, I had shifted his bloody great van for nothing and then lost the deal for a measly score. Mr Barber did not even have the common courtesy to ask me if I would care to match this price, or even to tell me himself that he had purchased his new car elsewhere.

I felt then – and still do today – that for a company director his behaviour fell a long way short of acceptable business ethics, and I was cross, *very* cross. I drove straight down to head office, ignored reception, hammered on the door and demanded – and got – an audience. Mr Barber, while not used to a young salesman barging into his office, was nonetheless visibly embarrassed when I pointed out that having provided assistance in regard to the Saurer van for nothing, all the assistance necessary in respect of demonstration runs – which had been expensive in both time and effort – I did not expect my company to be done out of a deal for coppers. To cover his discomforture, of course, he pulled rank and blustered. His company, he told me, was in a competitive business and people often visited his shops, used the facilities and then bought elsewhere. I had a lot to learn, he said. Further argument was pointless. So I walked to the door and opened it, turned round, and with as much dignity as I could muster said: "The difference between your business and mine, Mr Barber, is that when you sell a lady a pair of knickers you are not expected to accept the old ones in part-exchange", and with that I hoped crushing observation I departed, resisting the temptation to slam the door.

On the credit side, however, I had been taught two valuable lessons, and before the end of my career I would be making a good living on two occasions retailing, if not quite the unsaleable, the so-called hard-to-sell goods which few others would touch. Also, throughout my commercial life, while I have always endeavoured to provide a good service, I have always charged in proportion. It is a formula which usually leads to appreciation. Some two or three months later I received in the post a further order for a new Ford 3-ton chassis/cab typed neatly as always by Mr Barber's attractive secretary, together with a compliment slip on which she had written the cryptic note: "Sorry, no part-exchange!!!"

I was not able to spend every day on the territory for there were other jobs to be done such as the inevitable paperwork and ensuring that my cars were available for delivery as required. There was also some trade to be had from the petrol forecourt and from customers who had cars in for service or repairs. It was during the course of some of these activities that I had the opportunity to observe Jack Carpenter at work. He was perhaps 10 years older than I and a man of good looks and much personal charm, and as such he had a way with clients, particularly the lady clients. He took his car selling very seriously and if he failed to complete a deal for any reason he would spend a great deal of time analyzing the transaction, trying to find out if he had perhaps made an error in presentation, or said something out of turn. I think we were both to learn something as a result of these discussions, which became valuable in later years when the competition was stronger, but at the time, when it was usually a matter of trying to persuade the client to accept the colour and/or specification that happened to be available, I don't think we lost a great deal. By now I was able to assess the value of all but the more specialized cars that were offered to me by applying a simple logical thought process, but the trade was less complicated then and make and model availability considerably smaller than today. Nonetheless, valuations of our used cars had to be very accurate for I was not expected to lose profit on the new-car transaction, discounting being unheard of. Most of the used cars were sold to the trade in Warren Street through Ches' old contacts and the fact that it was little over a mile away. One of his old cronies – a likeable man by the name of John Grey, who lived in nearby Hampstead – bought the sports cars and exotic machinery that we took in from time to time, and we had a list of local bomb-site traders who bought the bangers.

At this point a short description of Warren Street in the Fifties is called for, if only to nail a few myths and endeavour to provide some insight into the unique atmosphere of what at the time was a most important, in fact well nigh indispensable part of the national retail motor trade. I cannot claim to be an authority on 'The Street', a full history of which would provide meat and drink to any enterprising historian who had the time and facilities to research the subject and produce his own book. That it would be a volume seller there is little doubt, if only for the many larger-than-life characters who have trodden its pavements before and since the war. Today, Warren Street is but a pale shadow of how I remember it during its heyday in the Fifties, killed-off by parking meters and all the other factors of modern-day life as the motor trade itself has undergone so many changes.

The popular image of Warren Street during the two decades or so after the war was as a street populated entirely by 'Arthur Daley' characters selling dodgy used cars to gullible members of the public, this myth being propagated by music hall comedians and the popular press. In truth it was a trade clearing house. Mind you, should Joe Public wander by chance or curiosity into the street with a pocket full of fivers, searching for a car, he would be relieved of his money with pleasure, and might well have found that he had purchased a very good car indeed. As for value for money, well that would be quite another matter, for most buyers of secondhand cars who visited Warren Street were hard-headed professionals buying on their own behalf.

In other words, Warren Street was a trade market which had come into existence prewar when Great Portland Street and the Euston Road were to the motor trade what Harley Street is to this day to the medical profession. In those days there were a number of well-known firms in the immediate vicinity selling and distributing the new cars of the time. Names such as Henlys, The Car Mart, Pass & Joyce and, of course, Arthur Gould all had showrooms in or close to Great Portland Street, which also accommodated dealers for other makes, together with a selection of palatial showrooms specializing in the more expensive and exotic secondhand cars. Prewar, the trade in cars nationally had still been quite small and these West End firms would tend to deal almost wholly with their respective 'stock in trade' and would not wish to soil their hands with run of the mill used cars accepted in exchange. In consequence, and as far as can be seen almost by accident, used-car traders began to move into the adjacent Warren Street area, thereby establishing a clearing house for cars that were then moved on into the provinces and to the rural used-car dealers for eventual resale.

In the Fifties Warren Street was at its peak, parking meters not yet heard of and the used car business brisk and ever-growing. The huge car auctions which were eventually to provide exactly the same service to the trade, albeit on a vastly increased scale, were only just beginning to expand under the capable hands of David Wickins, who had only recently started up his second auction at Alexandra Palace and had yet to take over Measham. The Street was an institution, and proud of it, and many were the stories that originated there, some true and some apocryphal, for any street of this nature will generate its own folk law. Indeed, The Street enjoyed some sensational publicity when one of its inhabitants, Stanley Setty, was murdered and his dismembered remains were dumped in the Thames Estuary from a private aircraft by Donald Hume.

While some of the older-established firms had showrooms, the majority of the regular inhabitants had premises little larger than an office containing a desk and telephone. Outside would be a blackboard on which would be chalked bare details of the day's stock, which would be parked on the pavement or somewhere in adjacent streets. A number of less affluent dealers would lay absolute claim to a pitch comprising a length of pavement, from which they could buy or sell one or two cars. That particular length of roadway they would consider to be theirs by divine right, and were you to innocently park your car on a pitch that happened to be vacant you would at once be approached by a tough looking character with the query: "Ow much, guv?" On advising the gentleman that your car was not for sale and that you simply wished to park, you would immediately be requested to "go forth and multiply". Should you be so misguided as not to comply with this simple request, your car would be worth considerably 'under book' by the time you returned!

One of the more conservative organizations in The Street was a partnership by the name of Short & Glass, and Sam Chesterfield's favourite and oft-repeated story was of the time when he actually purchased a car from Mr Short at one end of Warren Street, later to sell it at a profit to his partner Mr Glass in the local pub, *The Goat & Compasses*, over a social drink! It was quite usual for the cars to be sold and resold throughout the length of Warren Street for small profits before finding a more permanent home, which is not as daft as it may seem; often dealers would have personal contacts where they knew they could place particular cars on the telephone for better than average prices. Therefore, if dealer A was to find himself with say, a Humber Hawk purchased on spec from a contact, he might well find on return to The Street that he was approached by dealer B, who was prepared to provide a quick profit, as he knew in turn that dealer C had a contact 'up north', who was always interested in luxury cars, from whom he would obtain a good profit. Cars would change hands for profits as little as a fiver a time. Mind you, a fiver at that time would represent something like 20 per cent of the average weekly wage!

The late Noel Whitcome, a popular columnist of the *Daily Mirror*, once set out to do a feature on Warren Street in the erroneous belief that they dealt with the public at large. He was recognized at once as his picture headed his column every day, and in due course one or two of the 'elder statesmen' took Noel to view a locked shed wherein, he was informed, dead pan, was hidden the Tyre Machine. Several large scotches later, at the entire expense of the *Mirror*, it was casually leaked that after a speedometer of a used car had been adjusted to a false mileage, the Tyre Machine would be pre-set to wear in a set of new tyres to the exact degree appropriate to match the new reading. Noel swallowed this nonsense hook, line and sinker, and a day or so later the story, suitably embellished, appeared in his column. Warren Street could have had a field day with Esther Rantzen – bless her!

During my employment with Ches I was to dispose of quite a few used cars in The Street, mainly to a highly respected company which had been established for many years. The Bercow brothers, Charles and Ralph, were arguably the best-known and certainly the most liked among their contemporaries, with a reputation of being as straight as a die; two nicer Jewish gentlemen you could not expect to meet in any company. Elder brother Ralph had served in the Royal Air Force with some distinction during the War, but was to die tragically from cancer in the Sixties. My dealings were mainly with Charles, a charming, precise little man with a unique gift of expression. We became very good friends right up to his death some 30 years later, and we had a valued business relationship in that we trusted each other throughout. I was to deal with the Bercow brothers for several years both as a seller and a buyer of used cars, and within this relationship I was to witness the gradual demise of The Street as those iniquitous parking meters arrived with their attendant traffic wardens to make life intolerable and the earning of an honest living impossible. It really was the end of an era, but of course it is hard to imagine how The Street could possibly have functioned under present-day trading conditions now that the motor auctions have taken over the function of marketing and finding homes for surplus used vehicles.

By now I was doing pretty well for myself at Chesterfield Motors. I had a good area well sewn-up, a good range of cars to sell, with just enough built-in shortage to make life comparatively easy, and my income was such that I was able to enjoy a good standard of living and to save at least something each month towards the eventual purchase of a house of our own. Mind you, this was not easy with the temptations of the many pubs and superb restaurants in Hampstead, just up the road, and the West End not two miles away. Each weekend in the summer we were able to join Albert Chidley's brother Bob and his lovely wife Audrey at Burnham on Crouch, where they kept a boat and a caravan. There being no trade on Saturday afternoons, Jack and I would take it in turns to have the morning off so that we could enjoy long weekends.

One of my regular clients at this time had a large pet shop in Haverstock Hill. One day, on delivering a new van, I was presented with two budgies, one green, one white, complete with birdcage and accessories. They were christened Percy and Omo. Both had the run of the flat and could fly around as the fancy took them until, on delivery of a further van some six months later, I was presented with a tabby kitten, whereupon the birds' flying excursions had to be restricted. Not that the cat seemed to take the slightest interest in them way or the other as they flew around while we were watching TV in the evenings. One sunny afternoon I was called from my lunch as a client was waiting for me in the showroom, this being one of the disadvantages of living on the premises. By the time I had sorted him out it was too late to bother, so I settled down to catch up on some paperwork. Much later in the day I remembered that I had left the birdcage open, and the cat was somewhere in the flat. Leaping from my desk and mounting the stairs two at a time I shot through the door wondering what kind of carnage I would find, and it was with considerable relief that I found the birds sitting on top of the cage as large as life and perfectly happy.

It was some time before I found the cat. It was curled up and fast asleep in the bottom of the birdcage. Just as I was trying to figure out how to get the cat out, Omo decided to take off and fly into the cage where it then perched on the swing above the cat's head. The cat opened one eye, yawned and went off to sleep again, at which point the phone rang. "The old man has arrived and is looking for you", a voice said, so I had no choice but to leave them to it. When I went up some time later the cat had made its own way out and was waiting to be let out via the rear window and the fire escape. Both birds were back in their cage This strange event had an odd sequel, for several weeks later there were signs of panic from a private house across the road and I wandered over to investigate. It would seem that the house budgie has escaped through an open window and was perched in a tree in the front garden. Ladders had been brought and folk were trying to coax the bird back. It must have got the wind up, for without warning it flew out of the tree and fluttered down onto the front lawn. Our cat appeared from nowhere and, to horrified screams from the kids, shot across the grass and grabbed the bird in its mouth. Without much hope for the luckless budgie I called out and the cat just wandered over to me with the bird in its mouth and handed it over shaken, but otherwise unharmed. That little excursion was worth two columns in the local rag for free, and that was the sum total of our advertising during the whole time I was employed at Chesterfield Motors.

One morning Jack Carpenter found in his mail an invitation to make use of the training facilities available at the British Motor Corporation's sales school, something that was now being offered to retail dealers. Jack gave me the opportunity to attend what was to be a four-day event, starting on a Tuesday morning and ending on the Friday afternoon, and would include a tour of the car and commercial vehicle production lines. I was delighted to accept as I hadn't been on a factory visit since I had been to Ford at Dagenham, apart from which the best part of a week off at the firm's expense sounded fine to me. There were seven or eight of us staying at the same hotel, all hell bent on having a good time whatever else. On the first day, after an early breakfast, we set off for the factory in two cars and I found myself in the one driven by the course comedian – there is always one in any group. We duly arrived at 'The Austin', as it was known by the locals, and pulled up at the huge and imposing main entrance with its array of magnificent illuminated signs everywhere advertising the company and the products it made. A dignified commissionaire with two or three rows of medal ribbons on his immaculate uniform approached the car from the gatehouse. "Excuse me", said our driver, "is this Austins?".

The course was run by a well-meaning elderly gentleman named Lamb, who of course was immediately nicknamed 'Larry', as no doubt he had been by scores of other young salesmen before us. As an aggressive sales course it was a non-event, and I can remember nothing of the daily routine apart from the visit to the production lines, which is always fascinating, and a memorable afternoon devoted to 'the part-exchange problem', which was a classic, and indicative of the general standard of the course as a whole. This was about the time that most cars had become more or less available and there were distinct rumbles of competition in the air. The lecture was composed of two parts, one dealing with general used-car appraisal, and the other to 'the making of an offer'. It soon became clear that as far as the BMC were concerned, this was the problem area.

The solution put forward in all seriousness was that, having shown and hopefully sold the new Austin car to the client, you should invite him to the sales office for further negotiations. I didn't think it tactful to venture that perhaps it would be unwise to take a client away from the product at the very zenith of his interest. However, Larry's view was that he should be seated in a comfortable chair and asked the question: "How much do you want for your present car, sir?", to which the client would doubtless reply: "I don't know" – true enough so far. We all waited with baited breath for the solution to all of our future part-exchange problems as Mr Lamb beamed round his audience. "Right, gentlemen. What we would suggest at this point is that you should ask your client to write down on a piece of paper how much he would like for his car, and at the same time you write down on another piece of paper your price. But do remember to keep it on the low side. Then, ask the client to compare his price with yours and say: 'Can we split the difference?'. The comedian looked at me, I looked at him, and we raised our eyebrows. For perhaps the first time in his life he was speechless. That anyone, least of all a factory instructor, should offer this charade as a credible method of dealing with an intelligent customer was beyond belief, but that was exactly what was proposed. From that afternoon the catchphrase guaranteed to raise a laugh from our group at breakfast or dinner was: "You show me yours, and I'll show you mine!" The waitresses must have thought us quite mad, apart that is from one rather buxom blond, who took up the offer in the back seat of my car after an evening out, but that is another story

The trip round the factory was fascinating insofar as it was at about this time that the line had become part-automated, and two or more different models were being completed on the same line, all the correct bits arriving to meet the appropriate bodies. I remember the seemingly casual spot-welding of the A30 roof section to the boot and rear quarter and resolving never to drive one at speed again, but of course the weld was more than ample, at least I never heard of one coming apart at the seams, and there are still quite a few A30s on the road today. A phenomenon I shall always remember was the feeling of animosity that prevailed throughout the entire workforce, on whom even our tame comedian failed to make any impression. One old boy to whom I spoke was working away at a bench behind which, on the wall, were pinned details of some moderate football pool successes. My polite and friendly inquiry produced no more than a surly: "Only way to get any brass, mate, no future in standing here all day for 27 quid a week". Although this sum was considerably ahead of the national average wage at the time, clearly he was not a happy man.

The comedian did have one moderate success, however, when we discovered in the commercial vehicle section an old gent, obviously very near retirement, screwing Morris or Austin nameplates on the trucks and vans, for by this time both were being 'badge engineered' in the same factory. No doubt the old man had been a bit of a pain to the younger workers in his latter days, and they were considerably amused when the comedian, after watching for some time, said quietly to the old boy: "I see you've put 'AUSTIN' on the front of this one." The old chap looked up with an expression which suggested it was barely tolerable for a man of his age and experience to respond to the comment of a thick young car salesman. He pointed to a worksheet stuck on the windscreen. "Says 'AUSTIN' on there, don't it?" The comedian paused for a moment. "Sorry, I just wondered why it had 'MORRIS' on the back, that's all." It hadn't, of course, but the old boy shot round to the rear to check up while the lads in the shop fell about laughing. On our final night we had a good dinner and a booze-up, and next day, with a kingsize hangover, I bade a fond farewell to the blond waitress at breakfast, after which we shook hands all round, swearing to keep in touch, which of course we never did. Then life returned almost to normal.

However, at various periods in my life, just when I had every reason to believe that everything in the garden was rosy, fate has provided me with a salutary kick up the bum when I least expected it. This particular instance, which was to generate a long-term chain reaction, at least came with some warning of its possible consequences, thereby leaving me reasonable time to plan ahead. It all started on a sour note. One afternoon, soon after my return from my rounds, Jack Carpenter told me he had had a row with his brother-in-law, had resigned as a director and would be leaving at the end of the month. This was sad news indeed for Jack was a good boss as well as a good friend. But there were more serious implications. Jack had always taken care of the administration side of the business and I couldn't see the old man coping with that under any circumstances. Ches never showed his face before opening time morning or afternoon, and even spent the greater part of these short periods in *The Castle* pub across the road.

Sure enough, no sooner had Jack departed to join the Rootes Group in their magnificent West End showrooms than the old boy told me that I was now sales manager, and as such I would have to look after the showrooms and run the business. I managed, with difficulty, to get an increase in salary, but I knew full well that sooner or later my income would deplete through a fall-off in commission, for my trade was dependent on regular calling. True, I could use the telephone for a time, but at the end of the day it's the personal contact that gets the business. I also reasoned that Sam Chesterfield would lose interest sooner or later; he was now well into his sixties and a wealthy man with no use at all for the problems that might arise as new cars became ever more readily available. It seemed likely that he would seek to sell the business, and there would be no telling if I might suit the new owner or *vice versa*. Within a year events were to prove me right, and my eventual move was painless. However, that was for the future, and in the meantime life had to go on. By this time we had acquired a much-needed service manager by the name of Arthur Barker, and his long-term interests being exactly the same as mine we had both come to exactly the same conclusions.

Arthur was a bit of a card and he had two passions in life, one of which was his violin, which frequently he would play in the workshop office during his lunch hour. It must be said that he was pretty good, but his choice of music, being a touch on the heavy classical side, didn't do a great deal for the fitters or the pump attendant. His other devouring interest was crumpet, of which he was never short, and he used to entertain his ladies late into the night in the back seat of any convenient car in our workshop, to which, like me, he was a key-holder. As I used the workshop to garage my car I was obliged to drive in at nights by the street lights to save the ladies any embarrassment – Arthur just didn't give a damn. He was a short and physically unimpressive man in his forties with sparse hair and an engaging grin; whether it was the fiddle or the grin that pulled the birds I never found out, but those I was introduced to in the cold light of day were quite attractive and most certainly not 'bought'.

With Jack gone the whole daily routine changed. I now had to take care of all the administration for the elderly secretary Ches employed for bookkeeping could never have coped. Not only had I to sell the cars, I now had to ensure that orders were placed with the various distributors as well as look after the sales records. But every cloud has its silver lining, and the experience gained was to prove invaluable in the years to come. It was not just a question of writing out orders for new cars. It was now entirely up to me to choose the colours and specifications which could be sold, and there were some pretty odd specs around during that period. For example, some manufacturers had been experimenting with medium-size family cars with automatic transmission, for which it was believed there would be a demand. They were not a success, being mainly of a clutchless, semi-automatic variety. Rootes had Easidrive in the Hillman range, which for some obscure technical reason required the addition of iron filings to the works at regular intervals! The manufacturer we represented, Standard-Triumph, had Standrive, which was offered as an option on the Standard Ten. It had no clutch pedal, this being replaced by a press-down solenoid switch on top of the floor-mounted gear-lever which 'broke' the drive when pressed with the thumb, then took up the drive upon release so the gearchange could be completed. The problem was that the drive was either in or out – there were no half-measures – which worked fine on the open road, but manoeuvring in a confined space was, to say the least, difficult. As our showroom entrance was tight and up a slight incline, the only safe way we could back one into the showroom was to push it, which was hardly satisfactory. Furthermore, we were experienced professional drivers, so how elderly ladies coped with awkward garages and driveways could only be guessed at. In the event these comic-cuts gearboxes had a very short life and were soon abandoned. It was to be another 10 years before Alec Issigonis was able to introduce his successful Mini and 1100 ranges with an acceptable and wholly reliable automatic transmission.

To return to the realities of 1956, with all this extra workload I was hardly able to leave the premises apart from visiting a client to obtain a specific order or deliver a car. I was still getting orders on a reasonably regular basis from my existing clientele, but these were gradually diminishing as I was not continually cultivating or following up new prospects. On the other hand I was picking up the orders which Jack had dealt with in the past from our regular petrol customers, so for the time being at least I was maintaining the personal financial *status quo*. During this period Ches was not a great deal of help. Each day he would arrive around 11am in his Wolseley 1500 with the inevitable question: "How many have you sold?" He would wander around for a time, look through the accounts and his post, then in due course I would see him crossing the road in the direction of *The Castle* pub, where he would stay until around 2pm. He would return, well sloshed, then drive home to have his lunch and sleep it off. If any of his old motor trade friends were to arrive he would remain in the pub till closing time, or after. There were a few afternoons when I literally had to assist him behind the wheel of the car and start the engine for him he was so paralytic. But somehow he always made it home and not once did he have an accident of any kind!

One lunchtime his particular friend John Grey arrived. John was a wealthy local motor dealer with whom we did a fair bit of business one way or another. After a lengthy session in *The Castle* they both departed in Ches' Wolseley in the general direction of the West End. The following day Ches arrived in a taxi to tell me that he and John were off for a while on a tour of the clubs to see if they could find the car! I heard from Jack some time later that his sister had been woken by the doorbell in the small hours and had found Ches outside with the local bobby who, knowing perfectly well who he was, had kindly brought him safely home, rather the worse for wear. In any event they somehow found the car, which was as good an excuse as any for a further binge. At Chesterfield Motors it was practically a condition of employment that Arthur and I should join the old man each evening for a few rounds in *The Castle* after we had closed so that he could indulge in his favourite sport . . . the pinball machine. This particular one had flippers with which, if you were quick enough, the ball could be returned to the top of the table. Each night it was the same routine, we took it in turns to buy the rounds and played the machine for 6d (old pence) per head, highest score wins. He seldom won, for Arthur's reactions and mine were far faster than his, but he never seemed to mind in the least. I often wonder how much we took him for during those evenings, when a sixpence would just about pay for half a pint of beer.

One evening Ches had wandered over to the pub at 5.30 for a quick one as usual. Arthur and I usually closed the shop at 6pm, depending on whether we were busy with late clients, and followed on. On this particular evening, however, Ches was back within 15 minutes, muttering that the machine was out of action and he would see us up the road in another pub. It being a quiet evening, Arthur and I were ready for the off on time so we walked the 50 yards or so up Regent's Park Road together. By the time we arrived Ches was in fine form once again; it seemed that he preferred this pub's machine to the one in *The Castle*, not that he played it any better, and for a few nights we changed our venue. All went well until the night that Ches ran out of money and the landlord refused to cash his cheque, which was a bit daft, for everyone in Regent's Park Road, including this landlord, knew perfectly well who Ches was and that his cheque was as safe as houses. For a moment Ches was speechless, then, picking up his chequebook he grunted: "Would you accept a cheque from the Bank of England then?", and walked out.

We got our own back, however. The company who owned most of the games and fruit machines in this part of London had an office and a workshop in the yard at the rear of our showrooms. Alf Manzie, the Italian proprietor, was a client and a good friend of mine who would lend me his superb 1940 Buick convertible at any time on request. The very next day I called on Alf and told him what had happened. Within the hour the machine had been collected and re-installed in *The Castle*, to the delight of Ches and the considerable relief of mine host at *The Castle*, who had no wish to lose Sam Chesterfield's considerable custom.

That year, 1956, I had taken in part-exchange from the pet shop a very pretty 1952 MG 1½-litre saloon. Based on the Midget and the Morris Eight Series E, it was known as the Y-type and was notable for being the first MG to be fitted with independent front suspension. For me it was love at first sight, and I managed to catch Ches in a particularly good mood and persuade him that I could use the car for personal transport. Now cars to me are a commodity, and as I have already mentioned, at Chesterfield Motors I was able to use any car that happened to be in stock at the time. In any case, living on the premises meant that I usually only needed a car at weekends and some evenings during the week. But this little MG was something else. For a start it was red, with leather upholstery and a sunshine roof. The dashboard, with the familiar octagonal instruments, was in real wood, and it was a pure delight to drive with its short stubby gear-lever. It boasted an opening windscreen, which was quite useful in fog if you could stand the draught, and it had a Jackall system, which comprised two pairs of built-in hydraulic legs, front and rear. Under the bonnet was a valve marked 'Front', 'Rear' and 'All'. By simply setting a pointer to the appropriate mark and placing a wooden handle in the valve, which could be worked from side to side, you simply jacked up the car as required. Even the most helpless of lady drivers could work that system while waiting for some gallant gentleman to arrive to change the wheel. Needless to say the car was kept in a highly polished state and was my pride and joy. Alf Manzie had somehow obtained a Rolls-Royce mascot which he promptly gave to me, and we agreed that it looked very smart on the MG radiator cap.

Later in the summer we had arranged for a holiday with Bob and Audrey Chidley; it had been proposed that we might even take the boat to France if the weather looked suitable. A week or so before we were due to depart I had been formally introduced to a Mr Horsefield, whom Ches had been seeing a lot of during the past weeks, and was told that he would shortly be taking over the assets of Chesterfield Motors Ltd. Mr Horsefield made it clear that my services would be required, together with Arthur Barker's, and that he hoped we would stay on. For my part I reasoned that at worst I would have a situation to return to after my holiday, so I had nothing to lose by playing for time and seeing what might occur. We were due to leave for the East Coast on the Saturday at lunchtime, and during that week Ches had told me that the takeover was due to happen while I was away. He suspected that Horsefield was short on cash and might not have enough to cover the car stock. Obviously Ches didn't want to be in a situation where he would have to retain title to complete the deal, so he asked what the situation was. As it happened, it could hardly have been better; all but one of the new cars on the premises were sold and awaiting delivery, while those coming in part-exchange had trade buyers waiting. There were other new cars awaiting collection and payment at the distributors, but these could be comfortably left for a while, so responsibility for payment would pass to the new owner. The only car available for sale was a new Standard Ten, which by pure chance I was to sell on the Saturday morning of my departure. By the time Ches arrived I was feeling quite pleased with myself and ready for a welcome break.

When I gave him the glad news he simply looked round the showroom and grunted. "Well, we can't have the showroom empty, can we now? Put the MG in and I'll get my daughter to drive you to the station." For a moment I could scarcely believe my ears. When I had pulled myself together I told him exactly what I thought and didn't mince my words. Without a word he turned on his heels and I watched him cross the road to *The Castle*. I was sorely tempted to grab my wife and the luggage and just drive off, but commonsense prevailed; you simply cannot load a car up for two weeks' holiday in moments, and in any case we had yet to farm out the cat and the birds. Ches was back within 10 minutes. On the back wall was a plaster MG plaque about 2ft across; Ches looked up at it: "You had better put that in the middle of the floor if the place is to be empty then." With that he was gone, back to *The Castle*. He could be an odd person on occasions.

When I returned from holiday, Horsefield had disappeared, never to be seen again. I didn't ask, but I guessed that the cash had failed to materialize. On the whole it was an unsettling time because on top of my uncertainties in regard to my personal future, in October that year there was the Suez crisis and the return of petrol rationing. For the motor trade this was to be the first of many postwar recessions, and as such it should perhaps have been a salutary experience. New-car sales and used-car values tumbled virtually overnight. While the British Motor Corporation immediately sacked hundreds of workers, other manufacturers hastily reduced their prices and chaos reigned supreme. Yet it all ended as quickly as it had started, so quickly in fact that I remember trading a car on a Friday for a price well below what I could have obtained for it on the following Monday. Nobody, including me, learned anything, for in no time at all everything was back to normal, and it was all going to last forever. BMC took back all the staff and production restarted, pending of course the next strike. On this note we moved into 1957, which was to be my last year with Ches. One way or another I was managing to keep the new cars moving, and Ches seemed to be well-pleased. No-one else showed any interest in the business and the year passed quickly enough with no more than the usual local and domestic problems which govern all our lives.

One of the perks of my situation was that I was able to attend on behalf of the company the many annual dinner-dances and functions held by the car makers, their distributors and the finance companies, these mostly being held during or near Motor Show time. On October 10 I attended the invitation dinner for the London Morris & Morris Commercial Dealer Team organized at the *Dorchester Hotel* by Stewart & Ardern Ltd, the old-established London distributor. The guest of honour was Viscount Nuffield, CBE, FRS, DCL, with entertainment by Charlie Chester and others. The toast: 'The London Morris and Morris Commercial Dealers' was proposed by one K H J Sinnott, home sales manager of Morris Motors Ltd. Sitting close to him on the same top table was R R Holditch, the home sales manager of Wolseley Cars Ltd. Of all the many functions which I attended it was purely by chance that I kept the programme of events from which this information now comes. Little could I have guessed the part which those two jokers were to play in my future! On a lighter note, I obtained Charlie Chester's autograph on that programme; 33 years later almost to the day I was invited to a 60th birthday celebration where the guest of honour and proposer of the toast to our worthy host Mr David Hamblin (one of my past employers) was the same Charlie Chester, from whom I solicited a further autograph on my menu for old time's sake!

Motor Show time in the Fifties was always exciting. The first show I attended was in 1950 and from then on I went every year without fail. In those early postwar days showtime was for viewing exciting new models, meeting old friends on the various stands, which all boasted a bar of one kind or another, and the inevitable social rounds. One of the major finance houses held a huge cocktail party each year, taking over the Great Room of the *Park Lane Hotel* for the occasion. If you failed to receive an invitation to that function you were certainly not one of the motor trade 'in' crowd. *Raymond's Review Bar* was packed nightly with motor trade people from all parts of the country looking for a good time. The comedian's jokes were slanted at the motor industry, while the ample naked bosoms of the ladies of the chorus were slanted in all directions, to the delight of the then largely unsophisticated provincial motor dealers. Paul Raymond's establishment was always a favourite venue in those days, offering a first-class meal and good entertainment at reasonable prices.

One night we decided for a change to patronize one of the sleazy back-street establishments on the off-chance that we might see something which by law we were not allowed to. There were perhaps eight of us, and we negotiated a special price at the door of 10 bob each. We were taken upstairs to a dingy, ill-lit room, complete with a makeshift stage and a few rows of wooden seats. Centre stage was a grubby couch on which reclined a somewhat tatty bird, stark naked, but showing nothing at all worth looking at. After a suitable interval the stage lights went out, and when they came on again another grim-looking bird had replaced the first in an 'artistic pose', and so it went on. By the third change we were becoming decidedly bored, and the bloke next to me, who was not with our party, leaned over and said: "Don't think much of this for three quid." When I innocently told him that we had only paid 10 bob I thought he was going to blow a fuse; while he was loudly calling for the management on a plate and a refund, we made our excuses and left. Another group of motor dealers, we found out later, had purchased tickets from a tout at the door for a blue movie show. They were told to go to the top floor, several flights up, where they found themselves at the flat of an elderly local prostitute. By the time they had raced down again the tout, of course, had departed. As I said, *Raymond's* was good value!

Following that 1957 Motor Show things went on fairly normally at Chesterfield Motors, but Ches was getting edgy, and even our nightly visits to *The Castle* were not the same. He must have been trying to sell the business, but no more Horsefields were to appear and worse, my sales were beginning to suffer as a direct result of losing personal contact. This situation clearly could not last. Arthur had elected to sit tight and to see what happened, but I decided to try and seek alternative employment. Each week, almost from the day I started in the business, I had my copies of the *Autocar* and *Motor* magazines, which served to keep me in touch with new models and developments in the industry and contained a fair bit of trade gossip. Present-day readers may be surprised to learn that in the Fifties and Sixties these publications, long-since merged, were but a pale shadow of the aggressive consumer magazine which it is today. Faults, particularly in regard to British-made cars, were ignored or glossed over, particularly during this period when the British Motor Corporation were producing a succession of so-called new models which were no more or less than existing cars wearing alternative marque names justified by some minor variations in detail – badge-engineering at its most blatant. Both magazines would faithfully introduce each new (?) car with a detailed specification and a cutaway drawing. In due course, comprehensive road tests would appear, the contents of which make for interesting comparisons with present-day test reports. Notwithstanding the fact that it has long been fashionable to knock the former British Leyland – and that consumer magazines must at all cost be fashionable – the road tests were, to say the very least, accommodating.

Both *Autocar* and *Motor* also carried detailed and well-documented reports on the motorsport scene, articles on general motoring matters and, inevitably, there was a comprehensive classified advertisement section covering everything from new and used cars to parts, services and, at the very back and of particular interest to me at this time, a trade situations vacant section, which I began to study closely. My preference, I thought, would be a situation in the broad North London area, where I was known and where by now had useful contacts. In the light of my recent promotion, of course, I was hoping for a senior position, being none too keen to work just as a salesman. There were all sorts of situations in all parts of the country, but I could see nothing that had any attraction. Each week I continued to study the section as soon as my copy arrived, then one day in early December I spotted an advertisement offering a situation for a general sales manager in Northampton. This was of particular interest because we had friends in both Corby and Wellingborough. What little we had seen of the county we had liked, so on this basis alone I decided to apply at once. This, however, was easier said than done, for I had never had to write an application of this kind in my life.

I decided after some thought to simply write a short history listing my situations since leaving school and my achievements to date stating, tongue in cheek, that I was presently employed as a sales manager at an establishment now up for sale; in this modern high-tech, buzzword world it would be referred to as a CV. At least I had some worthwhile experience to place on record. Thanks to a reasonable education, I had always been proficient at writing letters, furthermore I was a handy self-taught two-finger typist, so if nothing else I was able to compile a reasonable presentation. However, not having a great deal of faith in my suitability for such a senior position, I promptly forgot all about it and didn't even bother to mention the application to my wife. But to my considerable astonishment I was to receive a reply within a week.

CHAPTER SIX

PROVINCIAL SALES MANAGEMENT – 1958

Hamtune Motors Ltd had sent me a very detailed reply, covering two pages, which stated the duties expected of the successful applicant, a short history of the company and the facilities available, which included two separate car showrooms. Also of considerable interest, the fact that the previous incumbent's earnings had averaged £32 per week, which in November 1957 was an outstanding remuneration, more indeed than I had been averaging, and I most certainly didn't consider that I was being underpaid. The situation didn't offer any form of accommodation, though by now this was not too much of a problem for I had saved enough to at least consider buying some kind of home of my own. I reasoned that if I were to be successful in my application – and it certainly seemed to be a very big IF – the cost of a suitable property would be considerably less in Northampton than in London. The letter invited me to telephone for an interview if I was interested, so being very interested indeed the following Saturday found us heading for Northamptonshire, where we were to stay at Wellingborough with friends of my wife.

Meanwhile, I was able to study the notepaper containing some details of the company I was to visit. It was quite imposing, apart from the company name, which I considered was distinctly odd: Hamtune Motors Ltd conveyed to me an image of ham-fisted tuning, and I have to say that in my ignorance I felt the choice of name to be unfortunate. However, all was to be revealed when a friend of mine pointed out that Nord Hamtune was the original name of the town, and as such would make a great deal of sense anywhere north of Watford. For the rest, I noted that the company had a showroom in Northampton town centre, which I had assumed was their main office as it was where I was to report on arrival. They also had showrooms and a workshop at a place called Weston Favell, which I knew to be a little out of town on the main road to Wellingborough, so I would be able to have a quick look on the way in. The letterheading established that the company were distributors, no less, for the luxury Armstrong Siddeley cars, which made me cough, for these were on a par with the very big Humbers, and as such could hardly be classed as volume sellers. However, on a more down-to-earth basis the company were also retail franchise-holders for Morris, Wolseley and MG, which was fine by me as I had been selling them for the past three years or so. I also noted that there were just two directors – H H Frisby and M Frisby – so clearly this was a family concern.

I was not due for my interview until late afternoon, so on arrival at Wellingborough there was time for a freshen-up and change into the gent's natty, complete with immaculate white starched cutaway collar and meticulously arranged white breast pocket handkerchief. Then it was off in the MG to Northampton, pausing en route for a quick look at the Weston Favell showrooms. After dark and with the lights on it was quite imposing, so noting only that the showroom was appreciably larger than that at Chesterfield Motors and there was room for the display of used cars on the large petrol forecourt, I pressed on for Sheep Street, not wanting to risk being a second late. It was not quite 5.30pm when I arrived, and as Christmas was near there was a great deal of activity from late shoppers. But I was able to park with ease just short of the premises from where I first took stock. It was not as imposing as I had expected, doubtless, as I had now surmised, because this was certainly not the head office. It was no more than a converted double-fronted shop with glass sliding doors and room at the front for four cars facing forward in pairs. This then narrowed to a point where there were two more cars, one behind the other, and I was to find that behind all this the area widened at the rear so that a further three cars could just be placed side-by-side across the back and in front of a small office and a storeroom.

Having taken in most of this, I was about to get out of the MG when I found I was well-placed to witness a fracas that was to provide a unique insight into the most extraordinary character of my future employer. A huge broad-shouldered gentleman with the most luxuriant ginger RAF-style handlebar moustache I have ever seen before or since, was in the process of backing a black Vauxhall Wyvern with consummate ease into a vacant spot at the front of the showroom. Assisting him quite unnecessarily, but with much gesticulation and shouts of "left-hand down, old boy . . . watch that other car now . . . back a bit more . . . hold it! . . . ", of which the driver was not taking the slightest bit of notice, was another huge gentleman in a typical country town green tweed suit with rather baggy trousers. I watched the proceedings with amusement and appreciable interest, for it was clear that the owner of the baggy suit was none other than Harry Hawtin Frisby Esq, managing director of Hamtune Motors Ltd.

Through my father I had become a devotee of P G Wodehouse, and my first thought was bloody hell, it's Ukeridge come to life!, while for the benefit of readers who have never read this most humorous and descriptive author, Mussolini springs to mind as a possible comparison, but only in respect of build and general appearance. As indicated, he was a big man, and reasonably tall and well-proportioned apart from his head, which was round and a little on the small side. He had sparse black hair, a swarthy complexion, deep brown (almost black) eyes and a small bristle moustache. At some time he must have suffered from Bell's palsy for his mouth had a permanent upward twist which was particularly pronounced when he laughed, but gave him a kind of sinister expression at other times, causing him to look cross even when he wasn't. At present he looked very cross indeed, which I assumed was simply because the man he had been directing had ignored him.

At any rate, by now the car was neatly parked and as I got out of the MG and walked towards the showroom somebody slapped a 'SOLD' label on the windscreen, so it would seem that the effort and the shouting had been well worth the trouble. I introduced myself and a huge hand gripped mine in a vice-like grip and pumped it up and down vigorously. "Nice to meet you, old boy, this is John Hayes, now follow me up to Weston Favell and don't lose me or you'll never find it." Then like some pantomime genie he was gone out of the doors and into the night. John Hayes, the affable Irish salesman, grinned at me as much as to say, don't worry, he's always like that, the while warmly shaking my hand and guiding me back to the door. "D'ye see the old maroon Armstrong Siddeley, me boy?", he said. "Well, just you be following that, he only travels at 25, you'll keep up with him right enough."

So pausing only to thank him, I jumped into the MG and off we went. I was to learn later that Harry never went anywhere by the proper route for he had a compulsion for short cuts that was almost a fetish. My first thought was that Harry Frisby must have a call to make *en route* such was the tortuous trail that we followed through Northampton. But the old Armstrong Lancaster plodded on, trailing clouds of smoke at a steady 25mph, just as John had said, in the general direction of God knows where. The journey didn't bother me a great deal because I had all the time in the world to enjoy a tour of the town and area where I might have to live and to work. In those days Northampton was a lovely little market town, bearing no resemblance whatsoever to the ugly concrete city that it is today. My first impressions were of the number of parks and open spaces and the distinct lack of traffic after London.

In due course I noted that we had arrived somehow on the Wellingborough Road, and as we drove up a shallow incline I recognized on the left-hand side the green illuminated sign and Shell petrol insignia which was Hamtune Motors Ltd. The forecourt was deserted apart from a male petrol attendant sitting reading in a small white hut. Harry swung onto the forecourt and parked outside the workshop entrance at the far side of the showrooms. I parked the MG next to him and we all got out. "Right, old boy, follow me. By the way, you always want to come that way from town, it misses all the traffic." I made no comment; I could never have found that way in a million years!

We went into the showroom, which was almost a miniature of the one I had first entered all those years ago in Regent Street. In the base of the L on my right was an Armstrong Siddeley Sapphire 346 saloon, which looked super from outside under the many lights, although closer inspection revealed it to be rather sad and worn. In the stem of the L there was a new Morris Minor and a few used cars, none of which looked particularly inspiring, and at the top end were two offices side-by-side. The floor, paintwork and windows, I noted, were all fresh and clean. I followed Mr Frisby into the left-hand office, which had windows overlooking the school playing fields next door. Inside, behind Harry's desk and courteously rising to greet me, was Mrs Mary Frisby.

Mary was as slim as Harry was large, most certainly younger and with an air of charm and commonsense. She shook my hand, asking me to be seated, and I got the impression she was weighing me up very carefully. Firstly I was offered a most welcome cup of tea, and while Mary was somewhere at the back preparing it Harry and I talked of this and that; clearly no interviewing was to begin without Mary. On her return I started to relax a little, telling them the story of my commercial life to date while noting that Mary was quick to smile when I threw in a few of the more amusing incidents for good measure. When I had bought them up to date by explaining why I was now looking for a suitable position it was Mary who asked the questions and, I noted, answered most of mine. At the conclusion of these formalities I was shown round the premises which, after the dingy workshop at Chesterfield Motors with its tiny showroom, I found quite imposing.

I couldn't weigh up Harry at all because when Mary was around he didn't have a great deal to say. Mary, however, impressed me a lot and I got the feeling that while she might not know a great deal about the motor business, she had an instinct for what was right and what was clearly wrong. It was Mary, in fact, who had discovered that the previous sales manager was dishonest and told me bluntly that what was required above all else was a person of integrity. Without asking too many direct questions I discovered that Harry, having been left a great deal of money by his father, had gone into the motor trade somewhere in town with another person whom he was always to refer to as "my late partner, old boy". The partnership had not proved a success, so they had split up and Harry had purchased and refurbished Park Garage at Weston Favell, at the same time taking out a lease on the Sheep Street premises. Now that cars were having to be sold he was finding commercial life a problem. While Harry certainly had more than adequate premises, there was no way he would ever make a successful car salesman; I admit that at the time this was purely an 'off the cuff' judgment, but as will be seen, my opinion was prophetic, although for entirely different reasons.

On return to the office I was beginning to feel somewhat overdressed in my smart new business suit. I wondered if all country motor dealers dressed like Harry with his baggy tweeds, the trousers of which were held up by a large leather belt with the rim of his underpants doubled over the top. At least on him it all looked normal enough, and certainly was in keeping with the rest of his character. Inevitably it was Mary who drew the interview to a close; I had stated that I would like to be considered for the situation on offer, then after shaking hands all round I departed.

It was fairly late on Sunday evening when we returned to Regent's Park Road. On lifting the roller shutter I found that Arthur Barker was entertaining a lady on the back seat of a handy car. As usual I pretended not to notice, but this time as I drove in he was bounding across the garage with a message, still drawing on his trousers, to the considerable embarrassment of my wife. A Mr Frisby had telephoned several times, it would seem, and whatever time I returned I was to phone Blisworth 209 forthwith. It was rather late, but those being the instructions, telephone I did. There was no doubt it was Harry's booming voice on the other end of the telephone as I mumbled my apologies for the lateness of the hour. "Don't worry about that, old boy, Mary and I thought you were like a breath of fresh air after the others we had seen. When can you start?" It would appear that I had got myself a job, so I agreed that the first week in January would seem to be appropriate. Meanwhile, I would travel to Northampton again the following weekend to sort out the details, and on that rather satisfactory note we went to bed.

Harry knew quite a few people in Northampton and had agreed to look out for some suitable temporary accommodation for us. In the meantime he fixed me up in a small commercial hotel at the bottom of Sheep Street, which really was a godsend as the food was superb and the room comfortable, which when you have a job to do is about as much as you need. From the moment I arrived I liked Northampton; after 28 years in London it was another world. The lads in the hotel all worked for local firms, and once I was accepted they proved a great bunch with whom I was to enjoy many a night in the local pubs. One night they took me to one called *The World's End* and got me hooked on the local pub game, skittles, played on a table with a net over, like some kind of leather armchair with nine wood pins and round cheeses thrown from around 9 feet; very skilful and very noisy. This was the initial social life that was to keep me relaxed, for very soon I discovered that I had a problem or two. The first thing I noted was that the main garage was by no means trading as it should, bearing in mind that Harry Frisby was Northampton born and bred; new-car sales were almost non-existent. On going through the records it seemed that my predecessor had favoured used cars that had all originated from Scotland. Those available for sale were certainly a mixed bag, but the first to attract my attention was the Sapphire 346, which I had resolved to use as personal transport for a while for I had never driven an Armstrong Siddeley in my life. By this time a brand new one had arrived in stock, so some basic knowledge of the merchandise would not be amiss. In the event I was out of luck. Firstly it wouldn't start as the battery was clapped-out, and when a new one was obtained and fitted I began to wish I hadn't bothered. The engine sounded dreadful. I asked the service manager, a morose young man by the name of John Nicholls, what he thought and he told me in one word: "Knackered".

It couldn't just be left, so I asked John to do what had to be done to make it a runner and went to try the rest. Of perhaps six or seven cars at Weston Favell there were but two that I felt could be offered for sale – the remainder were junk – so I set off for Sheep Street. It was much the same there, only worse. Some of the cars taken in were actually prewar, the worst of which were locked up in an old garage round the corner that was rented. John Hayes was no fool, and he told me that Harry, while a bloody good bloke with a heart of gold, was no motor dealer. The last sales manager had been left entirely to his own devices, doubtless feathering his own nest, with disastrous results. There was no way I was going to start trading in a new area with cars like that, so at the first opportunity I cornered Harry in his office and told him a few commercial facts of life. At first he was inclined to argue, but after a while he promised that he would "discuss the situation with Mary, old boy". The next day Mary appeared at Park Garage, where I was requested to join them in his office. Mary quietly asked for my opinion of the situation. I told her as bluntly as I had told her husband, who sat dejectedly throughout without saying a word. I told her that amongst other things we desperately needed fresh used-car stock on which I could return the company a profit. The junk simply had to go. When I had finished she turned to Harry: "Well then, I suggest we leave it all up to Mr Owen." And that was that.

Up to that time I had worked only for experienced motor men who did not allow themselves to get into situations like this. I had learned the hard way that if you make a mistake with a used car you move it on quickly, for the first loss is always the kindest in the long run. Tatty old used cars never appreciate in value so you take your loss, write it down to experience and seek to re-invest your cash in more profitable transactions. With the best will in the world I could not see this lot under the blue light at Measham. John Hayes, however, had the answer, in fact John, bless him, usually had the answer to just about everything. He seemed to know everybody and could provide just about anything at all at short notice, as I was very soon to find in regard to a personal matter.

"Where on earth can we lose this lot?", I asked him as I stood viewing yet another fabric-bodied Riley and others in the old lock-up. I wondered for a brief moment if perhaps we might start up the Riley and leave it awhile on the off-chance that, like the other one, it might catch fire and burn out the rest at the same time! As it happened the Riley showed no inclination to start, so that idea was nailed at birth. John was twirling one side of his ample moustache, which he always did when the grey matter was flat-out, and frowning in a thoughtful manner. "Leamington", he said at length. "Every Tuesday, me boy, they have an auction full of bangers, mate of mine goes regular. I'll get all the details and give you a buzz." In due course vehicle entry forms were provided on which I read: 'ALL CARS OFFERED BELOW £100 ARE SOLD WITHOUT RESERVE'. Hell's fire, I thought, we should be lucky to get £100 for the lot. So it was that one cold day in January 1958 found us heading for the Royal Borough.

With John and his brother Jim, who worked for us at Sheep Street, plus a driver we employed for the day, we set off driving three and towing the Riley. I had decided to set an example and not to pull rank, so once again I had the doubtful pleasure of being at the wheel of what to me at any rate was a memorable marque. We had not proceeded further than the bottom of Sheep Street before we had a severe problem; the Riley doors, as was fashionable at the time of manufacture, opened from the front, and every time the towrope took up the slack both doors flew open. Jim Hayes sorted that out by the simple process of roping the doors to the windscreen; if this bastard catches fire, I thought, then I've had it for sure! So off we set again and after several breakdowns we somehow made it to the auction, where I dumped the lot and we came home by hitching lifts in pairs and on public transport.

Harry opened the mail, so I had no idea what the cars were sold for, and in any case I thought it best not to inquire. The following week three others went, but this time I stayed behind as I had more profitable work to do. One of my first telephone calls was to Charles and Ralph Bercow in Warren Street, from whom I was quickly able to buy some proper cars to display on the forecourt. To assist with these I engaged a young man as a trainee and taught him how I expected cars to be cleaned and presented. Between us we managed to make the Park Garage business look presentable. From that day on I was always to be personally involved in all used-vehicle preparation and the vast experience acquired has proved invaluable; after some 35 years I can state with some conviction that nobody can clean and prepare a used car for sale to the standards that my wife and I maintain. Meanwhile, the problem still remained as to why we were not attracting the new-car trade that was undoubtedly still about. The huge factory estates that exist today around Northampton were then not even a gleam in the architect's eye. Such business houses as existed were spread over a wide area, which precluded my calling even if I had the time; the trading conditions were far removed from those in the densely populated area of London.

It should be appreciated that at this time, while the car market was continuing to expand, it was only doing so in the business and professional sectors and of course amongst the reasonably well-off. The days when every council estate was to be jam-packed with personal wheels were still a very long way off. Furthermore, there had been another significant change in the marketplace since I had graced a showroom on a more or less full-time basis. Car dealers were having to advertise, a factor that the likes of Robert Chidley or Chesterfield had never had to consider; the philosophy had been car manufacturers advertise, then new-car dealers deal with the clients on their behalf. Hitherto local used-car business had been conducted through the showroom and car site direct, or via the many pages of advertisements in publications like *Autocar* or *Motor*. Now the Friday 'New and Used Cars' section in local newspapers had become the new growth area. Advertising expenditure was about to grow throughout the industry from almost nothing to a point where it became the biggest single overhead! It's an ill wind indeed, as many a provincial advertising manager must have concluded over the last 30-odd years.

As the company's sales manager, advertising was clearly my responsibility, but it was all too apparent that my early efforts were not bringing home the bacon. While I doubt they were worthy of an award, I must say that on publication they didn't seem that bad. As things turned out the problem had nothing at all to do with the advertising. During my frequent trips between Weston Favell and Sheep Street I had taken to calling on shops and business houses to at least introduce myself. I was received politely enough, but as soon as the name Hamtune Motors was mentioned I became aware at once of a distinctly embarrassing atmosphere. One call I had made was to the old-established Northampton firm of Jefferies & Co, who were a very upmarket furnishing house. I considered myself fortunate to have walked into none other than the old man himself. He really was a most charming and extremely courteous gentleman, straight out of Charles Dickens, and he listened politely to what I had to say. When I had finished he said quietly and almost to himself: "Harry Frisby, eh? Yes of course, bit of a card, Harry Frisby", and that was that. Odd, to say the least. The next off-the-cuff remark came from a tough-looking traffic policeman at an accident I chanced upon on the Wellingborough Road, where an American from one of the local bases had tried to take a short cut through a hedge; I had introduced myself with an offer of our breakdown truck to remove the wreck. All I got for my pains was a contemptuous grin and the comment: "Oh, so you're one of Master Frisby's boys are you?" In my business you do not argue with the police, so saying nothing I moved on.

The following week the truth was revealed over dinner at the hotel. Up to that time I had still not quite been fully accepted by the other guests, most of whom were permanent residents. Nonetheless there was always a good deal of chat and leg-pull over dinner during which, as the new boy, I had to ride the inevitable remarks about my chosen profession. I had given as good as I got and demonstrated that I could take a joke, so things had been looking up a bit. That evening, one of the permanents, who was head brewer at Phipps' Northampton brewery, said during a lull: "I understand that you work at Hamtune", and as he was already well aware of this I simply nodded. "Tell me", he said, "is Harry Frisby still a Fascist?"

Northampton had a population in those days of around 114,000, and it had not taken me long to discover that at my executive level and above everybody knew everybody. In consequence, the fact that my employer and managing director, along with Sir Oswald Mosley, had on one memorable prewar occasion actually been chased off the market square by an irate crowd of locals had most certainly not been forgotten, even though in these enlightened days Harry was a true-blue Conservative. No wonder I was having an uphill battle with the business and professional class. I began to contemplate him with considerable interest. He was most certainly a very well read man, and given half a chance he could talk at great length on political history. There was no indication at all that he might have been anti-Semitic or racist in his views. As far as I was concerned he was a man of great kindness and compassion, and I grew to be very fond of him indeed. He certainly was odd in many ways, as will be seen in due course, but he never did anyone any harm for as long as I was to know him, right up to his untimely death in 1965.

All this apart, I had a job to do and I was beginning to enjoy myself. Through an agent in Northampton Harry had at last found us a flat. South of Northampton is the Salcey Forest and slap in the middle is Salcey Lodge, a sort of microscopic Woburn Abbey, but complete with a mile-long drive and lots of grassland and a tied cottage at the top, hard by the cattle grid. It was over this grid that I was to drive one early spring morning and down the long drive. I had been directed to the rear of the imposing lodge, wherein lived my landlord. I had been told to go to the stables, above which was the flat. Being an ex-cavalry man the prospects of living over horses bore no fears, but on arrival it turned out that the horses were in reality pigs! This I personally regarded as only a minor drawback, though I was not so sure about my wife. Anyway, from the outside it all looked rather grand, running as it did the full length of the stables, which formed the rear part of a large courtyard; opposite were outbuildings, one of these being a sizeable garage for the tenant's car. Apart from a modicum of snorting and grunting from within, all was calm and peaceful. It was not a great deal different from Combermere Barracks, at Windsor, so I felt quite at home, and what a pad for anyone like me, 28 years old, London born and bred, straight from two rooms in Holloway and a small flat in Primrose Hill!

On the right-hand side of the building was a wooden open-tread stairway up to the main entrance. I opened the door with the key provided by the agent and found myself at the head of a long corridor running the length of the back of the building, with one door at the far end and others to the row of rooms overlooking the courtyard. I opened the first, finding myself in a large lounge with a huge open fireplace, all wood and distemper; very olde world and very pleasant indeed. Next on the left came a recess, at the rear of which were the usual offices comprising a huge iron bath, a basin and a wicker armchair, which on closer inspection proved to be the loo, built into a commode. The old *Sunday Express* was never to be the same again! Next, after the recess, a large kitchen complete with a real old kitchen stove plus a solid-fuel boiler to provide heat and hot water in the winter. This was beginning to look a bit tasty, so on to the next room, which I took to be the main bedroom until I tried the end door and found a kind of mini-ballroom with lots of light from windows at each end, opposite the courtyard end and with a view of open country for as far as the eye could see. Pigs or no pigs I had made my mind up – this lot was down to me. Within two weeks we were in; I don't recall if I had mentioned the pigs to my wife! From that day I became the complete country gent, with flat cap and walking stick, the only item now required being the 'woofer' to complete the picture.

The man to see, of course, was John Hayes. "Well, me boy, so it's a dog your after", the old tash being twisted like crazy. "It just happens that I know a party at Moreton Pinkney who have to get rid of a very nice dog." "What sort of a dog?", I asked in some amazement. You never could get used to John, he was a kind of poor man's Jeeves. "Don't know, me boy, but it's fawn and a very nice dog indeed." No further information being forthcoming, I departed for Park Garage, where I had an appointment. Later that afternoon I had a telephone call from John to give me the name of a farm at Moreton Pinkney, near Rugby, and to tell me that the party would expect me that very evening to inspect the hound. When we closed for the day I set off in the only car available with a bit of road tax, a two-door Morris Minor. I had been in the area long enough to know that to find Moreton Pinkney, the last place to go to would be Rugby, and true to form, so it turned out as it was on the west side of the county and nearer Northampton. The farm was not too hard to find and I drove in to find two very young children waiting to say that daddy would be back soon, but that the dog was in the barn. With that, one child ran over, opened the barn door and out bounded a massive Great Dane. Having never seen one before in the flesh, to say that I was impressed would be an understatement. "It's name is Bella", volunteered one of the kids, "mummy says we can't afford to feed it." "Hello Bella", I said in a sociable sort of manner, and immediately wished I had kept quiet. With one bound it jumped up and placing a huge paw on each shoulder looked me straight in the eye. Bloody hell, I thought, a touch apprehensive as it gave me a sloppy kiss with its huge tongue. "Coo", said the child, "she likes you!"

While the hound and I were conducting formal introductions a battered tractor had pulled up and the dog's owner came over to shake hands. He didn't seem a bad old boy, a caricature in fact of the straw-chewing yokel, but he came straight to the point. "If you don't want it the dog will have to be put down." That was enough for me. I told him that I would very much like it, while wondering what my wife would say. He went into the house and came out with a lead and a chain collar. "She ain't been in a car afore", he said, "you'd best put this on." We walked to the Minor, I opened the door and tipped the driving seat so the dog could get on to the back seat. Without as much as a pause she stepped gracefully into the back and hence to the front passenger seat, where she sat bolt upright, leaning against the far door without a care in the world. It didn't seem to be the time for argument, so replacing my seat I gave the kids a few bob, bade farewell to the old boy and off we went. After a mile or so Bella laid her great paws across my legs, placed her head in my lap and went to sleep.

As we neared home darkness had fallen and I started to laugh. My wife was expecting a dog, not a pony! Furthermore, our poor cat had been enjoying the quiet life and wanted nothing else; it had totally ignored the pigs. I drove into the courtyard and parked at the foot of the staircase just as the light was switched on at the top. As I got out a petulant voice said: "You're late, where have you been?". "I've got a present", I said, opening the passenger door. With that Bella slipped out, saw my wife at the top of the stairs and said "Woof!" by way of introduction. "Bloody hell", she said "what on earth have you got there?" "Come on, Bella", I called, bounding up the stairs two at a time. I was not, however, being followed. At the base of the stairs the dog stood looking mournful. She may or may not have been in a car, but for sure she had never been up an open-tread staircase. There was no choice; she would have to be carried. In those days I was pretty fit, but by the time I reached the top of the stairs I was panting a bit. The cat had come to the door to find out what the noise was all about, and as I put the dog down, gasping for breath, the poor cat, after one look of total disbelief, arched its back, spat and legged it down the corridor at high speed with Bella in hot pursuit. Halfway down it did a split-arse turn into the kitchen while Bella, being unable to comply with this manoeuvre, shot on into the bedroom. On returning to the kitchen she found the cat had vanished under the cooker so took no further interest. On closer inspection the dog, while not starved, looked like it needed building up a bit. A fairly substantial mixture of odds and ends that we managed to rustle up was gobbled down at high speed, even though I had been told she had been fed that evening. Having just provided cars to a vet and a pet shop owner I resolved the morrow to make good use of my contacts.

Having sorted out my private life and moved my wife and furniture up from London I was able to concentrate on the job in hand. By now I had cleared out all the junk and Park Garage had an array of used cars displayed on the forecourt that would have done credit to any West End showroom – the new Armstrong Siddeley was in pride of place in the 'L' and the remaining new Morris and Wolseley cars were all laid out in a clean and tidy condition.

One day I thought I was having a visit from Robin Day, the well-known TV personality. I looked up to find a gentleman advancing towards my office in a purposeful manner; complete with thick-frame spectacles and bow-tie, he would have passed for Robin Day anywhere. However, it was none other than Mr James Tye, of the British Safety Council, albeit virtually unknown in those days. He said he was interested in promoting safety, to which end he required us to purchase for one pound each some impressive looking certificates which stated that each car bearing this document had been thoroughly inspected in respect of several safety items such as steering, brakes, tyres, etc under the auspices of the British Safety Council. Now I am all in favour of proper trading standards, and every car that we sold at Hamtune Motors was properly serviced, inspected and tested prior to being offered for sale, so I was certainly interested in this official sounding organization. I took Mr Tye round our workshops, where I had my own mechanic exclusively for sales cars, and I was at pains to show off our facilities, for Harry spared no expense in regard to workshop equipment. Nonetheless I had the distinct feeling that there was not a great deal of interest in what I had to say, and to the question as to how the Council ensured that garages offering these certificates were monitored I received a vague and evasive reply. However, the British Safety Council did sound very impressive and official, so I asked Mr Tye to return that afternoon so that I might speak to my managing director. When Harry arrived later in the morning and I put him in the picture I experienced yet another side of his nature when, without preamble, he put a call through to the House of Commons and obtained with no difficulty whatsoever the ear of a very well-known Conservative MP.

With a great many "old boys", the inquiry established that the British Safety Council had no official recognition whatsoever at that time. However, Mr James Tye was not unknown. "Worthless bits of paper", said Harry on completion of his call, "best left alone." On Mr Tye's return I thanked him and told him we were not interested. Nearly 30 years later I read that he had been causing a rumpus outside a shop for some reason or another and I wrote him a polite letter, gently pulling his leg and saying with all sincerity how much I had admired his capacity for self-publicity and that of the British Safety

Council over the years. Unfortunately, in his reply he chose quite unnecessarily to be offensive.

The used Sapphire had been sorted out to some extent, but it was a very long way from being in good condition. They were not the sort of cars that attracted a ready trade buyer at the best of times, so there was no way I could hope to auction it, and in the meantime I had been driving it myself to get a general impression. There was no doubt that they were a fine car in the very best British tradition for fine coachbuilding, with lots of real polished woodwork and leather within, and a very pleasing shape with its long sloping back and rear-wheel spats. The petrol consumption for such a large car was remarkable for the period, being no less than a reliable 21mpg with a synchromesh box and 19mpg for the automatic version. Unfortunately, the one I was driving was fitted with the optional Wilson preselector gearbox, which would have been fine except that instead of being mated to a fluid drive, like those I had driven extensively in the Army in the Daimler Armoured Cars, Armstrong Siddeley used a centrifugal clutch. The gearchange was no problem, but the act of moving away from a standing start made the car jerk alarmingly and created the most odd tortured mechanical noises.

With a price tag of a little below £2,000 for the automatic version now on view in our window I didn't see us selling a great many. In the event I was quite wrong, as things were to turn out later, whilst unknown to me there were other factors in the background that were to help turn the tide in my favour. Not the least of these was a huge scar that was appearing across the countryside, part of it not 2 miles from my home near the village of Hartwell, this being the local section of the brand new M1 motorway. Apart from any long-term benefits, it was not long before John Hayes was telling me that he had a 'party' working on the motorway, me boy, who was looking for a big car to transport bodies here and there, so could he show him the Sapphire? He most certainly could, and to my relief he turned up at Park Garage the next morning with a large deposit and a request for a new radio to be fitted. I threw in the most powerful radio I could find for nothing, hoping that it would detract from the noises in the engine. There was a sequel to this: John Laing, the constructors, had to build temporary bridges to one side of all the roads which were to cross the motorway so that the new permanent bridges could be constructed, and on minor roads these for the most part were single-line Bailey bridges. One Sunday afternoon a few weeks later I was about to cross one of these when I saw a car coming towards me, so I waited. To my horror it was the Sapphire, gleaming like a new pin and sounding worse than ever. I sat there hoping that I might not be recognized, but I was. The car drew to a halt and the window was wound down. "Glad I ran into you, I'm off to Germany with the old car for two years next week; it goes like a bomb!" With that he was gone, thankfully never to be seen again.

So as the M1 proceeded I reorganized the business and slowly got things moving; we even started to shift the odd new car as I drew on my past experience to make friends and influence people. There is always a brisk demand for good almost-new cars from people who cannot run to a new one. We used to present ours in super condition, so before long we had acquired a good reputation, while Sheep Street was a valuable asset as an outlet for the older cars taken in part-exchange. John Hayes usually knew a 'party' somewhere who would be interested in whatever was available at any given time, so most of the cars over three years old went to him for resale. By far the biggest cross I had to bear was Harry Hawtin Frisby. He was a big man in every sense of the word, with a heart of gold. I wouldn't dare, for instance, to mention in passing that my wife might have a headache or a cold, for he would simply refuse to let me stay on the premises. "Your place is with your wife if she is sick, old boy", he would boom. " Off you go now, I can take care of things here." The problem was he most certainly could not take care of things. Not to mince words, in commercial life he was a well-meaning pain in the arse.

As already mentioned, Harry didn't have a pretty face. My office was divided from his by a thin partition topped with bobbled glass. On many occasions I would be at my desk discussing a deal with a potential client when we would become aware of Harry peering at us through the distorted glass like some monstrous fish. I had become used to it, but to a client it could be quite off-putting. On one occasion when he made his presence known in this manner I was actually in the process of selling a car. This time he tapped on the window with a "can you spare a moment, old boy?". I could hardly refuse, so making my excuses to the client I went next door where, by this time, Harry was seated behind his desk. Waving his hands in a conspiratorial manner, he said in a loud stage whisper which could clearly be heard next door: "Shut the door, old boy, I want to tell you something." I shut the door. Jerking his thumb in the general direction of my office, and in the same audible stage whisper, he said: "What does he want?" "The gentleman," I said somewhat heavily, "is interested in a new car." To my horror Harry drew a deep breath and continued: "You want to watch him, old boy, I knew his father." Not bothering to inquire as to the situation between Harry and my client's family, I returned in considerable embarrassment knowing that he must have heard every word. He simply shrugged his shoulders and walked out. Too angry to move, I lit a cigarette, and 10 minutes or so later Harry put his head round the door and as if nothing had occurred said: "How did you get on with him then?" "We did not, Mr Frisby, make a sale." He just grunted and departed without another word.

The next time he put a spoke in, however, I really lost my temper. It was a quiet Saturday afternoon at Park Garage, and as I wished to go early for some reason, I left the lad in charge and on the way home looked into Sheep Street, where John was in earnest conversation with a customer who had just tried out a car that we had had in stock for some time. It is by no means unknown in the motor business for a perfectly good car to hang about for some reason. It may be that the colour is not fashionable at the time, or perhaps it is the wrong spec, but the fact remains that it is money tied up and therefore it needs moving. This was plainly a job for management, so John introduced me to his customer. Now selling often requires a great deal of patience, and contrary to popular belief it does *not* require a stream of high-pressure talk. A good salesman is a good listener, who is able to direct a conversation in the manner most advantageous to him so that he might gain information by which the customer can be assisted in making his up his mind. The main problem with this gentleman was that he was without his wife, and simply not used to making up his own mind. As his wife had departed that day for the East Coast on a week's holiday with the kids, this was clearly a now-or-never situation.

It took perhaps an hour, but eventually the client was in the office and ready to go, a price having been agreed for his car in exchange and the paperwork all but ready for formal signature when the phone rang. It was Harry Frisby. "Anything doing, old boy?", while I held the phone away to protect my eardrums. "Yes, Mr Frisby, I have a customer with me just now, I'll call you back shortly." No such luck. "What's he want?", boomed Harry while I pressed the phone close to my ear and glanced at John Hayes, who raised an eyebrow to convey that he could hear every word. "Mr Frisby", I persevered, "we are just selling the Ford Consul – I'll call you back", nudge-nudge, hint-hint. But Harry was determined to be obstreperous to the bitter end: "What's he got to put in part-exchange then?" In vain I tried just once more: "Mr Frisby, may I *please* call you back?" But he would have none of it. "Never mind all that, old boy, I'm the managing director and I want to know what's going on." I gave up. "The client has a 1955 Austin A50 and I am just in the process of signing him up." By this time I was sweating. "How much did you have to pay for that?" Jesus, I thought, and told him. "You got that cheap, old boy, see you Monday", and he rang off. As it happened the car was not cheap, and in any case Harry wouldn't have recognized a cheap car if it ran him over, but the damage had been done. Pretending that nothing had happened I passed over the order for signature, but it was a futile gesture. With a predictable "Well, perhaps I should think about it over the weekend", the customer walked out, never to be seen again.

To have had all that time and effort ruined for nought was just too much. Without so much as a "Goodnight" to John, I got in my car and headed for The Limes, at Gayton, where the Frisbys resided, as Harry once put it, "in splendid isolation, old boy". I was bad-tempered when I left, and by the time I reached The Limes I was fuming. Mary took one look at my face and in silence showed me to the lounge, to be shortly followed by Harry, beaming all over his face. I came straight to the point. "We did not", I told him, "sell the Consul." Without mincing my words I told him concisely and precisely why we had not sold the flaming Consul. Mary walked out; it was clear that this particular situation was all down to HHF. He started to bluster. "You can't talk to me like that, I'm your boss." "Then try to act like one", I said, getting up to leave. "It took me a whole hour to sell that car, we needed to sell that car, you and me both, and you ruined the deal in one minute flat." I guessed that Mary was somewhere close at hand and that Harry was well aware of this. He deflated like a punctured balloon and put an arm round my shoulder. "I treat you like a son, old boy", was all he said, which was perfectly true. "I'll make sure it doesn't happen again." There was really no answer to that, so I left knowing for certain that before long he would put his foot in it again one way or the other.

Anyway, trade was about to take an unexpected turn for the better as far as we were concerned and I was to learn that some of the more inspired ideas in life occur almost by accident. In a corner of our showroom was a brand new Wolseley 6/90; not one of the quicker selling cars of the era at best, and this one had been in stock for some time. One afternoon a gentleman had walked in and he was viewing the Wolseley with, it seemed, rather more than a passing interest. I have said before that I often prefer to say little at the outset of a sales situation while I weigh up both the client and the possibilities. After the usual courtesies I contented myself with the odd indirect question while seeking information. In this seemingly casual manner I was able to discover that the gentleman was not local, that he was on his way to Wellingborough to visit a client, and that one of the reasons he had stopped was that he had noted that we were agents for Armstrong Siddeley cars. As it was a Wolseley that he had been viewing it was not hard to surmise that it was an Armstrong Siddeley he was trying to unload. At that moment I spotted a lady on the pumps for whom I had a message, so taking the opportunity I excused myself for a moment, walked to her car, and while chatting had a quiet look round. Sure enough, parked on the far side of the forecourt was a Sapphire 346 saloon, as large as life and very handsome indeed, finished in black over light beige. Any motor dealer will confirm that there are a few used cars on offer at any given time that look just right from any distance and from any angle. Close examination in these cases is a formality for you just know that when you open the doors the interior will not only look new, it will smell new, the carpets will be protected by rubber mats and the ashtrays will confirm the owner to be a nonsmoker. For the rest the coachwork will gleam on the most dismal of days and be it wet the car will be covered with globules of water confirming that every panel had been meticulously Simonized. As a matter of course the car will have all of the desirable options and extras. This Sapphire was just such a car, and even our dour, elderly petrol attendant was sufficiently moved to comment: "Not a bad old bus for a strong-arm Sid".

I returned to my customer; by this time he had seen all that he wanted to see and doubtless had convinced himself that if he were able to unload his four-year-old Sapphire he could live with a Wolseley. Unknown to him I had likewise convinced myself that, with all due regard for the capital invested in the new car relative to the probable value of his, Geoffrey was willing to stick his neck out. There were, however, some delicate negotiations ahead as this was plainly a capable businessman and I thanked God that Harry was on holiday somewhere in the wilds of Scotland. Nonetheless I took the precaution of telling the secretary that if Harry should call, I was out. Battle commenced when the client fired the first salvo: "I quite like this Wolseley car, I'm looking for something that is well-finished and a little smaller than the one we have now. "Innocently: "What are you running at the moment then?" "One of yours, a Sapphire 346." Suitable pause for effect: "Oh." He looked at me sharply: "Well, you take them in, don't you?" "Well we do, but usually in exchange for a replacement Sapphire." At this point he made his first mistake. "Well I certainly wouldn't buy another one of those, you lose too much money." In one sentence he had confirmed that he had tried other dealers and that he was prepared to be reasonable.

At this point I wanted to have a quick look at *Glass's Guide* to obtain some idea of what he might have had offered elsewhere. In those days the *Guide* wasn't flashed around in front of clients in the way it is today. "I'll just let my secretary know where I am, then we'll have a look at your car and see what we can do, just give me a moment." With that I dashed into Janet's office for a quick butchers, then strolled out to the showroom from where we proceeded outside to view the car. I made a show of a close inspection; as expected the whole car was superb, with a total mileage well below the average. I turned to the client: "Well, I'll say one thing, the car is a credit to you." The client beamed. With men of this calibre you do not waffle, so I named a price that was close to fair and reasonable and furthermore I knew that *he* knew it to be fair and reasonable. As expected he named a higher figure, but I simply shrugged my shoulders in a negative gesture. He went to get in his car. "Here's my card, give me a ring if you change your mind." I ignored the card and held open his door for him. "If you were to accept the car in the showroom I'll give you a bit more." He was too quick. "How much more?" I named a price roughly halfway and made it quite clear that this was the best on offer by politely wishing him a safe journey. We had a deal! That is a short version of what occurred; it took perhaps an hour and was relatively straightforward insofar as it was a deal between consenting adults each willing to sell and to purchase a particular car – at a price. It also illustrates the difference compared with dealing in cars at the present time, when there are so many special deals, discounts and nought per cent finance offers that nobody really knows the price of anything anymore.

While I was delighted with the transaction, I now had to move into stage two before I was anything like home and dry. So far I had moved a large chunk of metal that had been tieing up part of our inevitable bank overdraft, without which most motor traders would be unable to function; the injection of a substantial cash sum would enable this to be reduced at once. However, I was still left with a car to sell which many 'experts' in the trade regarded as a lemon in any condition. The temptation to use it for a day or so was irresistible; this Sapphire had the four-speed synchromesh gearbox and was a joy to drive. It attracted a great deal of attention, but no punters, at least in the pubs that I used at the time.

I decided to advertise the car nationally in either *Motor* or *Autocar*. It seemed to me that a few bare lines could hardly convey to a prospective client the very real quality of the goods that we had on offer, so I sat down and wrote out a description of this superb car that I hoped would transmit my genuine enthusiasm. I quoted an above-average price and stated that we *might* consider a part-exchange which, to my way of thinking, was a subtle way of saying: "We have a bloody good car, for which we don't want a load of old tat in part-exchange just to effect a sale." And it worked.

When it appeared in print even I was taken aback by its length as a classified advertisement. It certainly stood out on the page under the heading 'Armstrong Siddeley For Sale'. Little did I realize that I was starting a trend, for ads of this kind have been copied many times over the years, but the series I was to run were without any doubt the first and, incidentally, were the subject of a great deal of mickey-taking from my contemporaries. Of course, they were not cheap. The morning the advert came out I arrived to find my young trainee trying to deal with a someone who had seen it. He was aggressive from the moment of introduction. The car, he informed me, had had a complete respray, what was more the mileage was most certainly questionable. I made no comment, nor did I mention the fact that I had in my office a complete service history, for the owner had always taken the car to the maker's own service depot at Coventry. I had decided that rather than match rudeness with rudeness I would say as little as possible. He walked around the car with an air of contempt, trying to find something tangible to criticize. At length he voiced the opinion that the price was bloody stupid, but that he might possibly make an offer after a trial run.

Not on your flaming life, I thought to myself, and fortuitously I was called to the telephone before I had a chance to put this joker firmly in his place. The gentleman on the phone had also noted the advertisement for the Sapphire; he introduced himself and came straight to the point. "I have been in touch with Mr Brian Bramley" (he was the home sales manager of Armstrong Siddeley Motors Ltd) "and he tells me that you are a reliable dealer for the marque, so is this car all that you say it is?" I advised him of the service history that I held and assured him: "Yes, the car is exactly as described." "In that case you will have a call from my bank in 15 minutes confirming that their certified cheque by way of a deposit is on its way, and I would like to collect next week. That car is precisely what I require down to the colour. I trust this is satisfactory to you." There was something about this man that I liked! "That will not be necessary, just give me your name and address so that I can send written confirmation, and I will deliver to you as required. If you don't like the car on presentation I'll gladly take it back without question." He gave me the required details, thanking me profusely, and closed by saying: "I'll send you that deposit anyway." He was as good as his word.

There was now one small and pleasant task to be completed. Taking a 'SOLD' label from my desk drawer, I returned to the showroom where my young salesman, ever helpful, had removed the plastic descriptive labels from the windscreen ready for a demonstration drive that it had been my intention to flatly refuse even prior to being called away. There was no point in argument or recrimination, so without a word I licked the label – never had gum tasted so sweet! – and stuck it slap in the centre of the windscreen before turning on my heel. "Hey, hold on, what do you think you're doing?" I paused: "The car, sir", I said, loving every moment, "has been sold". I think he thought I was having him on, but I was in no mood to elaborate and strode off through my office to the secretary's office at the rear, closing both doors firmly behind me. "A letter and a contract of sale, young lady, if you please, but first a nice cup of tea while I tell you what happened." After a while the lad joined us. "Coo", he said, "he weren't half cross!" That, however, was only the start of things. The phone rang again with another inquiry and continued to ring for the next week. It seemed there was more than a passing interest in used Armstrong Siddeley cars.

Now one of the peculiar things about the motor business is that odd or unusual events unfailingly come in twos and threes. You get a warranty claim or a breakdown on a new car that has scarcely ever been known throughout its entire production life and you'll get another within a week or so. Sell a spare part that has been on the shelves for months and somebody will want one just like it within days. It has something in common with the phenomenon that you can be in your office all day, but go to the toilet and you will instantly be wanted on the telephone, or that the infallible way to attract customers on even the quietest of wet Saturdays is to get out your sandwich lunch and your newspaper and brew up!

Within a few days I was to be offered another Sapphire in part-exchange, but this time the client was interested in the new one in the showroom. Given confidence from the last deal, this presented no problems at all and I had the satisfaction of being able to tell Harry Frisby on his return that I had sold two very expensive new cars, and of course the part-exchange for one of them. While the second Armstrong Siddeley was not quite in the exceptional condition of the first, it was still a perfectly good car, and in fact in better than average condition. I had already advertised it at length in exactly the same manner as the first Sapphire and was waiting with fingers crossed for publication day. To my delight the phone started to ring, just as before, and the car had been sold satisfactorily by the weekend, leaving in its wake a number of very disappointed potential customers. It was becoming apparent that there was a useful market out there for good used Armstrong Siddeley cars; that day I decided that Hamtune Motors Ltd were about to specialize – in Armstrong Siddeleys and others.

I'll say one thing in regard to Harry Frisby: providing the business was going well and Mary was happy, he didn't interfere in the manner in which I ran it. When I told him I was proposing to specialize in Armstrong Siddeleys and why, his only comment was: "Sounds alright to me, old boy", leaving me with the impression that I could just as well have suggested we specialize in plastic ducks. On reflection I don't recall that he even queried the cost of the classified adverts. My first move was to place a small ad in both *Motor* and *Autocar* under the heading 'Armstrong Siddeley Wanted'. The result was almost overwhelming. Before long we were receiving inquiries from all over the country from owners who wished to sell or exchange their cars for one reason or another. Most told the same story: on offering their cars in part-exchange to local motor agents they had either been declined on the grounds that "nobody wants one of those", or been offered such a low price that they felt insulted. Not all of the cars on offer were suitable to my requirements because of their condition or high mileage, so these were quickly eliminated. The owners of those which sounded the most promising were first questioned as to the liklihood of their purchasing a replacement new car as these were obviously given top priority.

In this manner, over the coming months we sold several quite expensive new cars, accepting Sapphires in part-exchange, so we kept the workshop busy preparing these as well as the Sapphires I had been buying for cash. Inevitably some needed minor paint rectification to bring them to the standard that I intended to maintain, and these were sent to a local high-class coachbuilder. In no time at all we were carrying around six or seven used Armstrong Siddeleys in stock, plus two or three new ones. On the whole I had my hands full. One of the first Armstrong Siddeleys we were to be offered on a cash basis, with no replacement required, provided a particularly odd set of circumstances, not the least of these being that up to that time I had hardly heard of, let alone seen, the model on offer! The proud owner, who had driven some considerable distance to us on the strength of my advert, arrived one afternoon as I was completing a picnic lunch in my office. He advised me he wished to sell his Armstrong Siddeley 234.

Some four years back, one of the best kept secrets of the 1955 Earls Court Motor Show had been the introduction of two new cars from Armstrong Siddeley: the model 234 and 236 Sapphires. While they caused a great deal of interest in informed motoring circles they would not have warranted much more than a curious glance from me at the time, being 'out of my class'. Unfortunately, the cars had not been well received, the kinder of their critics noting that they were "not aesthetically pleasing", while Basil Cardew, the motoring correspondent of the *Sunday Express* at the time, felt that the design was "enterprising". Rumours had been circulating freely that one designer had been commissioned to create the front half, another the back, and the two had been mated prior to production. Whatever the truth of this, the final result certainly seemed to suggest that this had been so. On the credit side, the 234 had a performance that was quite outstanding for the time: 0 to 60mph in a creditable 15.5sec (*Autocar* road test), this being only 1sec slower than the Jaguar 2.4, the two having an identical maximum speed of 100mph. The 236, with some 30 per cent less power, was intended as a touring machine and had sold in even fewer numbers than the 234.

With an original price in the region of £1,600 the car was a non-event. As I was still with Ches at the time of its introduction I hadn't paid much attention to what had been written about the two models in the motoring press. Then along came Suez and the general panic throughout the motor trade; Armstrong Siddeley, doubtless already up to their ears in trouble with these models, slashed their price by almost a third to £1,066. This meant that the cars were significantly cheaper than the MG Magnette which, nice car that it was, was not in the same class as the hand-built 234 Sapphire, however unattractive; at the end of the day beauty is only skin deep. When the Suez crisis came to an end the 234s and even the 236s, which had been stockpiled, began to sell like buttered buns. However, there was no way that these fine-quality cars could be produced to sell at this price, so at the end of the run the models were quietly dropped.

Subsequent issues of *Glass's Guide* were to show the final list price as being £1,066 so future used-car values being calculated from this basis, the cars were grossly undervalued on the used-car market. None of this information being available to me at the time, I asked the customer to hang on while I repaired to the loo with my copy of the current month's *Guide* to get at least some idea of what the hell I was going to do without making a complete arse of myself. 'The book' didn't give a great deal of information, and I might well have taken the last list price as a misprint, but I remember that both trade and retail looked surprisingly low for what was undoubtedly a quality car. There was nothing for it but to try and bluff it out, so flushing the toilet out of habit rather than need, I went back outside.

The car sat on the forecourt in a very dark green and without question it was another outstanding example, if anything even fractionally better than the 346 that had started the process, for the mileage was still in the four-figure range. Now when a car is four years old the shape is not quite such a consideration, and while it certainly looked a bit odd, the vehicle somehow sort of grew on you. There was no question that a very great deal of thought had gone into the interior; two huge cloth individual seats in the front with a mean looking gear-lever in the centre. Highly polished walnut dash containing sharp black instruments with fluorescent green figures, thick carpeting and an appreciable amount of room for passengers in the back. I sat in the front seat, trying to look knowledgeable: "How much are you looking for?" He was not looking for a great deal, he knew the score, he said, but he had been posted abroad.

At that point the cavalry arrived. Just as I was getting out of the driving seat ready to say to the poor man something on the lines of "Don't call us, we'll call you", on to the forecourt drove the maroon-and-grey Armstrong with its attendant cloud of blue smoke. Hardly had it drawn to a halt when I heard: "Afternoon – can you spare a minute, old boy?" At this moment even Harry was a welcome diversion, so I went to greet him at the showroom entrance. "What's he want?", pointing to the owner of the 234. "He wants to sell his car." "Crikey, you want to buy that then, old boy, sell like hot cakes they do!", and off he went to his office.

So I came to an agreement with the owner on the basis of trade price plus a bit extra for low mileage, then I drove him to the railway station in his former car. I must say I was considerably impressed. My first reaction was that for a sports saloon it was the most comfortable car I had ever driven, from which point I was to discover superb performance and an ability to go round corners as if on rails. Then to add to my astonishment I was to discover, after using the car for a day or so, petrol consumption was close to 30mpg, which in 1959 was quite outstanding for a 100mph 2,290cc motor car. On arrival back at Park Garage Harry was thumbing through *Glass's Guide*. "What are you going to sell that for?", he asked. "Well", I began in my best considered opinion manner, "it's only done a few thousand miles, so I shall be wanting over book." "Over book, old boy? I'll say it's worth over book, the last one we had just before you came we bloody near got list price for!" He was perfectly correct, we did just that. Harry wasn't always wrong; he even told me to avoid the 236 like the plague. Over the next two years we always had a waiting list for any 234 models we managed to obtain. I recall one that we purchased had the registration number VSM 1; I just wish I had that one today!

Because of the nature of the cars, our stock was coming from all parts of the country, as indeed were our inquiries. Buying was not too much of a problem as most owners were only too pleased to send their cars to us on receipt of a firm underwritten price, but where the purchase of a new car was involved naturally it was expected that we should make the effort to visit. Furthermore, for the most part I had to be prepared to take our cars almost anywhere to conclude a sale. Mind you, this was always done after a great deal of careful qualification on the telephone, and of course our cars had to be precisely as described. Interestingly, we never once brought back an Armstrong Siddeley Sapphire unsold, but I was certainly covering a great deal of mileage. It became obvious that we needed help, for the Morris, Wolseley and MG side of the business was becoming neglected, along with the bread-and-butter used-car side, so I advertised and found Arthur Maynard.

Now Arthur did not know a great deal about Armstrong Siddeleys when we first met, but he certainly knew a great deal about Rolls-Royce and his experience of dealing with clients at this level was to prove invaluable. Arthur would perhaps be best described as a 'gentlemen's gentleman', who knew how to be courteous and had a fund of stories based on real life with which he could amuse us for hours on end. He had two favourite expressions: one, to express his extreme disapproval or incredulity, was "Well, stone me!" (he was a great fan of the late Tony Hancock), and the other, which became my old man's nickname for him – he always referred to Arthur as "Old by-and-large". He was a donnish character in his fifties, with thick wavy hair, a sharp nose supporting heavy spectacles, and piercing blue eyes. In general appearance he was not unlike Dennis Norden, and every bit as dry.

We shared a passion for being on time, which was almost a religion. It was Arthur's proud boast that no matter how far he took a car on demonstration he would arrive early, park around the corner until the appointed time and ring the bell on the dot. This simple courtesy never failed to impress. I particularly remember one occasion when we went together for some reason to demonstrate a car. I tend to be absent-minded with names, so having traced the address and parked around the corner with Arthur studying his wristwatch and calculating how long would be required to drive up to the house and walk up the drive, I interrupted his train of thought: "What did you say his name was?" "Lawn", said Arthur abruptly, "think of mower." Ten or so minutes later we walked up the drive and Arthur rang the bell on the second. An astonished client opened the door; he knew we had come almost 100 miles. "Good afternoon, Mr Mower", I said brightly, somewhat spoiling the effect.

We cleaned our own cars as a team; the young salesman and I would look after the coachwork while Arthur would sit for hours polishing the dashboard and the general interior. 'Freestone and Webbing' he used to call it as he worked away with his cloth and polish with the inevitable cigarette going, for we all smoked at that time. The end result would be well worth the effort and I would insist that all toolkits were complete to the last item and that each car had its handbook ready for the new owner.

It was Arthur who suggested that I really ought to purchase my own home. By this time I could well afford it, and while I loved the life at Salcey Lawn I could see that a house of our own would be an investment. Wilsons of Northampton were building property all over the area, and Arthur had bought one of their bungalows on the town outskirts; he introduced me to their sales manager. Inevitably I favoured the country life and one development under way was in Pilgrims Lane, in a tiny village called Bugbrooke, some 10 miles west of the town centre. This was no Salcey Lawn, but Bugbrooke was a pretty enough village at that time with a lovely church, later to attract some notoriety when it was taken over by an odd religious sect, and two pubs. As I remember it, when we moved in the population was around 1,000. For a brand new three-bedroom bungalow with a 30-yard garden I paid the princely sum of £1,050, which attracted a mortgage of £12 per month! The manager of the building society told me that the mortgage could only be granted subject to me taking out certain insurance policies in respect of the house value and the mortgage repayments, but that these, he advised me, would stand me in good stead should I require another mortgage in the future. I later realized that both policies were unnecessary, and indeed worthless, but no doubt were insisted upon in order to obtain commission from the insurance company. And they call the motor trade crooked!

So we moved to our new home and joined in the village life. Every evening I would walk Bella in the quiet lanes, and on Sundays we would go further afield, often covering the towpaths of the canal which ran nearby and always finishing up at my new local, *The Bakers Arms*, where I was honoured to be invited to play for the skittle team in league matches. It was a very satisfactory period of my life and I had hoped that it would last forever. But unknown to me at the time, there were dark clouds on the horizon.

Barry Wilson, our young trainee, had left and been replaced by another young man who was to prove his worth in the motor trade. My first meeting with Mike Logue was memorable if only because he was so painfully shy and hardly said a word. It must have been something to do with having two extrovert older sisters, but some instinct told me that he had potential so we took him on. He was to prove the best trainee I ever had and we worked closely together for many years. To this day he is still engaged in the Northampton motor trade, now a successful manager in his own right. He came from a good family, and his father was principal of the local agricultural college. For a start we sent him off to join John Hayes at Sheep Street, where he had a few edges knocked off him and became more forthcoming. Now that Park Garage had moved upmarket, Sheep Street was getting a better class of car to sell and John certainly had no complaints on that score.

By now Arthur was taking care of all the long-distance sales and quite a few of the Armstrong Siddeley purchases for which he was entirely suited due to his unique personality. Absolutely everyone liked Arthur Maynard on sight, also he was totally reliable and entirely trustworthy. This meant that I could devote more time to the increasing number of new-car inquiries which were coming our way, both for Armstrong Siddeley, as we were rapidly becoming the number-one dealer nationwide, and for the Morris, Wolseley and MG ranges as Hamtune Motors assumed a new respectability with the constant turnover of very expensive machinery going through the doors. Arthur had not been with us long before he was given a practical demonstration of the Irish Jeeves at his very best. Of course, he had already been told of John's remarkable ability to produce just about anything at short notice, so one afternoon, when we called in to Sheep street on the way back from somewhere, Arthur had an opportunity to put John to the test. His son, who was left-handed, had been pestering Arthur for a golf club. This, Arthur had thought, was the ultimate challenge, so on the way out he casually asked John if he knew of anyone who wished to get rid of a left-handed golf club? With not as much as a single twist of the ample moustache, John turned on his heel and with a "Just a sec, me boy, I may be able to help you there", vanished downstairs to the boiler room, returning after a suitable pause triumphantly brandishing a golf club, left-handed of course! "Well, stone me!", said Arthur. Well I mean, what else could he say?

Around this time three important events occurred. Firstly, Harry and Mary Frisby were blessed with a baby son, Graham. Second, they celebrated by appointing me to the board of directors with an increase in salary and an annual bonus, which was very welcome as this demonstrated both confidence and appreciation of my ability, and thirdly, the British Motor Corporation introduced the Austin/Morris

Mini, the trendsetting world-beater on which they were to earn virtually nothing and learn even less. Like the magnificent Jaguars and Range Rovers that were to follow, they were grossly underpriced from day one, with the result that the only significant profits went entirely to the dealer network, particularly those not hidebound by outmoded convention and shrewd enough to deal at over list price. And why not, indeed? So-called consumer associations which have been bleating for a *free* market, where price prevails over all other considerations, must accept that any shortage will create extraordinary market forces of its own. I would contend that any BMW, Mercedes-Benz or Jaguar dealer in particular (at time of writing, when all of these models are fetching a premium), or for that matter any other dealer who sells his product for less than its full market value in these enlightened times, is a fool both to himself and to his shareholders.

However, to get back to the Mini. Harry Frisby and I, together with representatives from the retail dealer network in Northamptonshire, were invited to Henlys, the main distributor for the county, where a small party had been arranged for a preview. The night was memorable, for me at any rate, but this had little to do with the car. It may well have been the wine, but I had never seen Harry like this before, nor was I to again. He was not just voluble, he was the very life and soul of the party. Bearing in mind that most of those worthy dealers regarded him as a bit of a joke due to his infamous past, I have to say that I was proud of him that night as he regaled his audience with tales from his prewar days and his Army experiences. He was undoubtedly the star of the show that night, and I recall one noted dealer, a Rotarian, a JP and an ex-Mayor, muttering to a crony on the way out: "Never knew the old bugger had it in him – what an extraordinary man!" While I was driving Harry home to Blisworth, he said to me casually: "I enjoyed that little evening, old boy", and he was genuinely surprised when I replied: "Mr Frisby, didn't we all!"

The Mini was to provide Mike Logue with a practical object lesson in the value of the very high professional standards that I set. I had no time then, nor have I now, for the airy-fairy manner in which so-called car sales executives value cars and accept them in part-exchange. These have to be resold, and as such they can so easily dent a company's bank balance or reputation. I had experienced for myself the potentially disastrous end results of this kind of third-rate trading when I joined Harry Frisby, and within a very short time I was to experience it again, only 10 times worse. I had worked throughout for motor dealers of considerable experience, who viewed every car offered with suspicion and carried out a methodical and detailed examination, culminating in a road test, before agreeing a price with a client. This may sound fanciful today, but in the Fifties and Sixties mechanical parts were by no means as reliable or as well-built as they are today, and the evaluation of a car for resale required experience and sound judgment. I admit that in today's high-tech market I seldom if ever road-test a customer's car, but nonetheless I still make a proper examination before committing myself to a price.

Mike and his sisters, who ran a car between them, had decided to invest in the new Mini, and as Mike was employed by us naturally he came to me for a deal. Now the Mini, being new and underpriced, was in short supply and consequently we were able to sell every one we could lay our hands on without being embarrassed by tatty part-exchanges. Mike's family saloon was decidedly tatty, quite apart from the fact that one of the girls had clouted the offside on the gatepost a week or so earlier. I therefore suggested a little sales training exercise. Why not run it down to Cooper and Lines, a rival BMC dealer in the town, and see what they had to say? Mike was back within the hour, a broad grin on his face, with an offer that would have been plain daft even had their car been half-respectable. "Bloody hell, Mike, did they look at it?" "Well no, I parked it across the road in the only place available and the salesman just got his book out and made me an offer." "Mike Logue, you're having me on!" This was just too unbelievable. "No, of course I'm not, they say that I can have one that's due next month. What should I do?" I drew a deep breath. "I'll tell you what to do, young man, you just pop back in my car, tell them it's your mum's, place an order and leave a deposit; you can't go wrong." He got his new Mini in six weeks to the day, paid the bill and drove off, but still nobody had bothered to look at his car!

Some years later I was to attend a week-long sales management course at the Ford Motor Company, my brief on this particular day being to visit a local Vauxhall dealer to examine the newly introduced HA Viva as a potential client and to report to the others on my return as to how I had been received, sales staff product knowledge, etc. It was a wet day and I had to park 20 yards or so from the showroom on the far side of the road. The showrooms were both warm and comfortable. I viewed the car and a salesman appeared after an acceptable interval. His product knowledge was good and he made an admirable effort to sell the car. So far, so good. "How much", I asked, "for my 1961 105E Ford Anglia?". *Glass's Guide* appeared as if by magic. "Where is the car, sir?", starting to thumb the pages. "Over there, by the post office." The salesman walked to the window and peered through the rain. "Yes sir, we will be pleased to allow £XXX for that", he said, naming a near enough reasonable price for the day. I made my excuses and left.

As stated elsewhere, all courses usually contain one comedian, and there used to circulate a story, which may or may not be true, of some joker in the late Fifties who was sent out on the same exercise. At the time there were some oddball car manufacturers trying to carve a niche in the marketplace with names like Bond, Berkeley, Heinkel,

Messerschmitt, etc, all faithfully recorded in *Glass's Guide*, if only for a short time. Having viewed the new car, he asked the salesman if they would accept his present one in part-exchange. "Oh certainly, sir", the young salesmen replied brightly, "what have you got? "A 1950 Kodak", was the deadpan reply, leaving the young salesman frantically searching his book!

Hamtune Motors was by now well-established as an upmarket dealership, and our BMC franchise was developing in tandem. Ironically this was to be the cause of my future downfall. The British Motor Corporation in the latter part of the Fifties were perhaps at their postwar peak, and as far as the chairman, the board of directors and senior management could foresee, it was all going to last forever. All management were utterly complacent and basking in an air of reflected glory. On occasions I had reason to visit the Cowley works and I well remember a lighthearted argument with Mr K H J Sinnott, the home sales manager of Morris Motors Ltd, as I was about to depart after a good lunch. We had been discussing some aspect of the Sunbeam Rapier I happened to be driving at the time. His parting remark, after some 20 years of turmoil at the British Motor Corporation – later British Leyland, later still Austin Rover Group and now just plain Rover – might well have become a fitting obituary but for the timely intervention of Michael Edwardes as the Corporation's new boss. Sinnott said: "I wouldn't know, old boy. We used to have competitors – once."

His contemporary, Mr R R Holditch, the home sales manager of Wolseley Motors Ltd, had exactly the same complacent attitude as regards the future wellbeing of Wolseley. On my placing on record a particular client's bitter dissatisfaction with his new Wolseley 15/50, he actually stated – and I quote: "Well really, Mr Owen, your customer is very lucky indeed to obtain and to own a new Wolseley." Several complaints and two replacement rear axles later, both of which were to prove difficult to obtain, the client purchased a new Sunbeam Alpine from another garage in the town. At the time such attitudes were by no means untypical at this level of management, but even allowing for the fact that BMC's share of the home market in 1958 was 42.9 per cent – almost half the total – this kind of complacency is beyond belief. It has long been my opinion that this attitude filtered through to the shop floor via a third-rate management structure at both senior and junior level, thereby assisting the trades union militants in their endless quest for the power that all but brought the Corporation to its knees.

By this time quality was becoming a joke and availability of specific models and colours all but impossible. Certainly I could obtain new cars, the problem was there was no choice of colour or specification unless my customers were prepared to wait for an indeterminable period, and customers were rapidly becoming less obliging in that respect and were no longer willing to take whatever car was in the showroom simply because it happened to be there. The British Motor Corporation's attitude, on the other hand, seemed to be that customers were being most unreasonable in insisting on a colour or one of the options being advertised, such as an overdrive or a sunroof. Who did these people think they were, for heaven's sake, interfering with production schedules? After all, they were lucky to be able to buy one of these fine (*sic*) British products! Meanwhile, I was becoming irritated.

But at least for the moment this was a minor irritation as the bulk of our turnover came from high-class cars, and the new Armstrong Siddeley Star Sapphire was due to be released for production any day. Arthur was demonstrating and selling cars all over the country, I was looking after most of the purchases, for we had diversified into a few Daimler models as well, and John still had a seemingly inexhaustible supply of 'parties' in the far reaches of Northamptonshire to whom he was able to sell the bulk of our trade-ins. Once in a while I would travel with Arthur to keep my hand in, or just for a day off, for we usually had some adventure or other. Arthur was 'incident-prone' and was witness to several horrific road accidents on his many travels, but thankfully I managed to miss these. One trip we did to Manchester I had particular cause to remember. We had arrived with our car, dead on time as usual, the client had been taken on his demonstration run and expressed the desire to buy, but he had omitted to tell Arthur on the telephone that he had a car to part-exchange. Indeed he had given the impression that it would be a straight sale. In reality he was trying to be cute, for he was the owner of a virtually new Ford Consul convertible with an electric hood and almost nil mileage, which he had concluded he did not like. There was nothing wrong with the car, of course, but its probable true value relative to initial cost was unlikely to make this an easy transaction. However, both cars having been viewed, the client was in no mood to discuss business.

First we had to admire his electric train set, which was laid out in a huge room upstairs, there was no doubt it was an interesting layout and it must have cost a very great deal of money. After this we all went down to the lounge, where he produced a bottle of whisky and one of brandy. Well now, I thought to myself, so that's your little game is it? In those days I could drink a fair measure of scotch and stay lucid, while Arthur wisely chose not to drink at all, and so battle commenced. We argued the toss for the remainder of the morning and most of the afternoon, breaking off for a delicious meal prepared by his wife, who otherwise kept well clear of the negotiations. By late afternoon the old boy could hardly stand. While I could not claim to be sober, I knew exactly what I was doing as the argument now became quite belligerent, with him accusing me of trying to rob him blind, and me telling him that he had dragged us up to Manchester on a wild goose chase. "You think", I said at some stage, "that I won't take the bloody car back unsold, but I bloody well will, so there." It really got as bad as that. In the end we were some £25 apart. "Tell you what, I'll toss you for it", he offered. He did, and I won. While Arthur was making out a formal contract he fell asleep and we had to wake him up to produce a cheque book and sign. Arthur made out a cheque for the agreed amount, which he duly signed and promptly drifted off to sleep again. Then we couldn't find the keys to the Consul. His wife was nowhere to be found, but at length we found a set in the glovebox. The old boy was dead to the world, so we left a receipted invoice on his lap and drifted off.

We had just cleared Manchester when Arthur noted that the tank was low on petrol. It was then that we discovered that we had perhaps five bob between the two of us – no cheque cards or plastic money in those days. Arthur pulled on to a petrol forecourt, which was showing every sign of closing for the night. In the office we could see a very large, tough-looking gentleman and an equally large and mean-looking Alsatian dog. I prodded Arthur's chest: "Jush leave this to me". Up to the gills in scotch, I got unsteadily out of the car and made to knock on the door, which at once opened inwards and the hound rose to its full height. "Lo, Rover!" There was an ominous growl. "We're shut", said the man, his hand moving an inch or so to a shotgun near the desk. At this point Arthur appeared in the doorway, stone cold sober and courteous as always. The dog licked his hand. "Hello, boy", he said to the dog and the gent at the same time, "we have a bit of a problem." After this promising start, together with a fair bit of "by and large" and "stone me", the situation was explained at length. No-one could accuse Arthur of being a man of a few words, and by the time he had finished the gent was grinning from ear to ear and the dog had gone to sleep, bored to death. "Would the gentleman", concluded Arthur, "please telephone Mr Frisby, transfer charge, who would be pleased to verify who we were and guarantee payment, one petrol dealer to another. The call was duly made, and we both noted that when Harry came on the line the phone was moved from the ear a good three inches. In no time the tank was filled and we went on our way. I slept all the way to Bugbrooke, where Arthur finally dropped me off at God knows what time.

Everything, it seemed, was going my way because we had a good market for the used Armstrong Siddeley cars and we were able to sell competitively quite a fair number of new ones, enough to attract the attention of the makers, so when the new Star Sapphire was in the prototype stage Harry and I were one of the very few dealers invited to evaluate the model at the Motor Industry Proving Ground with its fine banked circuit at Lindley. The Star Sapphire was introduced at the 1959 Earls Court Motor Show and attracted much favourable comment. It was a great deal sleeker than its predecessor, with a longer and lower bootline. One of the options available on the duotone colour version was that the rear wings could be finished in the darker top-half colour, which gave the car an even sleeker look, so much so that we had some of our used 346 Sapphires painted in the same manner to good effect. With power steering and a Borg-Warner automatic gearbox as standard it was a lovely motor car, but unfortunately destined for a very short production life.

I attended the show that year on press preview day. The model on the raised stand was in gleaming white and looked a million dollars. It had already been sold to Richard Todd, the well-known film actor. There was another car on the stand, and both were fitted with the all-new steering wheel which could be adjusted for length by means of a small capstan nut on the column below the dashboard. However, there must have been a small production fault on this particular show car because when I arrived one of the sales staff, who must have been demonstrating this feature to the press, was sitting in the car with a look of pained embarrassment on his face and the steering wheel in his lap.

Harry Frisby had decided that we were to run a demonstration model and had asked me to "order a suitable specification, old boy". What he didn't tell me was that I was to have the use of the car for personal transport. He was still driving his dreadful old Armstrong Lancaster, from which he would not be parted, and there was I swanning round in the most expensive car I had ever driven. One Saturday morning when I had a day off I drew up at Park Garage for petrol, complete with vented tweed sports coat and matching cap, as Harry chanced by: "You look like the younger son of an Earl, old boy" was his parting remark.

One of my demonstration drives was provided on request to a Mr Marriott, a well-known shoe manufacturer in Rushden, Northants. After the drive I was invited into his palatial office where, without preamble, he gave me an order for his new Armstrong Siddeley with a very precise specification. All of his cars, he said, had been provided in a special Rolls-Royce two-tone grey finish and this one was to be no exception, Mr Marriott being quite prepared to pay extra for this service. Also, with regard to the front seating, he required this to be from a left-hand-drive model so that the wider part of the split bench would be on the driver's side, and in addition he required a quote for the provision of polished wood picnic tables, similar to those in the Rolls-Royce Silver Cloud. In view of the special requirements I organized a trip to the factory, where Mr Marriott and I were entertained by both Walter Henley and Brian Bramley, Armstrong Siddeley's director of sales and sales manager, respectively. Everything, of course, was arranged to the specification required; the extra cost of the special paintwork escapes my memory, but when it came to the picnic tables I can remember clearly Brian saying casually: "Sixty guineas be alright?", which was instantly accepted. In those days you could purchase a very good-quality dining room suite for that kind of money! In Robert Penn Bradly's book *Armstrong Siddeley – The Postwar Cars* (published by Motor Racing Publications Ltd) that car, chassis number 330706, is listed as the only one supplied with picnic tables of this kind.

Each summer Harry and his family would set off on their holidays, and most times they would put the car on the train and tour Scotland or drive down to the West Country, doubtless finding the short cuts. Each year, a few days before departure, we would go through the same procedure. Harry would wander into my office and sit down. "I'm off on holiday on Saturday, old boy, have we got anything that I could use? Mary is not keen on the Lancaster." At once I would offer the Star Sapphire; after all it was his car. "No, certainly not, old boy, you may well need that for a demonstration." We would then proceed through the stocklist, eliminating one after the other as being "too small, old boy", "not taxed", etc. When we had eliminated the lot I would once again suggest the Sapphire. "Now, you're absolutely sure, old boy? I don't want to rob you of your car." "Yes, Mr Frisby", I would insist, "you really must take the Star." "Thank you very much, old boy." Come the weekend and he would be off, and that would be that until the next year, when we would go through the same procedure once again.

With a price tag of just below £2,500 the model was by no means expensive in the context of the luxury range of the time. We were well able to exceed the numbers which we were expected to sell, but I suspect that many dealers were not meeting their targets. At any event we were quietly advised in 1960 that the Star was to be phased-out as Bristol Siddeley were to cease car production and the Armstrong Siddeley name was to be allowed to die. For me this was a cruel blow for it was obvious that the used market could only have a limited future, and the long-term effect was to exceed my worst fears, as will be seen. As one of the more successful dealers we were offered three of the final production run vehicles at a 40 per cent discount instead of the usual 20 per cent. I was pleased to accept these cars for I guessed that there would be a demand for the last of the series. The first arrived in two shades of green and I sold it at once to the Central Electricity Generating Board. They paid the full list price, and as the car was required in black they promptly sent it to an expensive London coachbuilder for a complete respray. Then they sent an order for one of the two remaining. Time went by and there being no sign of the second car I telephoned Brian Bramley at the factory to find out when it was likely to arrive; it was not going to arrive, for both cars had been re-allocated to other dealers. Harry Hawtin Frisby, it seemed, had got the wind up and quietly cancelled without consulting his director of sales. When I tackled him I asked if Mrs Frisby had had anything to do with his decision. Harry went purple, but I never did tell her, although my God, I was sorely tempted.

One morning I received an airmail letter from Australia which proved to be an inquiry for a used automatic Armstrong Siddeley 346. The writer was returning to England in six months' time and required the car for his homecoming. He had noted our advertisements in *Autocar*, he said, and concluded that we ought, given notice, be able to fix him up. I replied at once and quoted a price, and after a further exchange of letters he sent me a deposit and a date for his return. It could not have arrived at a better time for I was dealing with a gentleman in London who had just the car required and wished to exchange it for a new Daimler. I was able to kill two birds with one stone.

In due course I was able to present myself in a highly polished and most beautifully prepared Sapphire to meet Mr Latto and his family at Tilbury Docks. Now when a person shows that kind of faith it follows that you should go out of your way to ensure that the car presented is spot-on. Sod's Law being what it is, however, I was driving into the docks when an object rolled off a loading bay, bounced under the car, hitting the tailpipe and parting it from the rear silencer. Fortunately, no further damage was done, but the noise on restarting the engine was considerable and unpleasant, and it was with considerable embarrassment that I greeted Mr and Mrs Latto at the ship's gangway. As luck would have it, while I was loading the hand luggage and explaining the situation, a dockyard policeman came over to say that the company had accepted full responsibility and would be pleased to meet the full cost of the damage. He was also able to telephone friends at a local garage to arrange a temporary repair, which just got us back to Northampton. As the clients had arranged to stay in the town overnight *en route* to Scotland we had no problem fitting a new exhaust in good time to see them on their way the following morning.

For a year or so we managed to keep going while used models were available, and we also sold some Daimlers, but it couldn't last. We had reached the end of an era, for there were already a number of dealers specializing in the alternative low-volume makes such as Jaguar and Mercedes. I did, however, have one more success, albeit short-term, which came about in an odd way. I had continued to supplement my bread-and-butter stock from my old friends the Bercow brothers, in Warren Street, and one day Charles telephoned to tell me that he had the opportunity of buying a number of special export-specification Ford Consuls from a large self-drive company, which later turned out to be Godfrey Davis. The cars had been out on short-term lease to overseas visitors, and in the main had been driven by only the one customer; as a result the mileages of most cars were well below 5,000, with the remainder below 10,000. Charles had to agree to buy the lot or nothing over a period of time as the company didn't want to be bothered selling them on a piecemeal basis. These cars, of course, being generally in outstanding condition and with a specification rather better than the home-market model, would certainly not come cheap, although strangely enough for our climate none of them were fitted with heaters, so these would have to be added by the eventual purchaser.

"What's the numbers situation?", I asked. "Well, I have to buy five this afternoon and the remainder look like turning up on a four to five a week basis for the rest of the summer." "How much per car?", I asked, making rapid mental calculations relative to the current list price. On being told I made my decision. "OK, I'll take those and the others as they come." My word being good enough for Charles, it would not be long before my old acquaintance Redfern would have been told that his Consuls had been bought. I told Harry what I had done and got the expected "Sounds alright to me, old boy", so we were in business. That evening Charles and Ralph delivered the first two, Charles being the first to arrive. I can see that first car in my mind's eye to this very day; the colour was Ming Yellow, which in my opinion suited the Mk II Consul more than any other. The car had done very little mileage, and with the improved export upholstery and the extra trim fittings it was apparent even on a cursory inspection that if they were all like this one they would prove very desirable on the used-car market. Mentally increasing my proposed asking price as Ralph arrived in a dark green model, we went to my office to exchange cheques for paperwork. This may all sound very easy and laid back, but buying cars for resale in these numbers requires both experience and a flair for knowing what people will buy. Friends would often ask me which car I would buy personally, given unlimited financial circumstances, and be surprised when I said that I didn't know, the short answer being that in those days the only cars I liked were those I knew I could sell, and I was in no doubt whatsoever that these Consuls would sell if properly promoted.

So I booked a three-column by 6in ad in the local paper with a suitable heading on the lines of 'ALMOST NEW EXPORT MODEL FORD CONSULS' and devoted the rest of the space to a full description to provide interested clients with a mind's-eye picture, and it paid off. The advert appeared on the Friday, we had our first two sales on Friday evening, one each at Park Garage and Sheep Street, where John doubtless had a 'party' lined up. By close of business on the Saturday we had sold the four that had so far been delivered and accepted deposits on another on its way up plus a further one that had not yet been advised. Over the coming weeks we sold the lot from perhaps three or four adverts, more or less as they arrived. Some 25 years later I met the then advertising manager of that newspaper and he reminded me of that little campaign and the furore it had created among the town's motor dealers, not a few of whom felt sure that I would fall flat on my face.

The winds of change were blowing fast, and 1961 saw the end of what had been known as orderly marketing when retail price maintenance came to an end, at least in respect of consumer durables. Up to that time such competition as there was existed between manufacturers who were able to enforce their prices at the point of sale. Any retail outlet offering goods for less than the retail price would promptly have their supplies stopped. It is not for me to discuss the rights and wrongs in this book, but I have to say that on the whole I have never thought that the changes and the new 'free' market have always been in the customers' best long-term interests.

The year 1961 was to be my final one with Harry. My relations with the management at the British Motor Corporation had been less than cordial. The new cars were certainly not being produced to an acceptable standard from either a bodywork or a mechanical viewpoint. Customers were still unable to obtain the cars with the specification they desired and, as always, the dealers were having to take the flak. The management at the factory made it abundantly clear that they were not in the least interested in our problems. Indeed, they didn't even appreciate that we *had* problems; they certainly had no conception of the commercial world where I made my living and where, at long last, the paying customers were reacting against shoddy goods and the perpetual problems of non-availability.

There was a publication available at the time entitled *Who's Who in the Motor Industry*. From this I was able to trace the career of the aforementioned Mr Holditch of Wolseley Cars Ltd. It went something like this: Educated: (I can't remember). Army (wartime service). Joined Harrods as trainee floorwalker. Then: Articled to a Solicitor's Clerk. Joined BMC in export department. Chief instructor of sales school (!). Then: Sales manager, Wolseley Cars Ltd.

This was just about par for the course in management experience at the British Motor Corporation at this time. Such was the background and sales experience of the man who was to sit in judgment and be directly responsible for the termination of my employment, together with my directorship of Hamtune Motors Ltd. I had placed on record over the years numerous complaints on behalf of clients in respect of quality and availability. I suppose I must have become something of an irritation to their well-ordered lives, but things took a very different turn when I supplied a new Wolseley 1500 to a personal friend, his second. This man's car was his hobby and his relaxation in life, and it showed in the manner in which the car was kept; it was his pride and joy. The car that he purchased from me was a pain from day one. Quite apart from a succession of minor faults, it had no less than *three* replacement engines, each as bad as the one before, and to add insult to injury the London Wolseley distributor, while fitting the second engine, badly damaged the car and tried to placate him with a third-rate body repair.

For some part of this abortive rectification work we were sent a bill, which I promptly passed to Wolseley, together with an acrimonious letter in which I was not reticent. I was nonetheless factual, and stated clearly where this kind of lackadaisical treatment of clients was bound to lead the Corporation in the long run, were it to continue unchecked. That those words were prophetic was to be amply demonstrated over the next 25 years, during which Michael Edwardes, in his own words, had to bring the Corporation back from the very brink of self-annihilation, for which, incidentally, the trades unions were awarded rather more than their fair share of the blame.

Around this time the then British Motor Corporation chairman, Sir George Harriman, was appearing on the BBC TV *Panorama* programme, actually complaining bitterly about people who were so disloyal (*sic*) as to go out and purchase imported cars! What makes this all so poignant today is the fact that at that moment in time not a single model was being imported from the land of the rising sun! "Brother", as anybody could have told Sir George had they but realized, "you ain't seen nothing yet!" Meanwhile my client, of course, was doing some lobbying on his own account, part of which was to obtain an independent engineer's report. Not too many engineers were prepared to take on BMC at that time, but he found one in the end. That report made interesting reading.

A day or so later I had occasion to telephone our distributor on an unrelated matter. In the middle of a conversation with John Monk, their sales director, I was perfunctorily advised that our contract for Morris, Wolseley and MG cars would not be renewed in the coming year. Somewhat taken aback, I asked why? "Well, we all just have to do things BMC's way", was the vague reply. This was very serious news; Harry had lost his franchise for Armstrong Siddeley, so to now lose the franchise for the whole of his BMC content would wipe out a large proportion of the value of his business. Furthermore, there was nothing on offer that he could sell in its place, even if he had wanted to. Clearly he had to be told at once. There followed a very long telephone conversation with John Monk, of which I only heard part, after which Harry confirmed that they were quite serious in their intentions and that he was to attend an official meeting at Henlys the following week. Harry felt that in the meantime I should visit Cowley and offer some kind of apology. It was the very least that I could do in the circumstances, so I set off to visit Mr Holditch.

On my arrival he was supercilious, patronizing and clearly enjoying himself. I had been obliged to wait for 20 minutes before the great man would grant the interview for which an appointment had already been made. During the course of this unpleasant interview I was not invited to sit, but sat anyway. I did not grovel, but I did apologize for the tone of my letter, though not the content, which I claimed was both factual and a matter of record. When I had said what I came to say he read me parts of a letter that had been sent to Henlys the day before, which established that their minds had been made up before I had even set foot on the premises. The letter stated, amongst other things, that Hamtune Motors, through its directors, owed complete loyalty to the British Motor Corporation as part of its franchise holding and that in his (Holditch's) view a leopard did not change his spots. Having read these generalities Holditch added that Mr Frisby had been offered an alternative to the loss of his franchise, but he would not elaborate.

The week following, Harry returned from his meeting looking grim and clutching a letter which stated the alternative unequivocally: Harry Frisby could retain his franchise for Morris, Wolseley and MG cars – or he could retain the services of a sales director by the name of Geoff Owen. He could not, however, enjoy both. In reality there was no choice. I therefore resigned.

It took a day or so for the reality to sink in, and for a time I was in a state of shock. My customer was incensed and wrote a long personal letter to Sir George Harriman regarding the history of his car and the resulting circumstances insofar as I was concerned. In due course he received a reply from an underling containing the usual platitudes in respect of the car. As far as my position was concerned there was a categorical denial that a situation of this kind could possibly occur. But this was no ordinary client and he persisted, both in regard to the condition of his car and the situation in which I had found myself, which was real enough. In due course persistence paid off and he received a letter from the then deputy director of home sales, Mr T A Sangster, wherein it was clearly stated that: "In his (Mr Owen's) capacity as a director, his attitude and remarks concerning the dealership which his company held from us were by no means confined to the particular circumstances relating to your own Wolseley 1500, and the position was that none of the parties directly concerned felt that any good purpose could be served by continuing this relationship."

After the stick came the carrot: "I would like to be as helpful as I can in regard to your suggestion of exchanging your present Wolseley 1500 for a new one, but before proceeding further in this matter I would be most grateful if you would give me an indication of the source from which you would be prepared to consider the purchase of a new vehicle. It would be helpful to us and subsequently helpful to you if any suggestions or proposals that we *might* be able to make could be done through a London Wolseley distributor as you are resident in London. I would be happy to take the matter up and *see if it is possible to be of assistance to you in this particular matter.*" Not, one would think, a particularly subtle form of bribery. (The emphases in the quoted text are, of course, mine.)

By chance there appeared around this time an article in the *Motor Trade Executive* magazine highly critical of the high-handed attitude of all motor manufacturers in regard to their dealers. For interest I sent them details of my experiences and copies of the various correspondence, but at Mr Frisby's specific request I had to deny publication rights. Harry was no fighter, but I could not blame him for that. They did offer to take the matter up on my behalf, but I had to decline.

I did have a very powerful offer, however, from a totally unexpected source. One of my regular clients over the years had been the National Boot and Shoe Union. When I finally got myself another job I went to say goodbye to the general secretary. Inevitably he asked why I was leaving, and while I was telling him the story he listened intently with a grim expression his face. When I had finished he simply said: "Just you provide all of the details in writing, with all the evidence, letters and documents that you can lay your hands on. The TUC would be very pleased to deal with that little matter on your behalf." I must say I was tempted, and I have often speculated over the years on what might have been the outcome had I taken up this very sincere offer. BMC lived in fear of the trades unions, which at that time were all-powerful. However, as by then I was looking forward to my new situation I felt it best to decline.

Before I departed I was told, off the record, that a senior director at Henlys had expressed the view that it was high time someone had had the balls to tell British Motor Corporation where to get off, though he personally wouldn't dare! Meanwhile, my client had replied to Mr Sangster at BMC making it quite clear that while his good friend Mr Owen had found a new and satisfactory situation, he (the client) was keeping his options open and that should there be any doubts in their minds in respect of his car, a detailed report had now been obtained from an independent engineer, a copy of which was enclosed. Within three weeks an exchange was arranged through the London distributor for a brand new replacement car – and no money changed hands.

CHAPTER SEVEN

AN UNEXPECTED CHALLENGE – 1961

Harry Frisby had refused point blank to throw me out on my ear, so at least I had time to gather my wits and pull myself together. It was difficult to accept in a free-speaking country that this could be really happening. While a handful of trades union officials, hell-bent on causing havoc for whatever reason, could regularly close the factory down for weeks on end and get clean away with it, all I had done was offer blunt criticism, based on hard fact, and I had to be sacrificed like some poor bloody lamb to slaughter to placate the wounded pride of a couple of third-rate managers. This struck me as being particularly ironic.

In this frame of mind I sat in my car one Sunday morning, having taken Bella for an extra long walk, and after lighting a reflective cigarette I switched on the radio and heard one of the popular tunes of the moment with the lines:

"Hey look me over, lend me your ear:
fresh out of clover, mortgaged up to here.
I'm a little bit short of the elbow room so let me get me some
and look out world here I come"

And I found inspiration. OK, I thought to myself, you've beaten me this time, but no-one's going to screw me into the ground, least of all Messrs Holditch and Sinnott. I made up my mind that come what may I would never again work for any company selling products made by the British Motor Corporation – nor did I. Later, when I had my own business, I sold Italian cars – and anyone who tried to tell me that I should support Austin Rover, as they were known by then, got the appropriate answer!

Having made up my mind I faced life with renewed confidence and a change of luck. A good friend of mine, a local manager for one of the large finance houses, knew that his company had a very large stake in a Ford main dealership in Yorkshire, also that they were very concerned with the way that the investment had been performing in its first year. He felt that I was the right man to sort things out and said so to his superiors. The timing was right as the dealership was in the process of employing a new sales manager; it had been considered tactful at the time not to tell me why. So one bright Friday I headed up the A1 in the direction of the North Yorkshire seaside town of Redcar to attend an interview. As I had never been further north than Oldham, to where I had been evacuated during the war, I had no idea what to expect on arrival.

My first contact with Cleveland Motor Service Ltd, of Redcar, was to say the least memorable, if only for the somewhat novel interview technique. My appointment was for 3pm, so I was in the area well before time and took a trip round the town – notable for a rather derelict looking pier – before presenting myself to a young lady receptionist at 3pm precisely. I needn't have bothered about being so punctual. With a bright smile she told me that I was expected and there would be a cup of tea and food, if required, in the Zodiac room. This turned out to be a cafeteria on the first floor for the free use of customers (both service and sales) and of course it was named after a current Ford model. I was shown in, where I found three other men sitting around studiously ignoring each other and supping tea. I sat down next to a smartly dressed man some 10 years older than me, and after the usual preliminaries discovered that he and I plus the other two were all there for the same reason, and furthermore another candidate was being interviewed at that moment. I was not at all pleased; I didn't expect to be the only one under consideration, but I had assumed that in view of my recommendation by the finance house I would at least have been given an exclusive interview. The man to whom I was talking was already employed by a very large Ford dealership in Derbyshire, and he made it quite clear that because of his age and experience, the others – myself included – had no chance. Having driven some 200 miles to the appointment, there was nothing I could do but wait my turn. I had no idea when I would be called so I couldn't even go for a walk. In the event I was to be the last. I was invited into the sanctum at around 5.30pm by the same young lady I had met at reception – still with that bright smile

The interview room was fairly long and narrow. Down the centre was a large oblong boardroom table with a single chair at each end and three chairs down each side. I was welcomed by three gentlemen and invited to sit at the head of the table. In the single chair at the far end sat the company chairman and managing director, Mr Les Pinkney. Later I found out he was a well-known Middlesborough businessman and entrepreneur, and he looked exactly that, immaculately groomed in expensive perfectly fitting clothes. On his right sat George Wilkinson, a Middlesborough accountant and the only other director, who was rumoured to have been a member of the SAS in the war, although this was never actually confirmed as far as I was concerned. He spoke with a large plum in his mouth to conceal his Yorkshire accent. Opposite George sat Neville Smedley, the company's general manager. He came from a Ford main dealership in Blackpool and, it would seem, had brought half the staff with him. I was to find him a charming man, full of boundless energy; he was no motor dealer, but at the same time no fool. I understood he was a promoted service manager.

Mr Pinkney welcomed me and for the duration of the interview I was given a history of the firm to date. To my astonishment, apart from having to answer one or two questions I was not invited to say a word on my own account! "The Ford Motor Company, Geoffrey", I was told, "had advised us that it was unlikely that we would make a profit in our first year (just completed), but we are pleased to be able to tell you that we have." This snippet of information being at variance with what I had been told by the financiers, I made no comment. He went on for perhaps an hour telling me what would be expected of me if appointed and to give me a fairly good description of the set-up.

I just sat quietly taking it all in, making careful mental notes and appraising my interviewers. Neville sat throughout with a frown on his face. George fidgeted and chewed a pencil, while Les chatted on in a most friendly manner. He finally came to an abrupt end by telling me that the salary would be £2,500 per annum (it seemed that they didn't believe in commission at management level, but two and a half grand was very acceptable at the time), that a room had been reserved for me at the *Coatham Hotel* with dinner, and that they all looked forward to seeing me again at 11.30 next morning. Now that was quite unexpected, but Les' manner as he rose to signify that the meeting was at an end made it clear that there was nothing further to discuss. Neville escorted me to the now deserted Zodiac room and suggested that I might care to wait a moment and he would show me around. This was encouraging, for it was unlikely that any of the others had been given this tour, at least by the general manager.

He returned after a short while and we descended the stairs. The premises were a converted bakery on a large corner site and as such had some limitations. But what had been done had been done well, with imagination; the stair carpet alone must have cost a bomb! As we descended the enclosed staircase, on our right was a fair-sized new-car showroom with large windows on two sides of the corner. The only vehicle access at the rear of the showroom led into the workshop, which occupied the whole rear length of the building. On our left was an equal-sized used-car showroom, but without rear doors as this had access directly from the front of the building and the main road by glass doors. At the foot of the stairs was an office for three salesmen, from which they had a clear view of both new and used-car showrooms, not to mention the staircase which the office secretaries and lady clients had to use *en route* to coffee in the Zodiac room, this at the time when mini-skirts were, quite literally, at their height!

On turning left at the foot of the stairs and crossing the used-car showroom we entered a long corridor which, in fact, was the counter for parts and accessories, or stores area. As will be surmised, this area then conveniently backed onto the workshop. At the end of the corridor was the front workshop entrance, together with the customer service reception and workshop offices. The remainder of this very long building was fronted by a petrol forecourt and the 'grease bay', behind which was a body and panel shop, beyond which in turn was a further workshop area, part of it being utilized as a car cleaning bay.

This covered the whole ground floor area apart from a narrow walled forecourt fronting both used and new showrooms, where one could display perhaps eight used cars. On the whole a good square and compact area, with all sections fitting into place and handy for each other, but as stated, there were limitations!

The paint shop was upstairs, literally. It not being possible to drive cars up and down the Axminster, an ingenious solution had been found based, I imagine, on a part of the original bakery layout. A vehicle hoist had been placed in such a manner that it was possible to drive on a car, which was then hydraulically lifted to first-floor level. It was no problem going up, but coming down involved driving into thin air onto the two narrow metal tracks of the hoist. This was a hairy experience and certainly not for the faint-hearted. I never did find out if this novel arrangement had the blessing of the factory inspector!

However, first-hand experience of the building's shortcomings were for the future; these were just my initial impressions after my short tour, following which I departed for the hotel after bidding Neville goodnight. To my mild astonishment he said that he would be round to see us all later. At the hotel I found that everything had been laid on. All five of us were to share a table for dinner and our bill was covered. By the end of the meal, and after a few drinks, the initial tensions had inevitably disappeared. In the course of after-dinner small talk I was able to weigh-up the opposition dispassionately. I didn't think a great deal of my chances, the others being older than my 32 years, with more experience, two at least having been trained in Ford management techniques. In due course Neville arrived, as promised, and we all retired to the bar. He chose to say very little, but it was apparent that we were being closely observed. After a surprisingly short time he bade us goodnight and left. And that, so to speak, was that.

There was a private function in the ballroom that night, to which at least two of us managed to get ourselves invited. I enjoy ballroom dancing, and discos were for the future, so all in all I had quite an evening, eventually going to bed when the party ended and waking up feeling somewhat the worse for wear. To make matters worse the heating had been full-on, with no means of control, and the window flatly refused to open, with the result that I got very little sleep and woke early with a hangover. Nonetheless, I enjoyed a hearty breakfast, and after a brisk walk along the sea front I made my way to the showrooms at the appointed time in reasonable condition.

This time there was only one in the Zodiac room and he told me that the rest had been and gone. There was no time for further conversation because he was then called in and I was left to enjoy my coffee alone. I was not kept waiting very long when in came the same bright smiling young lady and once again I was ushered into the boardroom. The scene was exactly as the previous afternoon. Les Pinkney greeted me and I was invited to sit down and comment on what I had seen and how I felt about the situation as a whole. I remember nothing of what I had to say, but spoke for perhaps 10 minutes or so, at the conclusion of which Les sat back in his executive chair, looking me straight in the eye. He said that after a great deal of consideration (I thought to myself – here comes the bum's rush) we have decided to award the position to enthusiasm rather than to experience. Would I now care to join them all in a drink? It took a little while to sink in, and I must have looked rather foolish. A very well stocked cocktail cabinet was opened and the next thing I knew I was enjoying a very large scotch indeed and shaking hands all round. Had I then been aware what a frightful mess I was to discover on taking up my appointment perhaps I might not have been quite so ebullient. It was some time during these preliminary celebrations that I was told that my predecessor had committed suicide!

No-one was more delighted for me than Harry Frisby. On my last, rather sad day with him I was presented with an expensive real leather briefcase and allowed to purchase a quite respectable trade-in at cost price to provide transport until I received my new company car. The car was a godsend, living out of town, and with a great deal to organize in selling our bungalow, together with the endless problems relating to moving lock, stock and barrel. We also had many good friends to whom to say farewell. Meanwhile, I was to live in an hotel in Yorkshire and travel home on alternate weekends to complete arrangements.

Early one Friday afternoon I set off for Redcar in my faithful old Rover with a disproportionate amount of luggage; still following Arthur Barrow's example, I was a very snappy dresser and had a very full wardrobe. I also took a very bulky tape-recorder for personal entertainment (there were no micro-electronics then) and in due course arrived at the hotel, thoughtfully arranged by Neville in the old seaside town of Saltburn, at around 9pm, having stopped for a meal on the way, thank God.

As I drew up at the hotel entrance a body appeared from nowhere. "Are you for CMS? My name's Ted Danson", in a broad Lancashire accent. "Leave your luggage in the car, man, we can deal with that later – we're all in the Con Club." And so they all were, indeed, for it transpired that the greater part of management, plus the sales staff, met in the Conservative Club every Friday night, during which the custom was to consume a minimum of a gallon of ale each and discuss the problems of the week. In point of fact these informal meetings were very productive. In the motor trade it is rare indeed to find harmony between sales and service personnel, but we ironed-out and avoided many a potential problem at the Con Club and these weekly meetings were a sight more productive than those we were to suffer every Monday afternoon in the boardroom. But that was for the future.

Anyway, on that first Friday evening, apart from renewing my acquaintance with Neville I was able to meet and to drink with the service and parts managers, service reception (Ted Danson), shop foreman, cost clerk and both car salesmen – who were to be my particular responsibility. Not being used to the very strong North Yorkshire ale, it was quite an evening, and it must be said that I remember nothing of the latter part whatsoever. The following day I was told that I fell over the hedge at the hotel, complete with tape-recorder, and the greater part of my worldly goods were carted upstairs by Ted. I doubtless slept well!

The following day, my first in my new situation, I spent wandering around the showrooms examining the new and used-car stock, generally getting the feel of things. Neville was quite put out when I declined to go for a drink at lunchtime. It would seem that I was not expected to work on Saturday afternoons, but I needed to find out what made the place tick as soon as possible and to try to make some impression on the sales staff who, understandably, regarded me with a great deal of suspicion. I chose for the time being to let them carry on as normal and contented myself with watching and listening while I familiarized myself with the Ford model range and the prices. The range at the time consisted of the Anglia and the Classic, both with the odd rear window, together with the Mk II Consul, Zephyr and Zodiac range, shortly – as we were all aware – to be phased-out and replaced by the Mk III. At the very bottom of the range, and again soon to be phased-out, the Popular lived on, a cheap edition based on the old side-valve Anglia, and midway in the range, an all-new and rakish Classic Capri fixed-head coupe.

As the whole of the Mk II range was being phased-out there was not a great deal to learn at the present time, so I was a able to concentrate on the used-car situation. What I could see seemed reasonable enough; the used cars on show were certainly prepared to a very high standard and were all in an extremely saleable condition. There was nothing to criticize on this score. If, as Les had said, they were making a profit, why, I wondered, was the finance company so concerned?

My secretary was not available on Saturdays, I had no access to a stocklist and my office was in a mess, so I was unable properly to assess what might be going on. As far as I could see it all looked very imposing and I decided that first thing Monday I would clear out the junk and tidy my office for a start. Then we should be able to see the wood from the trees. The day passed quickly enough, and we certainly sold two or three cars, but I don't recall becoming directly involved.

There were two salesmen – Joe and Noel. Joe was the cartoonist's image of a car salesman: tall, very presentable, well-groomed and well-dressed – a complete extrovert in his early-twenties. Everybody liked Joe, who had style; even when sitting on the expensive stair carpet talking to a customer while eating a bag of chips, Joe somehow made it all look normal. Even later, when he had to be fired, I regretted his departure for a considerable time. Noel was the opposite: introverted and sly, with a watchful, foxy face and shrewd eyes. I never took to him and was not sorry to see him eventually leave of his own choice.

The weekend passed with deceptive quietness. I thought I had summed up the situation reasonably enough and was content to amble around taking it all in, including the town. Neville and his lovely wife Sadie had invited me to Sunday dinner, and late morning found Neville and me in the local Catholic Club, where he immediately saw to it that I was made a member, not that either he or I were of the faith – it just happened to be a bloody good club! Neville never ever talked shop away from the premises; his passion was the fruit machines, which he could read like a book! These were the old-style sixpence in the slot, mechanical machines with a pull-handle, which Neville taught me how to play to such good effect that later I kept a jar on the sideboard at home, which I would add to most nights, and this provided most of our beer money on our annual Norfolk Broads holidays!

All in all it was a pleasant introduction to life in the area prior to starting work on Monday morning, when I was to discover the magnitude of the task that I had taken on, and why the finance company had good reason to be so concerned about the validity of their investment. On reflection, and with the benefit of hindsight, I should have realized that sales managers do not commit suicide without good reason, and that no business of this size can be properly managed without a very firm hand at the point of sale. But I had been impressed by Les Pinkney, who gave every indication of being the successful businessman with his outstanding charm and manner. It was only later that I was to find that he was something of a showman. He had enjoyed some success in other fields, but he was totally naive as far as the motor business was concerned and, guided by an equally naive accountant, they had both been led to believe by the Ford Motor Company – desperate for additional representation in the area – that the motor trade was a licence to print money.

Both Les and George simply failed to grasp, as did so many others in these boom years, that elementary bookkeeping, with profit and loss accounts so dear to auditors, are quite meaningless in motor trade accounting unless proper regard is given to the true value of the car stock in hand, particularly when that stock is to a large degree secondhand. Just short of the famous Middlesborough transporter bridge on the south side there stood a building – it may still exist for all I know – with a large sign proclaiming: E & L B Pinkney Ltd – No 4 Machine Shop. The other three simply didn't exist. Such was the character and make-up of Les Pinkney; if nothing else he certainly had style!

I arrived at the showrooms on Monday full of enthusiasm and immaculate as ever, ready to take the reins and sort things out. In my office was an efficient looking north country lass by the name of Avril, who lost no time in introducing herself as the sales manager's secretary. Without preamble I stated my intention to change all the sales record systems. This was not at all well received, and it showed. However, I care nothing for popularity, neither do I expect to have to explain my motives; in my view that is not the function of management, which exists to manage and set the example, so I simply removed my coat, rolled up my sleeves and proceeded to sling out large amounts of collected junk under a somewhat frosty gaze.

By lunchtime I had created some sort of order and Avril at my request had produced a list of every used car held in stock in order of date of arrival, indicating the purchase price. I was puzzled to discover that the list was somewhat longer than I had expected, but for the moment this would have to wait as I had a date with Derek Whitehouse, our service manager, who was waiting in his office. From Derek I was to discover something of the catastrophic situation the company was actually in. It so happened that Derek was, as he put it, "just about to go on test in one of your better used cars, Geoff, so would you like to come for the ride?". We set off in a Ford Anglia that had been made ready for sale that morning. I was quite happy to sit beside him and enjoy the mid-morning sunshine and sea air but intrigued when he told me of his intention to take me to visit the 'Farm'. In my innocence I assumed that Les had agricultural interests!

After a short journey up a road leading out of town, Derek turned left into an almost derelict area fronted by equally run-down sheds. We drove into a large yard at the rear of the sheds and he pulled up, switching off the engine. "Right, young man", said Derek, "let's go and have a look round." Somewhat mystified, I climbed out of the Anglia and looked about me. The first thing I noted across the back of the yard was a row of perhaps a dozen or so cars that appeared to have been abandoned. At any rate it was clear that most had stood in the same position for some time, for they were all filthy dirty, the tyres were either flat or half-flat, and most had evidence of damage by vandals, not perhaps quite as bad as one would expect these days, but bad enough nonetheless.

At the far end of the row at right-angles stood two derelict tipper lorries and what at first sight appeared to be a rusting secondhand

Ford chassis/cab. All in all a sorry-looking collection of scrap vehicles. "Who's the proud owner of this lot then?", I asked Derek with mild curiosity. "You are, sunshine", he replied with an impish grin. "Apart from the Ford chassis/cab, which is new!, the others are the remnants of your used vehicle stock; some have been here for some time." "*New*?", I asked incredulously. "You're joking!" "Bloody well is", he said. "It's been down here since the day we opened." Still not really crediting what I had been told, I walked across through the profusion of weeds and nettles and took a closer look. It was new right enough, less than 10 miles on the clock, but with rusting chassis plates, propshaft and differential housing, not to mention the cab, which had only a protective coat of primer; it was a sorry sight indeed. "Derek, how could this possibly happen?" He shrugged his shoulders. "Simple, when they get fed up with anything they park it down here and forget about it; there's more in the shed." Jesus, I thought, what a way to run a business! "Do Les and George know what the hell is going on?" "I doubt it, they only look at the weekly figures and Neville hasn't much of a clue; come to think of it I don't think he has ever been down here."

Well, I thought to myself, having come this far I might as well see the worst. "OK, Derek, open up and let's have a look at the others." He fumbled with a bunch of keys and selecting one opened a large padlock, broke a hasp and pulled open the double doors. Inside, parked in a line, were three new Consul Classics, five new 105E Anglias (all covered in filth and grime as the old roof offered no protection), and at the end of the line the *piece de resistance* (in like condition) – a brand new Ford Consul convertible. It was just discernible, under a coating of filth, as being very pale powder blue with a white hood! This really was too much. "Derek, I have seen enough for one day, I think we had better go back."

What I had seen had been bad enough, but there was worse yet. On my return I took a long hard look at my stocklist and on checking registration numbers with those seen at the farm I found to my horror that not only had I assumed responsibility for a bunch of bangers, but that these bangers had at some time been taken in part-exchange for prices that would have been relatively high even had they been in reasonable condition!

That same afternoon I was due to attend the first of our weekly Monday afternoon meetings. It didn't take long to discover how this deplorable situation had come about and how the directors had managed to achieve a profit in their first year of trading. At 2.30pm prompt, Neville took me to the boardroom; we all sat in the same places as at my interview and I was formally welcomed as the new sales manager by both Les Pinkney and George Wilkinson. Les was his usual immaculate, bright and breezy self. George, plum in mouth, was grinning like a Cheshire cat, and even Neville looked reasonably pleased with life as we all sat down.

Les opened the proceedings. "In front of you, Geoffrey, you will find Mr Wilkinson's report for the week, which I am sure you will agree is most encouraging." Sure enough, I found the neatly typed sheet of paper headed 'SALES DEPT'. The first item was a list of the new cars sold the previous week in model order, and by each car was noted the gross profit per car. Below this was a list of the used cars sold, each with its gross profit recorded, both totals having been added together and an allowance made for used-car preparation and repair charges. The week's quite impressive trading profit was shown at the bottom of the page. We had not, it would seem, sold any trucks that week.

So, I thought to myself, that's how George does it. As already stated, this kind of basic bookkeeping is fine provided that the part-exchange vehicles are worth what is allowed for them (in a competitive market, even with top-class sales people, they very seldom are). With a sales manager at the top who had felt obliged to take his own life for reasons that I could only surmise at this stage, plus a couple of smart-Alec salesmen, this child's guide to accounting was a sure road to disaster. However, I had determined to say nothing at this particular meeting.

George waffled on for a bit about market trends, average overheads and this and that, Neville nodded sagely from time to time, while Les maintained the dignified posture of the chairman of the board. After a while George, who was a man never to use one word when three would do, ground to a close by stating that he felt certain we would all be highly delighted. Bloody hell, I thought, he really means it!

There was a pregnant pause. I felt that somehow Les was not pleased with my clearly negative reaction. He asked if I had anything to say. I took a deep breath, feeling very uncomfortable; never in my life had I expected to be faced with a situation of this kind. This was no blustering, but kindly Harry Frisby, with sensible Mary to provide moral support and encouragement. Confronting me that afternoon was a man who, for all his faults, had become a successful businessman with a large house, a large boat and substantial local status to prove it, and on his flank a local accountant who clearly believed that his true vocation in life was something approaching Chancellor of the Exchequer. I didn't feel that they would respond kindly to a 32-year-old sales manager, whom they hardly knew, telling them that they were hell-bent for 'Carey Street'.

So I decided to play for time and test the water. "Were they", I ventured, "quite happy with the quality of the used vehicle stock?" It seemed that Geoffrey, who for once in his life was endeavouring to be the very model of tact and diplomacy, had inadvertently struck a bum note. The immaculate Pinkney neck turned bright red, the colour gradually spreading to the whole of his features, a sight that I was to witness many times over the next two years. Les, it would appear, was displeased.

"Happy with the used vehicle stock, Geoffrey – have you not noted the condition of our used cars?" Indeed I had, and tried to say so, but there was no way that Les could be interrupted in full flow. I was silenced with a glare and treated to a long thesis as to how the finest used-car experts at the Ford Motor Company had trained the staff how to clean and prepare used cars to the famed A1 standards. "Why, Geoffrey, we even clean and polish the engines. So don't you come to us and tell us how to prepare cars." And so he went on. I began to wish I had never asked. To be fair, what he was saying was perfectly true. I had indeed examined all the used cars on sale and they were extremely well-presented. But where, I wondered, did he think the rest of the used cars were? While he was chuntering on I quietly went through the typewritten papers in front of me, and as I suspected there were figures relating to all aspects of the workshop, paint shop, petrol, oil and parts department, *but* there was no used-car stocklist. I resolved to rectify that omission before the next meeting.

After a time he wound down and abruptly went on to the remaining items on the agenda. As these were concerned with other factions of the business they were not at the time of much interest to me, so I was duly ignored and left to my thoughts. When the meeting eventually closed I collared Neville and asked him to my office. Having firstly given Avril the rest of the day off I told him what I had discovered that morning and provided an off-the-cuff estimate of the implications relative to profit and loss. To my astonishment Neville declined to accept any responsibility, showed little interest in what I had to say and wholly blamed my predecessor. He made it perfectly clear that whoever broke the news to Les it was certainly not going to be Neville Smedley. As the company's general manager I failed to see how he could possibly opt out, but did not say so.

The problem with Neville was that through the Ford Motor Company he had been promoted out of his depth. He had held a good job at Blackpool as service manager with a very large Ford dealer, where he had been quite outstanding. When Les and George refurbished the bakery, Ford, who were particularly anxious to establish a main dealership in Redcar, recommended Neville as a candidate for the top job. This was immediately accepted by Les and George, with the added advantage that Neville brought most of his key staff with him. It has long been my view that to be a successful general manager in this kind of greenfields environment requires successful sales rather than workshop experience. Vehicle sales is where the real money is made, or lost! And at the end of the day it is profitable companies which are able to provide the best back-up facilities.

To give credit where due, there could be no doubt that by his boundless energy and enthusiasm Neville had got that business off the ground. It was no easy task establishing a venture of that kind from scratch, as I was to discover for myself in later years. The fact that the building was a conversion rather than purpose-built would certainly not have helped matters, and for what he had achieved, with Les and George constantly on his back, I sincerely took off my hat to him. By the time I arrived on the scene he was showing visible signs of strain. I believe that he had guessed what was going on in sales and simply didn't know what to do about it. By now he was almost beyond caring. Neville had suffered very long hours and a rough ride for 12 months; now he was making it quite clear that the problems in the sales department were all mine, to be dealt with entirely by me, particularly at board level.

As it happened this suited me fine because there was no doubt that responsibility for clearing up this dog's breakfast and ensuring that it was never to happen again was certainly going to be mine. I therefore preferred to handle the situation in my own way on the simple basis that if it all went right I expected the credit. On the other hand I was quite prepared to take the kicks if it all went wrong. So, bidding Neville goodnight, I declined his invitation for a quick one at the club and instead, on my way to my hotel in Saltburn, I stopped off at *The Ship*, in Marske, for a quiet drink on my own before dinner. This proved to be a mistake; *The Ship* was one of the most popular pubs in the area and the haunt of most of the local motor trade. By chance, that night there were several propping up the bar. I recognized Hilton Armstrong as the proprietor of one of our sub-dealers; he promptly stood me a pint and I was introduced to the rest.

Most had at least a suspicion of what had been accumulating over the past year at CMS. These were longstanding, local motor dealers who had all lost deals due to clients getting silly prices for their cars in part-exchange for CMS Fords. When my predecessor committed suicide their worst suspicions were confirmed, or so they thought. Consequently I was the object of considerable curiosity, particularly as I was 'from the South', and I had to fend off many leading questions. I had the distinct feeling that they had all expected to meet some kind of high-pressure whizzkid, which clearly I am not. By the time I departed for a rather late dinner I had obviously been written-off, and I heard later that at least one dealer was intending to dust off his black tie and topper ready for the next funeral!

After dinner I retired to my room with a large scotch and had a long think prior to drifting off for a good night's sleep. I came to the conclusion that, having accepted the position, it was clearly my duty to prepare a professional report and opinion on the state of the company and to present this to Mr Pinkney in private as the dealer principal, together with a sensible strategy for both the short and long-term future of the dealership. The problems were not, after all, of my making, Following this, if I was still employed, I would have to get stuck in and start again from scratch. If I were to be successful it would be a considerable achievement. I had no self-doubts whatsoever after my achievements at Hamtune Motors, albeit on a smaller scale, so I decided that night that, come what may, I would immediately reorganize that sales department and lay down some professional ground rules for starters. With that I went to sleep.

I made a start next morning: I presented both salesmen with written instructions that until further notice no part-exchange deals were to be entered into with customers without my personal sanction. This was not well-received! My next move was to telephone Mike Logue and persuade him to prepare to move to Redcar to take up the post of senior salesman at a moment's notice. I then telephoned Mr Pinkney at his Middlesborough office and arranged for a meeting the following Friday morning. The remainder of that day and most of the week was spent, with Derek's help, in dragging the better of the used cars back from the Farm and making a close personal inspection with regard to the likely cost of reconditioning. The remainder would just have to be auctioned off.

By Thursday night Avril, sworn to secrecy, had typed my comprehensive report on the situation, accompanied by a detailed stocklist showing the cost price of every car, together with my considered valuation and the likely cost of reconditioning where applicable. The difference between cost plus reconditioning and possible value (even on a retail basis) represented a substantial loss to the company. At trade, or true value, the loss was staggering.

Meanwhile, the new chassis/cab and the Consul convertible had been brought back under cover of darkness and hidden away *pro tem* in the workshop following a good hose-down. The two tatty old tipping lorries had to stay where they were for the moment as I had no idea what they might be worth.

On the Friday I chanced to meet Les at the foot of the staircase, he gave me an encouraging grin and I was invited upstairs without preamble. I was never more glad of my self-confidence as we entered the boardroom and I was invited to "Sit down, Geoffrey" next to Les in the chair usually occupied by Neville.

I came straight to the point by calmly telling him that I had grave news. "And what would that be, Geoffrey?" he asked, with an edge to his voice. In silence I just handed him my detailed stocklist. He examined the contents with great care before looking up and asking me exactly what this meant. I explained that due to the condition of a large part of his used-vehicle stock, on my examination I had felt it my duty to conduct a professional valuation. It was my opinion, I went on, that he stood to lose a great deal of money. The profit he had been led to believe the company had achieved last year needed to be in excess of my bottom-line loss. It wasn't, and I didn't need him to tell me for I could see it in his face.

For a time he just sat staring at the typewritten sheet, then after a while he rose without a word and went through a door behind his chair, which led to his private toilet, leaving me to my own devices. Not knowing quite what to do I just sat and waited. In due course I heard the toilet flush and he returned to the boardroom, having regained some of his composure. He didn't return to his seat, but stood for a while gazing out of the window. At length he turned: "Geoffrey, this cannot be." I said that I was sorry, but that was the situation, and went on to tell him about the Farm, the condition of the cars now lined up at the rear of the building waiting rectification, but nothing about the dreadful state of the Consul and the truck chassis. He had had enough to contend with at the moment and I must say that I felt truly sorry for the man.

Shock then turned to anger. He said that he refused to accept that things were so bad. "On what basis do you justify this so-called valuation?" I stopped thinking and let instinct take over. "Fifteen years in this business, Mr Pinkney", I said quietly. "You employed me as a professional to run your sales operation; this is the true situation as I see it. If you do not accept it and believe it to be a nonsense, you must employ someone else." I had struck exactly the right cord; there was a moment's pause while Les looked thoughtful. "That will be all, Geoffrey", he said at length, picking up the telephone, "be ready to present your report to the meeting on Monday." As I departed I heard Les tell reception: "Get me George Wilkinson, wherever he is."

I heard nothing more from anyone until Monday afternoon when, climbing the stairs with Neville, he remarked that this was going to be one hell of a meeting as I had apparently caused one hell of a stink, and brother George was not amused. My impression was that Neville was not looking forward to the afternoon. For myself, commonsense told me that the very fact that I had heard nothing meant that Les had taken me seriously. Therefore, I had already quietly put into operation part of my strategy for getting the company out of the mess and planning for profit.

We entered the boardroom, Les was formal, with a "Good afternoon, Geoffrey". George gave me a frosty look and said nothing. Right ho, I thought, now we know the form let's get on with it. We all sat down and Mr Pinkney at once asked me to report on the situation. He was grave, but certainly not unfriendly, and his boardroom manner suggested plainly that he wanted the truth, the whole truth and no bloody waffle. That is exactly what they got, a clear and factual report based on what I had found at the Farm and elsewhere. By this time I had obtained precise estimates from Derek for individual rectification work on all of the cars. Also, for good measure, I described in some detail the state of the new Consul convertible and the new truck chassis, information that I had hitherto kept to myself. Les just looked shocked, but George, seeking a distraction from his responsibility, said just what I thought he would say: "My God, Geoffrey", outsize plum in his mouth, "those vehicles want bringing up here straight away." "They are already here", I said with studied calm, "what is more Derek is repainting the chassis/cab and the car cleaners are well on with the cleaning and refurbishing of the Consul." "Are they indeed?", said George with a nasty smile, "And on who's authority, may I ask?" "Mine", I replied, looking straight at Les Pinkney. "Absolutely right, Geoffrey, now what can we do to get out of this mess and see to it that it never happens again?", Les said, promptly shooting George down in flames. At that moment it became clear that I had acquired an implacable enemy.

Before anyone had a chance to speak I stated clearly that there was no chance whatever of the situation arising again as I had effectively closed the Farm. In future no vehicles would leave the premises for any reason until sold. George opened his mouth to speak and I was delighted to note that Les shut him up with one look, so I continued and said that we would repair and recondition the better of the cars as best we could to minimize the loss. The trucks I wasn't sure about at this point, but in future no deals would be completed without my sanction until such time as the sales staff had come to heel. I told them of my intention to restructure the commission system so that this would reflect profitability rather than sales, also that I had arranged to employ an assistant, who was used to my methods and high standards of trading. This last pronouncement drew an audible gasp from Neville, who later told me that it was not customary to make decisions of this kind without consulting the board. In other words, Les. To his credit, while Les looked surprised about my arrangement, he made no comment other than that he supposed that I knew this new man and could vouch for his capabilities. On being assured that I regarded him as the best of my trainees from the past, no more was said on the matter.

Les then asked exactly what I meant by the sales staff not being allowed to deal without my sanction. I explained that they had been allowed to "get away with murder" in that their commission was being paid as if they were achieving full profitability on every transaction, whereas in a great many cases (as could now be seen) they had been paid a reward for losing the company money. In future I intended to institute a system of training by personal example. I intended that every car accepted in part-exchange should be correctly appraised, and to design a system of commission payment that would the better reward profitability, but would at the same time affect the salesmen where it would hurt most, *viz* through their pockets, should they attempt to carry on as in the past. In short, where a deal in my opinion was uneconomic, it would be turned away – as simple as that.

What I had to say covered a good deal more, but that was the gist of the strategy. When I had finished there was a long pause. George was clearly out of his depth and said nothing; Neville looked quite cheerful, while Les gazed thoughtfully out of the window. It was some time before he actually spoke, and when he did it was obvious that he had weighed his words carefully.

"Geoffrey, it just won't work. We cannot afford to turn business away out of hand, and I do not think you realize that in Middlesborough there is an old-established Ford main dealer owned by Keith Schellenberg." (Of course I realized, I had visited all of the opposition.) He went on: "Now Keith doesn't like me – he resents us opening here – and has told me bluntly that he intends to sell every new Ford on Teesside, regardless." Sometimes I wonder how perfectly normal, reasonable and respectable people can be so naive. I mean, that is not what retail trading is about in any commodity. In our business it is suicidal.

After a while Les repeated again that he didn't think it would work. I said nothing, but to my delight Neville then rowed in with some worthwhile support. He may not have been sales-orientated, but he knew enough about it to follow what I was driving at, which effectively meant that there was no point in selling anything for the doubtful pleasure of losing money hand over fist. From that moment there was the beginning of a new dawn in the management of CMS, for Neville made it abundantly clear that he had faith in me and that I could rely on him to back me. This was just enough to convince Les that there might be something in what I had to say, not that it would have made the slightest difference to the way that I proposed to conduct the business in future – but it was helpful to have the support of at least one of the directors.

While Les had given Neville a hard time over the past year, he was well aware that he had worked miracles in general organization and he held him in high regard. So, for the time being at least, George had his nose pushed out of line. But from that day on he was to go out of his way to be a pain in the neck, and ironically the end result was to prove disastrous for the company that could well have provided him with a very sound investment for his old age.

The meeting seemed to have gone quite well on the whole, but I was to have one more brush with George before it drew to a close. Les asked if there was anything else I wished to add. There was. In future I proposed where necessary to write down individual used-car values against individual new-car profits to establish reliable profit forecasts and to maintain the integrity of the used-car stock value. This statement of policy was in fact actually recommended by Ford as standard dealer accounting procedure. The proposal, however, brought forth a howl of protest from George with a distinct echo of "don't you try to teach me accountancy, young Geoffrey me lad." In the end we compromised in that I would produce a stocklist and profit forecast each week based on my method, and George did it his way. It was to be several months before Ford sent along a business management team who were to recommend, among other things, this very system of profit-and-loss forecasting, and it was George, of course, who was to greet it as if it were the most original idea since sliced bread. But that was George. He was less than delighted when the same team put forward in a written report the unequivocal recommendation that the directors should leave the day-to-day running of the business to the present management team – or replace them *en masse*. But that was for the future.

Having established my position, I now had a clear-cut job to do and I set to it with a will. My most pressing problems were to get rid of the rubbish, sort out the sales staff and get things moving again. Shifting the junk was a formidable and very expensive exercise. Every car needed paintwork rectification, mechanical reconditioning, plus new and replacement parts and accessories before we were able to offer them for sale. Derek, of course, had his own workshop clients to take care of, and to a large extent sales had to take second place in the queue. But slowly we managed to get them to the showrooms in presentable condition and they went one by one at 'special prices'. We lost a great deal of money, but it was not all bad news, for one or two cars managed to produce a profit. This was certainly not due to the skill of the sales staff.

Tucked away in the paint shop I found a black Jaguar Mk VII which had been taken in part-exchange for, of all things, a truck, and the sales staff had failed to realize that at that particular time good Mk VIIs were very desirable cars on the used market. It was in for rectification, being a bit tatty on the bodywork, but the mileage was low and the interior immaculate. The bodywork blemishes had been repaired and were ready for painting. On impulse I directed Derek to respray the whole car in Jaguar Carmine Red, put it on offer at a substantially increased price and personally sold it for a handsome profit within a week of completion! Apart from any other consideration, this had a profound effect on Joe and Noel. By this time Mike Logue had joined the sales staff and from him I gathered that both Joe and Noel had been viewing the refurbishing of the Jag with considerable scepticism, convinced that I was to get stuck with the car, fall flat on my face and lose even more money. Mike knew better!

Nothing succeeds like success. When the car had been sold, foundations of respect were laid, flimsy foundations it's true, and tempered with a great deal of ill-concealed dislike for this jumped-up sales manager who had cut their income and was hell-bent on turning the whole place upside-down and inside-out. I was beginning to enjoy myself!

The Consul convertible had survived its ordeal remarkably well, requiring only minimal paint rectification, but the white hood required considerable elbow-grease, and even then we felt that the car could only be offered as 'shop soiled'. Work was still proceeding on the new truck chassis.

Three of the used cars on my list were missing altogether, nobody seemed to know where they might be and nobody, including Neville, seemed very much bothered. Indeed, it was not until some two or three weeks after my arrival that they all turned up in a rather unexpected manner. I had arrived a little late one morning, having been house-viewing in Middlesborough, to find one of our low-mileage used cars sitting on the front with the price removed from the windscreen and fitted with trade-plates. Round by the workshop door in my personal parking space was one of my three missing cars: a one-year-old four-door Consul Classic in a disreputable condition. I assumed that the used car was going out on demonstration, but the Classic was something of a mystery.

On entering the new-car showroom from the service department rear entrance I went to my office. Comfortably ensconced in my chair, with his feet planted on my desk, was a nondescript-looking man in his mid-fifties with iron-grey hair. He was chatting away to Avril, enjoying a cup of coffee, obviously without a care in the world. He all but ignored me as I walked in. I was not very pleased, and it showed. "Who the hell are you?", I asked. He turned his head in my direction, making no effort to get up. "I suppose that you are Mr Owen." "Too bloody right, and what's more this is my office, my desk, my chair and my bloody secretary, so what are you doing in here anyway?" "Oh, I thought you knew", he said, somewhat put out. "I'm McKinney, your commercial-vehicle salesman." Are you indeed, I thought; nobody had taken the trouble to tell me that I had one.

"Right then, I have enough to do for today, so if you would be so kind as to vacate my desk I'll see you tomorrow at 9am sharp, and by the way, where have you been for the past fortnight?" He moved his 'plates' off the desk and stood up. "I work from home and come in once a fortnight, so there's no way I can come in tomorrow morning, in any case, I have to deliver that car to Hartlepool." "What car?", I asked. "Why, the Ford on the front. I know just the bloke to sell that for us." By this time I was really cross. "Well so do I, Mr McKinney, and that happens to be me."

With that I told Avril to get the Ford back in the used-car line-up sharpish and shut the door. I told McKinney to sit down, indicating a visitor's chair, while I went behind my desk. I intended that this should now become a more formal interview, for it was becoming clear that this was the man responsible for the two derelict tippers I was lumbered with, and I had a suspicion that he might be able to throw some light on the other two still missing cars.

I was dead right. In answer to my questions, McKinney admitted that his 'bloke' had both cars on a sale-or-return basis and that he had been promised the Ford that Avril was now reversing into the line. "Right", I said. "You get on to your mate right now and tell him that you and I are on our way for those two cars, no ifs, buts or maybes. I'll borrow a driver and trade-plates; by the time I get back I want it organized".

McKinney looked for a moment as if he was going to argue. "Use my phone", I said, and walked out. Clearly this was not the Cleveland Motor Service that friend McKinney had come to know and love. It later turned out that this motor dealer mate of his had been having the pick of our stock, at no cost to himself until sold, and while I couldn't prove it I reckoned that McKinney was having a back-hander for his pains. On my return McKinney was still on the phone, and it seemed that the dealer friend wanted to speak to me as he had sold both cars.

There wasn't a great deal I could do about that so I told him that I would provide an invoice and McKinney would be over to collect a cheque for (naming a fair return on each car) in the morning. As I surmised he expected to pay rather less, so I innocently suggested that I should look up our copy of the sale-or-return agreement and call him back. There was, of course, no such agreement, so by bluff and some obscure legal threats, which I was by no means sure I could substantiate, we eventually agreed a suitable price and I packed McKinney off in his grubby Classic to collect.

This, then, was another loophole plugged from the past management. It was a pity about McKinney, for he could well have been a top man at his job; he knew trucks and he knew a great many truck users in the area. His problem was drink, and an unlimited expense account that nobody had bothered to check. When I put the screws on he eventually left for pastures new, but not before he had managed to sell the new (reconditioned) Ford chassis, for which I was eternally grateful.

In the midst of these trials and tribulations Mike Logue and I were managing to get the sales department on a proper footing and creating some order. We still had cars to sell which were losing money, but gradually new part-exchange cars were coming in from more profitable new car deals. Slowly but surely, week by week, the depressing overall loss returns on car sales began to diminish. It was to be almost three months before the tide turned and each week George was having a ball with his snide remarks, and I couldn't help but notice that it was *my* written-down figures he was quoting to Les at the meetings as, of course, they reflected even bigger loss figures at the bottom line. He did just the same when we went into profit!

Les on the whole was not too bad during these difficult times; he had endured a nasty shock and had lost some of his confidence in our George. Testy and sharp at the meetings he might have been, but I think he realized two things: one, that I had a clear-cut plan that I was following without deviation, and two, that Neville had the utmost confidence in me and as such was a changed man. It was really a question of time, for Les was not a patient man. And, of course, I still had the problem of Keith Schellenberg and his declared intention to sell all the Fords on Teesside.

To understand how this problem was overcome it is necessary to appreciate something of the situation *vis-a-vis* CMS and Neashams of Middlesborough and it is also useful to know something of the geography of the area. Redcar sits four-square at the mouth of the River Tees on the south side. Seven miles to the west is the city of Middlesborough, covering both sides of the river. Between the two a trunk road with dual carriageways provided easy and convenient communication between the two respective Ford main dealerships, Cleveland Motor Service Ltd, of Redcar, and Neashams Ltd, of Middlesborough.

Keith Schellenberg was the larger-than-life proprietor and managing director of Neashams, a well-known international sportsman, perhaps best known as a member of the British bobsleigh team, and latterly an intrepid entrant in a Great Britain-to-Australia Marathon car rally with a prewar open Bentley. It is a matter of regret that the whole time I was at Teeside we never met, for we were locked in a well-publicized price war from which the punters were able to take full advantage, and why not indeed?

Keith resented the fact that Ford had appointed a brand new dealership in Redcar, which he doubtless had come to regard as a suburb of Middlesborough and as such his own exclusive territory. The only way he could hit back, he thought, was (as stated by Les) "to sell every damn new Ford on Teesside". Keith, like Les, was new to the motor trade, and as such just as naive. They had both landed themselves in an impossible situation in which the customers were winning hands-down, particularly those with high-mileage cars in worse than average condition. Neither business was earning a profit and both were accumulating a collection of over-valued secondhand cars simply to try and move more new Fords than each other. By the time I had arrived on the scene the war was the talk of Teeside, and by then even dealers in alternative franchises were forsaking cynical amusement for real concern because, inevitably, where a better-than-average trade-in price is available, particularly to a Yorkshireman, even the most dedicated British Leyland fan will decide to live with Ford on cost price alone.

Fortunately for most of the opposition, Ford were not then in the same league as they are today, thus providing a degree of protection to the other dealers. To some extent Ford had been prepared to turn a blind eye to this suicidal trading in the early days, expecting it all to blow over as the market grew and commonsense prevailed. After all, Ford were doing OK. But this kind of cut-throat competition is bound to be counter-productive sooner or later. Whether they lectured Keith we shall never know, but they were most certainly to become very disturbed about CMS.

The popular method of buying a new Ford in Teeside was simple enough at the time I started. If you lived in or near Redcar you went first to CMS, obtained a price for your car in part-exchange for the model of your choice, then off up the trunk road to Middlesborough where, if you were really crafty, you would let slip that you had obtained an offer from CMS of 'X' pounds for your car. Without argument or preamble, Neashams would immediately offer more, whereupon you returned down the trunk road to impart this information to CMS, where the chances were you would finish up with even more, just to steal the business from Neashams. Of course, if you happened to live in or near Middlesborough, you went through exactly the same procedure, only in reverse order.

To put it all in perspective, during the early-Sixties the motor trade was nothing like as competitive as it is today, so there was simply no need for this kind of cut-price marketing. Even with the depression that existed at that time in the North-East due to problems at the Dorman Long steelworks and in shipbuilding, there was more or less *status quo* in the supply and demand for new cars of all types. People who bought either new or used cars up to, say, four years old were still in the house-owning and professional classes. This certainly excluded steel and shipyard workers, most of whom could not even aspire to a fridge or a washing machine until John Bloom came on the scene in the latter half of the decade.

It was still generally accepted nationally that where part-exchanges were not involved, car dealers sold new vehicles at full list price, inclusive of delivery charges, number-plates and road fund licence. You might, if you tried hard enough, get a spot or foglamp thrown in, but only commercial vehicle buyers got a discount of any sort.

Consequently, to effectively give a discount simply to become the owner of an over-priced tatty used car, or even a nice used car for that matter, was crazy in the extreme. Many of my contemporaries in the South at the time simply refused to accept that I had to face this kind of problem: what kind of tight-fisted Yorkshire motor dealer, they would ask, not unreasonably, throws good money down the drain on a regular monthly basis? Answer: Our Les Pinkney and Keith Schellenberg.

By the time I arrived the situation was beginning to get completely out of hand, with dark threats of at best solicitor's letters, at worst legal action. CMS' advertising agent was some kind of big wheel at the local TV company. His speciality was promotional newspaper advertising, and while he cost Les a fortune in the first year, there can be no doubt that he achieved a very great deal by humorous promotional advertising, with excellent photographs and copy, to put CMS on the map. Whether it was entirely cost-effective, of course, was quite another matter.

One of his efforts I recall was made up around a photograph of a gentleman driving round Middlesborough in a kind of motorized bathtub, while another depicted a very young child in a somewhat battered pedal car at our petrol pumps telling the attendant that "Daddy says this is a good place to buy a new car." All heady professional stuff, which attracted a great deal of attention. One day, however, he came up with the idea of two brand new Ford Anglias accelerating away from the traffic lights, one with a prominent CMS number-plate marginally ahead of the other, with the bold caption: 'YOUR NEW FORD IS BEST BOUGHT FROM CMS'.

This was the last straw for Keith, who promptly phoned Les in a foul temper with dark threats of legal action on the basis that the advertisement clearly suggested that Neashams were failing to properly prepare their new cars for sale. In truth it would not have been difficult to argue this point as the picture was taken in Middlesborough at a well-known road junction practically on Keith's doorstep. While it was certainly not the intention to imply any such thing, Les had his back firmly to the wall. The whole incident left him with a bright red face for a week, but the threat of the law never materialized – Keith had other dark plans afoot.

The CMS premises stood on a corner at a roundabout opposite Redcar race course. One Saturday afternoon, while minding my own business with a cup of coffee and a bun in the Zodiac room, I became aware of the sounds of a brass band, and on walking through to another room at the front of the building I looked out of the window and witnessed an astonishing sight. Going round and round the roundabout, to the delight of an amused crowd of locals, was a new Ford truck covered with Neashams posters and their distinctive motif, while in the back the band was playing *Colonel Bogey* at full blast! Now I reckon that any form of publicity is good publicity, particularly when it's on your own doorstep. In any event, we were all highly amused and suitable insults were being traded freely. All, it might be thought, jolly good fun.

But Les was not amused. When he heard about it on Monday all hell broke loose and the line from CMS to Neashams nearly caught fire. At the afternoon meeting we were told that nobody, Geoffrey, but nobody must set foot in Neashams for any reason under pain of instant dismissal. It really was all getting rather childish.

Nevertheless, CMS was beginning to show distinct signs of improvement. All the old cars had now gone and we were starting to show a profit each week on new and used-car transactions, and this based on my presentation with the fresh part-exchange cars written down to prices on which we could be certain of a return on investment. George was as pompous as ever, making snide remarks at every opportunity, but as yet making little impact on Les, who seemed to be pleased enough with the way things were going.

All I had done really was to re-educate the sales staff, with Mike's help, in the proper use of *Glass's Guide*, and at the same time find new ways of promoting the company as a reliable used-car dealership so as to create a constant demand for every good part-exchange that we could get our hands on. The history of the much-maligned *Glass's Guide* and a similar publication is dealt with in the next chapter. For the moment, though, it should be realized that most young salesmen failed to note the title on the cover, indicating that the name of the game was to use it as a guide.

With regard to the fairly limited range of cars likely to be offered to a Ford dealer in part-exchange at that time, it meant that a really good car in better than *Glass's* average condition could be resold for a better-than-average price. Those, however, that fell short of these minimum standards were not only worth considerably less, but quite often were virtually unsaleable without disproportionate expenditure. Failure to observe these simple ground rules had been the whole cause of the problem which had confronted me on arrival; while the good cars had been sold, and if the truth be known probably undersold, the junk had been allowed to accumulate. This situation simply could not be allowed to happen again, and the solution was really quite simple.

I was quite prepared to allow Neashams to sell all the new Fords they could to clients with sub-standard, high-mileage cars who were simply cashing-in on a well-promoted price war. We quietly began to dispatch them off to Middlesborough when it had become apparent that our price would not be acceptable, with very clear and precise instructions as to what sort of price to suggest they might have been offered! On principle, in most cases Neashams salesmen would almost always offer more, or alternatively some extra inducement such as a free road tax to secure the deal. That was fine by me. Those clients who had already been to Neashams and secured a price that I considered to be uneconomic were promptly returned with a strong recommendation to accept. In this manner I was ensuring that Neashams were taking in the below-standard cars for an above-average price!

Clients with above-average or low-mileage cars to exchange were dealt with in an entirely different manner. In the initial stages they were handled entirely by Mike Logue or myself. Both salesmen were encouraged to hand clients over in this manner on the basis that as long as they were learning their trade from our example the client remained theirs for commission purposes; the way to a car salesman's heart is always through his pocket! This, however, was certainly not a matter of 'money for old rope'. I expected my sales staff to learn in the process; it was what today would be termed 'on the job training'. It had been conceived as a matter of dire necessity, but it enabled me to train several salesmen very successfully in later years.

The system that Mike and I devised was one of progression. To succeed it depended, like most good schemes, on certain base disciplines which were built into the commission system. The system paid a good commission to a salesman on all of the profit generated from his new-car transaction. What this meant was that where a used car might be written-down by management to guarantee the remaining first profit in the new-car transaction, if and when this profit was subsequently recovered, or even added to, on the sale by any person of the used car, all of that profit was credited back to the salesman who had sold the original new car. He was then paid his commission on both the recovered profit and any extra profit in full.

However, in the event that money should be lost by the company during the transaction, the salesman had to sacrifice commission in the same proportion. There is nothing quite like the loss of commission to encourage a salesman to use his head! On the simple basis that the proper marketing of used cars was the prerogative of management, all used cars carried a fixed sum of commission regardless. Having established the discipline, we were all set to encourage the sales staff to progress step-by-step through a thinking process, the end result being that we should all be working along the same lines and to the same ends – sales and profits.

The first job of a salesman is to establish if he is dealing with a potential short-term purchaser or a long-term 'looker'. I would not accept that there exists what many salesmen term a time-waster, for *any* person who takes the time to visit your premises, even for a chat, may well become a customer in due course. However, no salesman should spend too much time with a 'looker' if there are people around who might wish to spend money. Nor should a salesman ever attempt to judge purely on sight! Most salesmen are capable of classifying customers in the course of a short chat by asking one or two indirect or leading questions. If they have time they chat on, if not, they should move on to the next likely client. This, therefore, was the first and most obvious step.

Given that they had a prospective client looking for a price on his car, their next step was to appraise the car in a methodical manner, give it a test run and then, excusing themselves, report to Mike or myself, where they were expected to provide a concise report on the client, a description of the vehicle offered in part-exchange and, most important, an opinion as to its value both as a part-exchange and its probable retail sale price. On this basis both salesmen were perfectly well aware that I was prepared to pay commission, even though Mike or myself might well complete the transaction personally. In voicing these opinions they were demonstrating that they were thinking and learning, depending, of course, on the eventual validity of their valuations. Afterwards, and particularly where a deal was completed, we would hold an inquest, when I was quite happy to argue or be proved wrong, especially where the salesman's retail valuation of a car was greater than mine! In this manner, over a period of a few weeks salesmen were taught to think the way I would think in a given situation and they would progress steadily towards completing their own transactions.

During the initial stages of the price war, however, only applied experience was to win the day, and to win we had to ensure that CMS sold every new Ford to the clients with the best of the part-exchange deals. Where a salesman felt he had a car that fitted this category I would make a careful appraisal, at the same time talking to the client to gather a few observations of my own regarding the possibility of him obtaining a price elsewhere, or how soon he might be prepared to place an order. Indeed, we might even return with the client and his wife to discuss further the car in which he had expressed an interest and restart the selling process again, rather than the valuation of his car, which might for various reasons be put off until a later date.

Whatever the outcome, I would have classified my man and be ready to close the deal, having obtained as much background as possible. When the new vehicle had been chosen and the question inevitably came: "How much then for my car?", I would not hesitate for a moment. I would hit him with what I knew to be a comparatively high price *providing* – and in this respect I was ruthless – the deal was completed there and then. Keen observation coupled with experience on my part would pick up some kind of reaction. Most times my instinct told me that I had a deal; most times I got away with it. Inevitably in some instances there were genuine reasons why a deal might not be concluded on the spot, but these were there to be overcome if at all possible. For instance, a wife who was not with her husband at the time might wish to choose a colour. "No problem sir, place the order now, choose the colour later." But at all costs we tried to get that order on the spot.

This way, while our friends in Middlesborough were no doubt building up stocks of expensive sub-standard used cars, we were taking in and aggressively marketing good-quality cars which might appear a bit over-priced 'on the book', but were selling without difficulty because they were superb cars, beautifully presented and prepared by Mr Pinkney's Ford-trained A1 car cleaners who, led by their redoubtable foreman Stan Kinson, were good – very good.

It being my intention to build up a reputation for good used cars, I promptly made a further enemy in the shape of our advertising agent, a smarty pants if ever I saw one. Policy adverts were one thing, but when it came to used-car advertising, with the experience in copywriting I had gained with Armstrong Siddeley cars I was not at all interested in the pictorial suggestions he was forever putting forward, and said so. The problem as I saw it was that at the end of the day it was my responsibility to sell the cars, not the agent's. While I agreed that his expertise in layout and smart eye-catching headings might be superior to mine, I now felt that expensive photographs of gents in bathtubs, etc, had outlived their usefulness. I wanted to try something else. There was no question that the agent took Les Pinkney for a ride, even though some of his creations were very good indeed. But at this time there could be little doubt that the company was well-known, perhaps in some instances too well-known, and I was concerned about nothing other than selling cars.

At about this time Ford introduced a new truck range called the 'Cost Cutter'. Many were the meetings between Les and the agent to decide how CMS were to introduce this to the waiting haulage contractors who, of course, would be perfectly well aware of its existence from their trade magazines. I have always held that in matters of national promotion the advertisements produced by the huge agencies on behalf of the manufacturers are far superior to anything we might be able to produce. The dealers' function in life is consistently to promote themselves, together with their association with the product, by good service, fair dealing and an acceptable public image. Successful promotion at dealer level depends on the ability of management and the dealership staff, not on fancy adverts. Nonetheless, the format eventually agreed by the directors took the form of another expensive advertisement showing the new Ford truck, complete with dolly-bird, a bowl of fruit and a bunch of flowers. I don't remember how it was all laid out, but I do remember seeing the final account listing: hire of dolly-bird with expensive photographer, the agent's valuable time – and one bowl of fruit and a bunch of flowers. I never did discover what became of either the flowers or the fruit! In any event the advert failed to sell a single truck.

The upshot was that I felt both determined and indeed entitled to design and produce my own advertisements. When the agent failed to influence me he inevitably tried to influence Les and George, with the result that one afternoon I was summoned to the boardroom for a meeting. The agent put his views to Les, as he had already done in private, and when he had finished I took the wind out of his sales by agreeing with almost everything he had said. What is more, I went further and praised in particular one specific advert he had produced that had cleared our stocks of an old model. Having said that I pointed out that spasmodic new-car promotion was one thing, but that used-car advertising was something else. The selling of cars was my sole function at CMS, and as long as I was responsible for results and profit and loss I intended to call the shots in the sales department, calling on the agent for his valuable assistance as required. If, however, the agent wished to relieve me of that responsibility, that was another matter, in which case I did not care one way or the other. This was not quite true, but at least it was an irrefutable argument.

Les was in a quandary. He thought that Bob was the greatest, but at the same time he was obliged to be realistic as a businessman and deep down he had to accept that what I had to say made commercial sense. He tried a compromise: "Are you saying, Geoffrey, that you are prepared to leave the new-vehicle promotions to him and that you simply wish to handle the used-car adverts?" "No, Mr Pinkney", I said firmly, determined to clear this once and for all. "What I am saying is that I should value his advice in regard to advertising and, if he cares to, I would be pleased to consider his suggestions at any time. *But,* at the end of the day it is my neck that you will be after if things go wrong again" – pause for effect – "and as long as it's my neck I intend that the final decision should be mine." Put like that there was not a great deal more to be said. The agent could see that his days at CMS were numbered; it had been a valuable account and he was not pleased. Les asked me to leave, so I don't know how the meeting finished, but I was never bothered again and in due course the agent faded away, having as his final task the shortly to follow promotion of the new Ford Mk III Zephyr range, for which he had already been engaged and for which, unbeknown to me, detailed plans were already afoot.

Some weeks later there was an odd sequel to this. With my experience with the classified ads in the *Motor* and *Autocar* magazines I decided to try this format in the local evening paper. Today, most used-car dealers use the classified pages at one time or another, but in 1962 almost all of them used weekly display ads in the newspapers' motor section. One midweek evening I wrote and presented individual classified ads for all of our used car stock ready for sale. By chance, on the same evening our supporting finance company had organized a drinks and buffet evening on the premises for the directors and the sales force, which was due to start at 7.30pm. By 9.30 the sales force, led by myself, were at last able to report to the directors and our hosts for a well-earned 'jar' and some grub, having sold every car advertised bar one on the night!

What was now required was a boost for the new Mk III Zephyr range shortly to replace the ageing Mk II Consul, Zephyr and Zodiac. With this brand new model range to supplement our present sales I felt that success would be within my grasp, but whether I could achieve sufficient profit to compensate for the first-year losses was another matter.

Noel found that he couldn't stand the pace and had departed; I was not unduly sorry. Good salesmen are hard to find in this business, and in any event I prefer to train my own, so an idea began to germinate. I had long felt that anybody with commonsense and the right personality could sell cars providing they had associated experience; I reckoned I knew just the man.

As we had expanded at Hamtune Motors the workshop had been unable to cope with the volume of sales work. I therefore persuaded Harry Frisby to let me set up my own service area, with my own fitter, John Stafford. I had never got on with the service manager anyway. John was ex-United Counties bus company, a top mechanic and above all a nice guy, with whom I became a good friend. I had seen him with our own clients on occasions and it was clear that he was a man very much liked and respected, almost on sight.

Harry by then had sold out and departed, so there were no problems there, so one evening I mentioned the idea to Mike, who to my surprise was very much in favour. John was presented with the opportunity of a lifetime and accepted, with some reservations. At worst he had his trade to go back to, so it was an acceptable gamble as far as he was concerned, but it did involve a substantial house move. As he said, he had never sold anything in his life. But John knew cars, he had personality and he could talk to absolutely anyone. He was a large man with a kind, friendly face and a permanent, but genuine smile. Les took one look at him and the cut of his Burtons suit and promptly wrote him off. But Les was wrong, very wrong: the customers had never seen anything like John Stafford in a car showroom before, and for no other reason than he was clearly no 'super salesman' the clients liked him, and more to the point, they trusted him. Given time to settle down, he became a notable success, to such an extent that when his clients returned to the showrooms to place their order they would oft times refuse to discuss it with anyone else if John happened to be out at the time or otherwise engaged. Some would not even speak to me, the sales manager! I was unconcerned, for if they would not speak to me then they most certainly would not speak to the competition!

Around this time I also acquired a trainee salesman, a personable young man in his late teens, very anxious to learn and to make a name for himself. It was Les who asked that he be given a chance – he was the son of my predecessor! With Noel out of the way we created a team in sales. Mike and John obviously got on as good friends from the past, between us we soon had John settled in, and by helping him to sell the odd car or two we gave him confidence in what must have been a novel situation. Joe and Mike were two of a kind, and poor old John had a bit of a rough time for the first few weekends when we were always busy. He always seemed to get the duds. The problem was that lacking experience he was unable to sort out the 'lookers' from the likely buyers. Even when it became obvious that some were just passing time until the pubs opened, or had nothing better to do, John was far too polite to excuse himself and move on to more interested clients. When you are quiet it doesn't matter so much, even time-wasters buy cars sooner or later, and in John's case any form of communication was good sales training, but when there are folk around with money to spend it is they, of course, who must be given the priority.

I enjoyed my Saturdays at CMS for they gave me the opportunity to get involved. I enjoy selling and dealing with customers, and there were plenty of those for this was the beginning of the 'never had it so good' society and the so-called 'Swinging Sixties', with the mass market in motor cars which was to follow.

Much of my day-to-day routine involved harassing Derek and trying to push my sales cars through the workshop ready for sale. Derek had his own retail clients to look after, and because patience is not one of my virtues we had a few ups and downs. Fortunately a mutual respect matured and flourished due, in no small measure, to our Friday meetings at the Con Club, so on the whole we got on well. We both owned dogs, so most Sundays would find us tramping the wild moors or the beach, where we would finish up at some pub or another dissecting the week's problems over a pint or two.

It was during these long walks that Derek told me something of the first year at CMS. One way or another it had been quite a time. Derek confirmed that the sales manager had had his hands in the till up to his elbows, with the tragic result that one night he drove his car onto the moors, where he ran a pipe from the exhaust and left his problems behind. Joe and Noel had been able to carry on just as they pleased, earning stacks of bogus commission doing any kind of deal that came along. My late friend McKinney had a company car, free petrol and an almost unlimited expense account, so he worked only when he felt like it, and Neville simply did not have the experience to realize or understand what was going on under his nose. He preferred to interfere with Derek in the organization of the workshop and the stores because this was the section of the business that he really understood. Neville valued my friendship for he realized that with all my apparent arrogance I knew exactly what I was doing. Neville, in fact, had told Derek that he was happy to act as a buffer between Les and myself to help contain some of my worst excesses!

With hindsight I really must have appeared a bit over the top on occasions. The problem was that I had taken over a tremendous challenge without realizing the magnitude of the task and found to my delight that I could cope. But to explain – if not necessarily to excuse – my perceived arrogance at this time, I have to return, if I may, to my childhood. As I think I have already indicated, in my early days I had had to endure and learn to overcome an inferiority complex due to my own shortcomings and the attitude of my father. He had failed to understand – and why should he – that I hated school because I had a practical rather than an academic frame of mind. Such a phenomenon, identified freely enough today, was not recognized in state schools of the Thirties when 'little boys were to be seen and not heard' and 'speech was silver, but silence was golden'; many the time I wrote out those little gems 100 times! Because I rebelled, my teachers, with one or two notable exceptions, either chastized or ignored me, and because they all knew I could be bright on occasions, I was written-off as being lazy, this being reflected in my reports: "Could do better." I must have caused the old man a very great deal of pain, for he had been a first-class scholar.

But his reaction to the school's verdict served only to make matters worse. He began to take the view that I was not capable of anything. Consequently, if anything were to go wrong in the home, such as a fuse or a tap washer, both of which I was perfectly capable of replacing, he would call in a tradesman, for he certainly was not practical himself. Because I loved and admired my father I was constantly eager for the recognition that he rightly considered I didn't deserve. It left its mark. But after I had left home and then returned, our relationship changed and we never looked back. Marriage, with its attendant responsibilities, helped, but now I had claim to real success, for had I not single-handedly turned a comic opera into a well-organized dealership? In the course of this I had secured the respect of the senior representative of the finance house with an appreciable stake in the business, plus those representatives of the Ford Motor Company whose job it was to guide the fortunes of their dealers. I was not intentionally arrogant, but that kind of success at 32 years of age is bound to intoxicate. I suppose it must have shown.

I just had time to get properly organized when the new Mk III Zodiac, the first of the new range to appear, was announced. I had been told many times by Les how the Consul Classic had been launched by CMS at a midnight party, when the showroom had been converted into some sort of garden complete with huge working waterfall. "Everybody, but everybody who mattered in Middlesborough was there, Geoffrey", Les told me with some pride. As the time drew nigh and arrangements, which had been afoot for some time, started to gel I began to realize just *why* everybody had been there: CMS was preparing to foot the bill for yet another gigantic booze-up, and few people can resist that kind of invitation. Whether they buy cars as a result is another matter, as will be seen.

Many were the frantic meetings with the advertising agent, now on his last assignment and making the most of it. It was decided that the waterfall was a non-starter as it took up too much room. In essence the idea was to hold a straightforward booze-up and buffet in the new-car showroom with the new car holding solus pride of place.

Used cars were relegated to the workshop, and remaining new cars to the used-car showroom.

The plan, as devised by the agent, was that the party should begin at around 10.30pm and the Zodiac kept covered under a dustsheet in the centre of the showroom. At midnight precisely all lights were to be extinguished without warning, a brief announcement would be made, the cover whipped off and the lights switched on – to suitable gasps of admiration. Les was at his most pompous, determined that this was to be the night of the year and that absolutely no expense was to be spared. As I recall, some 250 invitations were dispatched to the mayor, the chief constable, the town council (*en masse*), all of Les' many business friends, together with their ladies, etc, and most turned up, along with the inevitable gate-crashers. The showroom was completely blacked out for the day and the new car, wax polished and gleaming, was placed dead-centre under its oversized dustsheet. The salesmen had been given data to memorize and Les personally held a meeting at which technical questions were fired at all of us to ensure that product knowledge was at its peak. Les wanted to be sure that we all knew the car from back to front and issued dire threats in respect of slackness in this direction. This was to have an amusing sequel, for Geoffrey was to play an innocent little joke on our Les at a later date.

At our final management meeting just prior to the night, someone had pointed out that with 500 odd people drinking and talking we would be hard put to make our brief announcement heard when the lights went out. It was the agent who solved this problem in a unique way: during the evening the volume of the music would have to be constantly adjusted as the room filled up. At 11.55pm it would be further increased until it became almost intolerable, then abruptly switched off just a second or so before the lights went off – and it worked.

On the big night we all had our best suits and our badges on. Les was fussing around like an old dame at a garden party, and soon after 10pm the first of the revellers arrived. I had rigged up my tape recorder through an amplifier with suitable taped music for the event; it was also to be my function to provide the brief announcement. A great deal of my time was spent that evening popping in and out of the office to gradually turn up the volume. By 11.30pm I don't suppose I had had time for more than two drinks, and the party was going with a swing. Mike and Joe had been stationed at strategic positions to whip off the cover on cue, at 11.55 I started to 'screw up the loud pedal' and by 11.59 it was possible to observe the discomfort of such guests as were still sober, and as the music blared on even Les was becoming irritated. At dead on midnight, offering a silent prayer, I hit the switch. The music stopped and out went the lights. You could have heard a pin drop, the abrupt silence so completely astonishing that I nearly forgot my lines: "LADIES AND GENTLEMEN – THE

DIRECTORS AND STAFF OF CLEVELAND MOTOR SERVICE ARE PROUD TO ANNOUNCE THE ALL-NEW FORD ZODIAC MK III."

This was the cue for the cover to be whipped off. There was a whispered "Ready, Joe" from Mike, followed by a piercing female shriek, the crash of breaking glass, then all the lights came on. If nothing else it was dramatic: some idiot had parked the best part of a pint of beer on the roof of the car which had shot off with the dust cover and soaked a lady guest!

This, however, proved to be no more than a minor diversion; with great presence of mind somebody dragged the offended lady off to the toilet for temporary repairs and we all settled down to discuss the merits of the car with anyone who cared to listen, and serious drinking among the guests resumed in earnest. I actually heard one well-heeled lady demand a large double scotch on the basis of "Well, it's free isn't it?". What time it all ended I do not know, but eventually they all departed and Les invited management and their wives to the boardroom for a nightcap, giving his considered opinion that the evening had been a great success. That proved to be something of an overstatement, for with what had been consumed in food and drink, plus a crate of scotch that vanished without trace, the evening had cost a fortune. We didn't sell a single car.

Some months later Ford introduced the first Cortina, in many ways a much more important car than the Mk IIIs, being a completely new venture by Ford into a middle-range market with an all-new package. At my insistence we sent the same invitations to exactly the same people, but with a difference: coffee and light refreshments were to be available. We had the same midnight party arranged, the showroom was blacked out for the day, but instead of a dramatic display we simply displayed three cars on the showroom floor. By 10.30pm we were so bored with our own company that I ripped off the covers from the showroom windows and threw open the doors to catch people as the pubs turned out. By midnight the showroom was crammed with local folk munching sandwiches, who most certainly had not received an official invite, and we sold four cars on the night. There were no more booze-ups at CMS after that.

The Zodiac had been followed by the Zephyr Six and the Zephyr Four and we were back in business with a full range of cars once again. Les was running a Zodiac, while Neville and I had a Six and a Four, respectively, so we had a full range of demonstration cars. All had a rather novel parking light, for at the time it was still illegal to park anywhere on the highway at night without lights. This took the form of a small switch fitted below the dashboard which, when the side and tail-lamps were on, would extinguish the side and tail-lights on the nearside, thereby conserving the battery. For safety's sake it also cut out the ignition and starter circuit, so it was not possible to start the engine and drive off with only half the lights working. One night, shortly after the Zodiac launch, Les held a little cocktail party at his home for Neville, Derek, myself and one or two others, together with our wives. Les was an excellent host and we had all consumed a fair skinful one way or the other, so when the time came to leave (and noting the Pinkney Zodiac in the drive) I decided to play my little joke. Slipping unnoticed to the car, I surreptitiously depressed the parking switch prior to departing for home and bed.

Predictably, all hell broke loose next morning and I ran into Derek flying around the workshop organizing jump leads, fitters and tools. "What's up?", I inquired innocently. "Les' bloody Zodiac won't start, that's what's bloody well up!", muttered Derek. This was too much for me and I all but collapsed laughing. Derek asked what was so bloody funny?, so I told him. There was a long pause: "You little sod, this is one breakdown that I shall attend personally."

Derek later told me that on arrival Les had led him to the car, muttering dire threats about the state of his service department, the quality of the work, and what chance could the customers possibly have if he, the managing director, was unable to rely on his car, etc, etc. Derek had made a great show of switching on, scanning the dashboard and casually flicking the parking lamp switch. He turned the key to start and the engine burst into life. There was an awkward silence. Les asked Derek how he did it, and Derek told him. Another silence. He then thanked Derek and said he would see him later. Les was no fool; he knew he had been got at, the question was – *who*?

With the Cortina range added to the new Zephyrs and Zodiac things were really moving, even though Teeside was going through a severe recession. The once mighty Dorman Long steelworks were in all kinds of trouble, shipbuilding yards were closed, or likely to close, due to lack of orders and only the huge ICI plant at Billingham was offering any form of salvation for the growing army of unemployed.

Having seen this unemployment in the North-East during the Sixties, I was unable later to relate this sad experience to the well-publicized mass unemployment in the South and the East Midlands in the Eighties. When we required an extra car cleaner, for instance, we had to advertise under a box number to avoid being overrun with applicants. Advertise in the Bedfordshire area in the mid-Eighties and you were lucky to get a reply!. It was by no means unusual to see raggedy arsed little kids running around parts of Middlesborough and Hartlepool without shoes or socks, and wherever you went there were signs of real poverty. Nowadays it seems to me that the great unemployed have ample money to spend in the pubs and the betting shops and fill the remainder of their time watching films on their video recorders. Maybe I'm being cynical, but having witnessed real poverty and visible hardship, it really does make you wonder!

Just around the time of the Cortina introduction news started to filter through that Neashams' sales staff had received written instructions that *no* used cars were to be accepted in part-exchange without management approval and that cars were not being accepted above *Glass's* bottom trade price! This effectively meant that for the time being they had stopped trading. It was clear that somebody had discovered they were up to their ears in used cars, probably of doubtful quality, and that enough was enough. I knew from bitter experience just how they felt. Now we could all trade in a sensible manner, and I heard through the grapevine that all franchise-holders were breathing sighs of relief, for they had been affected to one degree or another. The battle had been won and with the Cortina, which was an outstanding car, and the continued popularity of the 105E Anglia, now also available in De Luxe form, plus the Mk III range (the Classic had been dropped) we began to record a worthwhile monthly profit.

One would have thought that the directors would have been delighted. Yet as the weeks and months went by they became more and more difficult to live with. Without any doubt George was the bugbear; he would carp and complain at any opportunity, and this to our faces, so what he said to Les behind our backs we shall never know. I remember selling a car to one of George's clients; he had no sooner taken delivery than George was on the phone complaining that the client had been promised a free radio – which he most certainly had not – and that the car had been delivered in a dirty condition – which it most certainly was not. The client was so astonished when I arranged for the most expensive radio I could lay my hands on to be fitted free of charge (it was Les and George's money, not mine) that he admitted freely that he hadn't even mentioned the condition of his car to George, but that in view of the size of George's fees he felt he should have had a free radio, and had said so.

The weekly meetings became a nightmare. I knew I had done a first-class job in pulling the dealership round, and I failed to understand why Les was not appreciative. On reflection it could only have been jealousy – I can think of no other reason – for both Neville and I were being criticized for the most petty and irrelevant things, while each month the figures got better! I recall with bitterness one particular gripe that George brought up at a Monday meeting which actually caused me to walk out.

I have always been meticulous with my showroom and vehicle display area; both new and used-car showrooms were always immaculate. We had a walled frontage where we could display half a dozen used cars, each one spotlessly clean, laid out at precise angles like a row of soldiers, and all neatly priced in exactly the same manner. Since we had disposed of the Farm we had always had a space penalty, and it took a great deal of ingenuity to make sure that there was room to display the clean cars and space to park the dirty ones until the cleaners could catch up.

On the morning of this particular meeting two new cars had arrived from Dagenham by train. British Rail, not unreasonably, expected us to accept vehicles immediately on advice, so they had to be collected and brought back. In the main we could rely on Derek for a space or two, but on this day he was full to bursting, with several new cars ready for delivery to clients. It happened that there were two temporary vacant spaces in the used-car showroom, so as the cars were fairly clean we all mucked in to give them a quick wash to clear the travel stains, after which we ripped off the adhesive tape which Ford then used to protect the chrome bumpers. This left behind a sticky residue, which would later be removed with white spirit when the cars were properly cleaned and prepared for the new-car showroom as space permitted. That day George arrived early; I noted that he was having a look round but thought nothing of it as I wished him a "Good afternoon", in return for which I received his usual sickly grin.

During the afternoon meeting George indicated to Les that he wished to raise a small point in regard to showroom presentation. With that, the man who had presided as joint managing director over a situation where a quarter of the used-vehicle stock had been allowed to rot away in a farmyard, where a brand new Consul convertible and a chassis/cab had been treated with the same criminal neglect, proceeded to lecture me in regard to a couple of new cars on display with sticky on the bumpers!

When he ground to a close I forcibly restrained myself from saying "a*******s", gathered up my papers, made my excuses to Les and walked out. Neville told me later that Les had assumed that I had been ill, but that he, Neville, had ventured that he felt that George was being a little unfair, and with that the topic had been closed.

For me this was the beginning of the end; there had been tempting overtures from down South and these were followed up with renewed interest. In any event my wife had never really settled in the North-East, so we decided to sell up and move back to Northamptonshire. By pure chance Neville Smedley and I handed in our resignations on the same day. Within two years Cleveland Motor Service had closed its doors for the last time.

CHAPTER EIGHT

INTERLUDE – CLOCKS, GUIDES AND JUNKETS

During the latter part of the Fifties, throughout the Sixties and into the Seventies, when the practice was finally outlawed, there is no doubt that a great many postwar-manufactured used cars were bought in all innocence by the general public with mileometer readings that were so totally false as to be meaningless. Even now, when simply to offer a car for sale with a false mileage is a criminal offence, it still happens, although not to anything like the extent that some pundits would have us believe. Today, car mileometers are turned back purely for greed in a cynical attempt to gain easy money, but in the Fifties, Sixties and Seventies they were turned back as a matter of necessity to avoid loss of custom and to protect *bona fide* commercial profit from being passed on and handed on a plate to the less scrupulous. And that, I submit, is a very different kettle of fish.

First let me emphasize that I am not making excuses, either for myself, or for the motor trade as a whole. The practice was as dishonest then as it is now insofar as it is calculated to deceive. But – and this is a big but – all historical events can only be viewed with total accuracy in the context of the situation and circumstances prevailing at the time. For example, the direction of Bomber Command by Air Vice-Marshal Harris, particularly in respect of the destruction of cities like Dresden, is viewed very differently by those of us who actually endured and survived the haphazard bombing of London, Coventry, Birmingham, Norwich and other British cities than by the well-meaning critics who were born long after the event and consequently never had an indiscriminate V2 rocket all but drop down their chimney pot on a cold dark night.

The most significant change in the motor vehicle market, apart from sheer volume, has been in customer attitudes. Today's car buyer is far more knowledgeable and streetwise than those of the Sixties, due in part to the vast amount of information available from magazines, the national press and informed TV programmes plus, of course, the simple fact that the majority of the population now learn to drive as soon as they become old enough to hold a licence. Furthermore, there is feedback resulting from mass family car ownership and endless car talk in the pubs and the clubs. This in turn has resulted in a wider and indeed more critical approach to car purchase, particularly in the field of secondhand purchase. (Nevertheless, even now a surprising number of people foolishly set out to buy a car on the basis of price alone – all too often from shady dealers with little or no facilities – and then wonder why they finish up with a lemon!)

In the Sixties, your average used-car purchaser was relatively ignorant of what he was about, particularly if it was a first-time purchase. Few had even the most basic knowledge of the workings of engines, gearboxes or rear axles, and fewer still had ever believed that the time would come when personal transport would be within the reach of virtually every household. Consequently, when the moment arrived and the purchase of a family saloon became a reality, most buyers found themselves in a commercial jungle, with a bewildering choice of vehicles and nothing whatever to guide them in their purchase other than perhaps the shape of the model under consideration and whether or not it offered sufficient room for grandma and grandad, or mother and father-in-law, on the back seats.

Having made a choice in the required price range, the question inevitably then arose as to the state of health and probable reliability of the vehicle under consideration. Most used cars on display, of course, appear to be in superb condition – even more so to the novice – after being professionally prepared for sale. How, then, could one be reasonably sure that the vehicle that *appeared* to be in first-class order was not in fact worn out? Almost without exception, the buying public would rely wholly on the ubiquitous odometer, to give the instrument its proper name.

Worse still, the apparent recorded mileage was to take precedence over almost every other consideration apart from aesthetic design and practicality. Today's well-educated car buyers might well find it beyond credibility that excessive wear and tear, poor-quality body and paint repairs, noisy axles and noisy, smoke-emitting engines were no barrier whatever to the eventual sale of a used car by the bomb-site dealers, always provided that the speedometer showed an acceptable mileage. With a low recorded mileage they could be certain of a nice little earner. Anyone inclined to take this with a pinch of salt should seek out someone who was selling cars during this period and ask how many times they were even obliged to provide a customer with a test drive, or demonstration run as it was then called!

For some reason never satisfactorily explained, the ultimately acceptable mileage on any vehicle over four years old seemed to be around 30,000, and newer cars, of course, proportionately less. In the Fifties and Sixties it mattered not whether a particular car was manufactured postwar or prewar, was an old banger, or was a two-to-four year old car in the most splendid condition imaginable, anything with over 30,000 miles on the clock made it totally unacceptable at any price – end of story.

Now a great many people who buy new, or low-mileage almost-new cars tend to use them for business purposes as well as leisure activities and the average mileage in the affluent Sixties was perhaps a touch less than today at around 10,000 per year. Nonetheless, this meant that by the time most vehicles were more than three or four years old, their mileage was already above the used-car market's self-imposed acceptable limit. It very quickly became all too clear to most new-car dealers, well used to collating subtle market trends, that they were losing used-car business to the wide boys and bomb-site traders, who had long since found a ready market for the high-mileage cars they had bought on the cheap direct from franchised dealers or car auctions and subsequently 'clocked'.

It also has to be appreciated that most motor dealers are much influenced by the monthly findings of *Glass's Guide* in respect of current used-car valuations. While the publishers were basing their valuations on a realistic annual mileage, this was not a great deal of help if potential buyers of used cars, not having access to a comparable book as they do today, failed to respond with their cheque books. More to the point – and this was the root cause of the dilemma – the owners of good used cars wishing to part-exchange them for replacement new vehicles were not in the least concerned about their dealers' used-car disposal problems. They usually had an excellent vehicle to part-exchange, they were prepared to spend money, so not unreasonably they expected an excellent part-exchange price, *pro rata* condition. By the late-Fifties most new cars were available almost immediately, so franchised dealers were all too aware that they had to keep the metal moving as further supplies were nearly always in the pipeline from manufacturers anxious to maintain and improve their share of the market. When dealers were faced with this situation, and a potential client appeared with a perfectly sound and presentable used car to trade in, they knew there was nothing to be gained by explaining to the proud owner that because he had covered an above-average mileage he would have to accept a proportionately reduced part-exchange allowance. The man would simply drive away and buy his new car somewhere else.

So what was the dealer to do? Obviously in a supply-and-demand situation he couldn't allow a customer with a perfectly sound car, of which he had probably taken a great deal of care, to drive off for no other reason than the car's speedometer revealed a total mileage in excess of many potential used-car buyers' acceptable limit. Unless, that is, he could be quite certain that every other dealer in the immediate area would regard the transaction in a like manner. So providing the car was basically sound we all endeavoured to complete the deal at the best price we found, by trial and error, we could get away with, and another new car was moved on. Faced then with owning yet another used car that might well have proved impossible to retail, we were left with the option of rectifying the situation or selling the car through the trade or at auction, thereby providing meat and drink for some used-car dealer who would undoubtedly wind back the clock the moment it arrived on his premises. This meant that we had lost not only a useful extra profit, but the chance of creating another valuable long-term customer for the dealership, for there was a great deal of customer loyalty in those days. Most dealers I knew chose to reset the mileage excessively, blatantly on the very low side, then saw to it that the sales staff disclaimed any knowledge of its authenticity or otherwise if asked. Oddly enough, in my experience, we seldom were asked, which tended to confirm that the exercise was probably more psychological than practical.

Henlys, being a very large dealer group, had the speedometer of every used car they handled reset to zero prior to sale. In doing so they endeavoured to shine in an aura of respectability, notwithstanding the fact that, like the rest of us, they were deliberately concealing the true mileage. I wonder if the directors imagined, or ever bothered to consider, what their commission-hungry staff were telling clients who, it is reasonable to assume, made inquiries about the previous usage of the zero-mileage cars they were seeking to purchase? By the time the cars were into their third or fourth ownership, many speedometers had been turned back for the second or even third time by those dealing in older cars. At least Henlys precluded the need for this in most cases.

Nowadays both of our trade used-car guides include suggested trade and retail valuations for high-mileage cars, and indeed not a few dealers even specialize in the sale of these. But to fully appreciate the argument it still has to be emphasized how incredibly naive prospective buyers were in those far-off days. In the mid-Sixties I took an elderly couple's Vauxhall Viva HA in part-exchange for the new model. The car was three years old, had been purchased from us and serviced throughout in our workshops. It had completed just 14,000 miles, had been kept in a heated garage and washed with loving care, whether used or not, each Sunday morning. Inevitably, when displayed on the front, it very soon attracted a potential buyer. His much older car was as tatty as mine was immaculate, with the result that, to put it mildly, we had to agree to differ over its likely valuation on a part-exchange basis. The gentleman's parting shot on leaving the premises was that I was "an effing idiot".

He purchased on the same day, from a local competitor, an identical HA Viva – indeed it was the same colour – for three reasons. One, that the price was competitive to mine; two, that the part-exchange allowance was rather better than mine; and three, that the car seemed to have had only marginally more use with just 23,000 miles on the clock. All of this was later related to me by the client, in a rather less restrained manner, because he was unable to resist the temptation to brag, having spotted me one day near the petrol pumps while he was having a fill-up. As it happened, we had supplied that Vauxhall Viva to the local minicab company, whose proud boast was that they only serviced their cars when something actually fell off, and merely topped-up the levels once in a while on slack days. The car in fact had completed 123,000 miles! Obviously it had been felt there was little to be achieved by winding back a clock that only recorded to five digits. I decided not not to enlighten him!

There were so many clients and so much business in the Sixties that we even had time to play the odd practical joke, one of which I devised and used both for amusement and as an object lesson to trainee salesmen. Given a four or five-year-old family saloon in really super condition, having been regularly serviced, carefully driven, garaged nightly and treated almost as one of the family – but, horror of horrors, with around 40-50,000 albeit genuine miles on the clock – I would have it prepared for sale, sensibly priced and awarded pride of place on centre spot of the used-car lot, and then await results. Usually we didn't have to wait long. A prospective buyer would very soon be drawn to it like a moth to a flame; after all, this was the most attractive car on the front. Crouching behind the venetian blinds in the sales office we would watch as the client walked in a seemingly casual manner towards the car, nervously glancing round to see if there was a salesman waiting to pounce. He had no worries on that score! On reaching the vehicle he would walk around it slowly, feeling the immaculate paintwork and kicking a tyre or two *en route*. You could sense the interest and the desire building up. Eventually he would reach the driver's side, and with a final cautious look round to ensure that he was on his own he would open the door, head and shoulders would vanish as the speedometer was examined; abrupt end of examination, straight out of the car, slam the door and walk away, all interest being at an end. At this point one of the sales staff would appear as if by magic, open up a conversation and probably sell him a marginally inferior car of doubtful mileage for rather more money. Any motor dealer of the Sixties who says today that he never once sold a clocked car is a fool or a liar. Or both!

Glass's Guide was founded in July 1933 by the late Mr William Glass. There had been a trade guide to used-car values in America from as early as 1910, but Glass's was the first successful guide for the UK market. Mr Glass, who had been trained as an engineer, was originally in motor car manufacture but later became involved in sales, where he decided to develop the service which still bears his name. During his early days he had acquired a reputation as bit of a tearaway having twice been convicted, once in 1899 for 'furiously riding a bicycle', and again in 1903 for 'driving a vehicle at a speed greater than 12 miles per hour on a public highway'! Six years after he founded the company it had to be suspended due to wartime conditions, following which the struggle to build up the list of subscribers had to start all over again. When William Glass died in 1949 his publication comprised just 120 pages. I wonder what he would have thought of the phenomenal growth in demand and the sheer size of *Glass's Guide* today, which runs at a tad over 1,000 pages. At the time of writing, the circulation is no less than 37,000 copies per month!

The Glass family withdrew in 1962, since when the company has been owned jointly by the International Thomson Organisation and the Municipal Journal Group. In addition to the monthly guide to used car values, sister guides were established for motorcycles (1950), commercial vehicles (1951), and in 1971 a quarterly guide for caravans was acquired and has been published regularly since. The group also produce similar publications in Australia, France, Austria and Germany. All this from the fertile imagination of a man who once got nicked for driving at 12mph! *Glass's Guide* has been much maligned over the years, generally by people who ought to know better. "Cars are making silly money" (according to *Glass*) is the oft-heard moan by so-called motor dealers at car auctions, when cars are making what the market is prepared to pay in busy times. If this be silly, perhaps these dealers should enter their own stock for sale! Car valuations, like those of any other commodity, are governed by the basic laws of supply and demand. The *Guide* may only be obtained by subscription, the bulk of the circulation, of course, being to the motor trade, although other approved subscribers include finance companies, insurance houses and police forces. At a Rotary meeting not long ago, our then President, a police superintendent, announced that Rotary were collecting unwanted books for old people's homes and hospitals. Not quite under my breath I said to a fellow member: "I've got a few old copies of *Glass's Guide* he can have". Quick as flash came the reply: "It's bloody fact we want, not fiction." And he was not altogether jesting!

People outside the business often fail to appreciate that there can be no such thing as a definitive 'book' price for any used car, indeed the wide difference of valuations in different circumstances, or even in different parts of the country, can often appear totally out of proportion and consequently misleading. At the end of the day, the value of anything is the price for which you can actually sell it, or indeed buy it. Certainly as a general rule the trade will value a run-of-the-mill average car with average mileage for the year at around the current *Guide* trade price. Whether they will be prepared to actually buy at that price or, conversely, whether they are indeed able to *buy* at that price is quite another matter, and depends on a host of different circumstances as well as fluctuating market conditions.

Bernard Braden, with Miss Rantzen in tow, once appeared on his television show *Bedtime with Braden*, gleefully brandishing a confidential copy of *Glass's Guide*, illicitly obtained, from the contents of which he then accused the motor trade of profiteering, citing the difference between the trade and retail prices then quoted. I didn't feel then, and I do not feel now, that the man making a black fortune from sponsoring consumer goods on commercial TV was quite fitted to censure others, who at least had to work and invest considerable sums of money for their profit. However, he certainly had an obligation, if only in the interests of journalistic accuracy, to point out that the *Guide* refers to this margin as a *gross* profit, which contains an allowance for the preparation of an average car purchased for stock for resale. Furthermore, as indicated above, because a used car may be listed in *Glass's* at a price, it doesn't mean that a dealer may actually be able to *buy* at that price. Neither does it follow that the public at large will necessarily wish to buy at the published mark-up price once the dealer has invested his money. If the motor business were that simple everyone would be in it. Nonetheless, it brought suitable ooh's and aah's from the captive audience as the wicked profiteering motor dealers were suitably exposed. The gross margins being quoted at the time represented *12 per cent*!

Throughout my years in the motor industry I managed to miss all of the more exotic new car introductions, and there were some really fantastic launches in foreign parts in those far-off tax-allowable days. I quote from the autobiography of Lee Iacocca, one-time president of the Ford Motor Company in America:

"In September 1966 we leased the SS *Independence* at a cost of $44,000 a day and set sail from New York for the Caribbean. At sunset on the second day, we assembled all the dealers at the stern of the ship. At a predetermined moment we released hundreds of helium balloons, which floated skywards to reveal the 1967 Mercury Marquis. Two nights later, on the island of St Thomas, we unveiled the new Cougar. At a beach lit by clusters of brilliant torches, a Second World War landing craft pulled up to the shore and lowered its ramp. The audience was breathless as a shining white Cougar drove out onto the sand. The door opened and out stepped singer Vic Damone, who began to entertain." Now, that's what I call style!

In contrast, the most bizarre that I attended was Vauxhall Motors' introduction to the quite important Vauxhall Victor FD range in 1968. The shindig, if one could call it that, was organized on a regional basis for groups of dealers, ours being at the *Billing Aquadrome* on the outskirts of Northampton. Too late it had been discovered that the car would not go through the doors into the main conference hall, and Sod's Law ensured that it was pouring with rain. Some 40 main dealer principals, together with their sales managers, were invited to inspect the new car on the lawn by torchlight in raincoats under umbrellas. It was not an auspicious occasion.

The most memorable had nothing to do with the car – a later Vauxhall Victor FE Series – which was introduced at the army cross-country training area near Bagshot. I had drawn a raffle ticket to ride two laps with racing driver Gerry Marshall while he 'demonstrated' a rally Firenza. Of course, I had realized that my own driving ability fell well short of his standards, but until then I had believed in my ability to handle a car reasonably well. Having been carefully strapped into the comfortable passenger seat and assured by Gerry that there was nothing to worry about as we would be well short of rally speeds, we took off – literally. My immediate impression was that the driver, far from having a leisurely afternoon warm-up, had gone stark raving mad! In no time we were through the box and proceeding flat-out up an incline between some formidable looking trees to an all but right-angled turn formed by a sturdy looking rock bank. Gerry did at least drop a gear but, doubtless as he was only 'cruising', he didn't bother to drop as much as a single segment on the speedometer. I closed my eyes. Before I could gather my wits I became aware that we had somehow turned left with a smoothness and total lack of fuss or drama that was wholly astonishing. By lap two I had relaxed and was enjoying the experience of being transported at very high speed, in cross-country rally conditions, in perfect safety by a master of his craft. All too obviously he certainly was *not* trying – by his standards. All young tearaways in their GTIs showing off in the high streets ought to have the opportunity to try an experience like this just the once; they might then come to realize what absolute prats they really are!

CHAPTER NINE

ROBERT DAVID HAMBLIN – 1964-70

It was mid-1964. Ford had just introduced their all-new Corsair, but like the Classic which had been introduced just prior to our move up North, it was not an outstanding success. *Radio Caroline*, with Tony Blackburn, would set me up each day as I drove to work, it was the early Beatles and Rolling Stones era, it was the 'Swinging Sixties', and even at the ripe old age of 34 it was a great time to be alive.

While exploring the various options open to me we had moved in with my parents in North London; there was a depression in the North, so the house was not going to be easy to sell. After Cleveland Motor Service I really wanted a fresh challenge and I had thought that with such a broad background and experience there must be no end of firms who would be glad of my services. The reality was that while there were quite a few jobs on offer they were all with well-established companies who had made it clear at interview that they would resist change. This was not for me. So to fill in time, keep occupied and earn a few bob I accepted one or two situations on a short-term basis over the next couple of years. One of the more interesting, and indeed lucrative, was with a used-car dealer in the Ilford High Road. This was real 'Arthur Daley' territory, and while my erstwhile employer enjoyed respect and a good reputation within his patch, some of the methods used and the short cuts taken quite literally made my hair stand on end. Used cars are an industry in that neck of the woods, and around and about there were various specialists making a good living from every facet of motor car usage. For instance, there was an electrical man who would overhaul and repair almost any starter, generator or alternator. A tyre man, who could supply cheap tyres or who on request would recut the treads on worn tyres! A speedometer man, who called nightly twice or three times a week to 'adjust' the mileage at 10 bob a throw. And last but not least, a dodgy MoT man, to whom the granting of the certificate was a formality on payment of the statutory fee plus a palm full of silver. It was during this period that we heard sadly that Harry Frisby had died in Barnstaple from a heart attack.

One weekend we visited friends in Northampton, and at a Motor Agents Association dinner I was introduced to David and Betty Hamblin. I knew from my time in Northamptonshire that David headed a group of five or six garages based in this part of the world; obviously we would all have been aware of each other's advertising in the local rags, but hitherto we had never met. David didn't mince words. We had a brief conversation during which he asked what I had been doing over the last three years and then the conversation was abruptly, though not discourteously, terminated with the blunt statement: "You should be working for me. Come and see me on Tuesday afternoon at my Vauxhall garage in Corby. Nice to meet you."

The following Tuesday I was at Hamblin's Stockwood Motors garage in Corby in my best suit. As interviews go it certainly was the shortest. I was given the distinct impression that as far as RDH was concerned there was no question that I was not to join the company; all that was required was the sorting out of the nitty-gritty. I was told that the garage was failing to meet acceptable monthly profits and David wanted someone to make it all "go go go", as he liked to put it. Well, that sounded to me like some sort of a challenge, always providing I had a free hand to run the sales department my own way. With a casual wave of the hand and a "fair enough, Geoff", that was settled. However, for me at least, there was one more fundamental problem which might not have been so easy to overcome. Besides holding a main dealership for Vauxhall cars and Bedford trucks, Stockwood Motors held a retail dealership for my old adversaries Morris and Wolseley, and there was no way I was prepared to get mixed up with that crowd again. When I raised the matter, to my surprise and relief David, who undoubtedly would have heard something of my background in this respect, simply said: "I don't blame you, get rid of them; it will certainly make Vauxhall happy – they don't like us offering competing cars." All that was left then was the important matter of my income, and as David had not raised it, I did. "I think you know what you want", was all he said to that question. In some respects he was dead right. I had already made up my mind that a set salary was not on after all the profit I had earned for the directors at CMS for nothing extra on my basic salary other than grief. I named a simple salary-and-commission structure, together with the usual fringe benefits, which was instantly accepted. And that, so to speak, was that.

Hamblins, as I was to learn later from David's father, had an interesting history. Robert Hamblin, or Bob, as he was affectionately known throughout the organization, was then more or less retired, but a regular visitor to Stockwood Motors. He loved nothing better than to reminisce about the old days when, as he often remarked, Bill Swallow ran Vauxhall Motors in a proper manner. In these days, of course, it was being run by a somewhat unusual American gentleman. Bob had started commercial life as a farmhand somewhere west of London. He had a reasonable enough job and a mate, who had been offered a better situation in the North Midlands. The mate had promised to get Bob fixed up if he could, and eventually, true to his word, a situation became available. This involved a long and somewhat exhausting train journey during which Bob fell asleep, finally finding himself stranded very late at night, almost penniless, at Leicester railway station. Feeling and doubtless looking somewhat at a loss, he was approached by a gentleman who, on hearing the sad story, took Bob home to his wife, where a hot meal and a bed were graciously provided, together with the offer of a job. The gentleman proved to be a haulage contractor and Bob started at the bottom, learning the ropes and how to drive and putting money away each week until he had enough to buy a secondhand lorry on hire purchase and start a business of his own. He told how the lorry had a plaque on the dashboard stating that it was the property of the Wagon Finance Company.

Through sheer hard work his business became successful, Bob married, and three sons were born, David, John and Peter. David, being the eldest, had the advantage of the best education at great personal sacrifice to his parents while times were still relatively hard. But in later years Hamblins Haulage was to prosper, eventually being purchased on very advantageous terms by a huge Norwich-based concern. Bob was then able to provide each son with a garage business at Uppingham, Corby and Rushden, respectively, this becoming the nucleus of the Hamblin Group of Companies, which went on to control several more garages in addition to entertainment and leisure activities worldwide; big oaks indeed from little acorns grow. When I joined the Group in 1966 the original three garages had expanded to six and an executive director had been appointed from outside the family. Stockwood Motors Ltd was the entire responsibility of younger brother John, who had been at court in connection with a dishonest employee on the day of my visit. Now while John was a nice enough bloke, he had resented – as I would have in his place – that although he had been advised of my appointment as general sales manager, he had not, thanks to David's usual casual manner, been given any indication as to the specific terms of my employment. Consequently, when I started to get the place organized to my way of working on day one, John was not pleased and said so. I had no choice but to stand my ground, insist on the terms agreed with the Group chairman, while adopting a position of limited liability. It was not an auspicious start, and it was to affect my tenure throughout. However, I was to be with John for four years, during which time I was delighted to be appointed to the Hamblin board of directors, so John and I must have got on reasonably well. When we terminated the agreement with Leyland for Morris and Wolseley the factory representative who came to clear up the loose ends asked if I was "by any chance, 'the' Mr Owen?" It seemed that I had left my mark at the factory somewhere!

Corby was certainly an education. Its modern history, as most will know, was steel, and the Sixties were the boom years. The country lanes that had led into and out of Corby when we departed to the North had become dual carriageways and by now the whole town had spread and altered almost beyond recognition, and there were more vast plans still outstanding. During those four years I learned a great deal about public relations at their lowest possible level. I have to say that I did not take to the area, which was known throughout the Hamblin Group as the salesman's graveyard. It was a period of my life – otherwise comparatively uneventful – over which I prefer to draw a veil; anything I were to write now about Corby, or the various happenings during those years, would be tainted, and therefore unfair to the many nice people who doubtless live there today.

One bright Tuesday morning in early January 1970 I was asked to meet David Hamblin at his Rushden office and was taken across the road to view the old *Palace* cinema. This had latterly been converted into a Vauxhall Bedford main dealership by a Wellingborough-based company. We all knew that it had not been a particularly successful venture, and now the building was deserted, so I was considerably surprised when David told me in his usual casual manner that he had bought it. In the same breath he then told me that I was to take over the business as managing director on the Hamblin Group's behalf on completion. What he failed to tell me was that none of the senior board members had expressed the slightest interest in the project, and that his brothers, in particular, had thought the purchase to be ill-advised. When they were told that Geoff Owen was to be handed the business, most directors went out to acquire toppers, black ties and grey gloves, ready for a funeral that was most definitely not to take place! It must be said that had I not been so desperate to get away from Corby, which was quite alien to me, I might well have given the situation rather more consideration. After all I was taking on a complete business for the first time in my life. Furthermore, it was not so much that the sales department had failed to come up to expectations, the whole bloody lot had failed ignominiously, with the result that all I was taking over was a totally empty building with neither staff nor equipment apart from a telephone, which was disconnected. At least I wouldn't have a used-car problem; there wasn't a vehicle on the premises.

I doubt that it ever occurred to David that I might turn the offer down, and we returned to his Rushden office, where he lost no time in lecturing me on his favourite subject, namely letting the manufacturers dictate all the terms and forcing overstocking of new vehicles and spare parts to their (Vauxhall's) benefit, etc. Meanwhile, he suggested that I should continue to make myself useful to John Hamblin at Corby, the while planning what I intended to do when the purchase was completed around March. All of this sounded fine except that I had not been asked, or really decided, if I could deal with this new responsibility. With David Hamblin, though, there was never much room for discussion; he provided the opportunity and the facility, then either you want it or you don't, and if you don't it will be a very long time before you get another chance, if ever. It was his very proper way of looking at life; if somebody like me thought they were pretty damn good, it was time to put up – or shut up.

It was the start of a new decade and, unknown to either of us at the time, this would shortly herald the start of a brand new Conservative legislation under prime minister Ted Heath. The timing could hardly have proved more auspicious. Tentatively I inquired about remuneration at the dizzy heights of MD. He gave me almost the same answer he had at Corby almost four years since: "I think you know what you expect." This time I was not at all sure that I did as this situation was a total surprise. Nonetheless, I named what to me was a reasonable figure as a basic salary, bonuses at director level being virtually automatic, but I pitched it on the high side relative (a) to the quite awesome responsibility involved and (b) that I did not see much chance of a bonus in the first year. At least events proved me right in that respect. I waited for David to argue. "Sounds about right to me, see accounts and get them to sort it out from today. But", with a grin, "don't expect any more salary from John, though you'll have to use one of his cars until you get organized."

I left Hamblins feeling both elated and apprehensive and drove round the one-way system, returning to the *Palace* to survey my acquisition. In essence it was simply a large oblong cinema building built on a downward slope at right-angles to the main road. On its left a wide drive was bordered by the old and now disused railway embankment, down to a huge car park area at the rear. The whole of the old foyer had been converted into a small glass-fronted car showroom with room for just five cars. A hole had been cut out of the side with glass sliding doors leading to a concrete ramp down to the drive; not ideal, but quite functional. Stairs at the rear led down to the old stalls area, which made for a very roomy workshop space right down to the old wood stage. I noted that the floor was completely level, unlike the old *Lyceum* ballroom in the Strand where, in my young days, you danced to the Oscar Rabin band downhill one way and uphill the other. Entrance to and exit from the driveway was by way of an electric roller shutter, hard by the stage. Adjacent to this shutter a new brick office had been constructed on the outside of the building, but with a connecting door, for the use of service reception and manager.

Stairs down into the old orchestra pit led first to the mechanics' parts counter, for the whole of the parts stores area was immediately below the stage, through to the rear of the building, where a self-contained entrance had been constructed for the customer parts counter. The main orchestra pit area also provided three handy purpose-built car inspection pits. Now while this was no Stockwood

Motors, it was nonetheless vastly superior to Cleveland Motor Service's converted bakery. From that moment all doubts were cast aside. Anything Les Pinkney could do, I thought, I can do 100 times better, and with this in mind I set off to explore upstairs. The old circle had been completely removed. Where the back row used to be had been repanelled and it looked very much as if there was more space upstairs once I had found the way. Back in the showroom I found a flight of stairs which led up to the old circle foyer and two half-decent toilets for ladies and gents, respectively. The area was huge and promised good facilities for new offices when needed, together with a balcony overlooking the main road, which was to prove handy on carnival days. Further exploration led to a narrow staircase right up to the original projection room. This proved something of an historical site. From here many a Hollywood epic must have been beamed over the years. Sadly, there was now nothing much to see, but I did find an old prewar wages book where the top salary was £2 18s 6d for one week's labour. I also found an historic Jeyes' Fluid wall mirror, which I have in my home to this day.

I had enough time to organize as we finally took over the business on April 1, 1970. By this time I had found two or three mechanics, a parts manager, a lady service receptionist who had been employed by the original company and knew both the ropes and the customers, a personal secretary and a junior car salesman. The telephone was working and we had some basic furniture and a typewriter. From my time at Stockwood Motors I knew all of the Vauxhall and Bedford people, so a single day at Luton produced sufficient information and the promise of vehicle stock to get us under way together with a starter pack of fast-moving spare parts to get the stores operational. David Hamblin had a redundant company, so it was decided that this would be reconstituted and the name used for the new business. Accordingly, in the latter part of March 1970 I found myself to be the managing director of Bedford Way Motors (Rushden) Ltd.

Given the name I could design, produce and order the paperwork, and this is where experience counts. I knew exactly what I wanted and, of course, I could do it all my own way. I shall always admire David Hamblin for one particular attitude, which was when he gave you a business to run the only discipline was profitability. How this was achieved was entirely your own affair. He could, however, be a mite impatient. One morning I chanced upon David's father Bob having a look round while various alterations were being carried out. I wandered over to wish him a good day. "Tell you what, boy", was his gruff greeting, "you'll never make any money from this bloody old cinema." I was a bit taken aback. "Well I reckon I shall", I said with more confidence than I felt. Bob grinned and made towards his car: "You do that and I'll see you get a good drink." There was later to be an amusing sequel to that!

I had been to Measham, now owned by David Wickins' British Car Auctions Group, and bought some used cars. I had also been to a bankruptcy sale in Northampton, where I purchased, with some other items, a large number of metal parts bins. Most unusually I was the only seriously interested buyer and I bagged the lot for a very low price. By now the word had got round and soon the oil companies wanted desperately to get in on the act. They wanted exclusive representation for what could well be a tidy drop of oil, in return for which they usually offered subsidized or even in some cases free equipment or, alternatively, long-term interest-free loans. The first caller was a representative I had fallen out with for some reason at Stockwood Motors, but I intimated that all was forgiven - as it doubtless was, for I seldom hold grudges - and suggested that he called again in a week or so when I had more time. Instinct told me that I should leave him until last. The next made me an offer I found easy to refuse; he managed to make it clear that in his opinion my forecast of future car sales and service business was pie in the sky. That it may well have been, but I objected to being told so by a bloody oil rep! Subsequent events were to prove us both to be wide of the mark. Astonishingly, the next to make contact needed the business very badly, which is rare amongst wealthy oil moguls, and I was made an offer that I found hard to refuse, but nonetheless resisted, by which time I was ready for the reappearance of the first. Without actually lying I managed to give the impression that caller number three had been rather more generous than he actually had, and I had hardly finished when 'number one' said, without any hesitation: "Oh, we can do much better than that!", and he did. In return for a contract to sell their oils and lubricants exclusively we received two hoists, on a long-term written-off loan, together with free bulk lubrication dispensers and various items of equipment on a heavily subsidized basis.

By around day three of opening we had a selection of new and used cars, we had staff, we had tools and equipment and we had paperwork. We did not, however, have the promised initial load of Vauxhall Bedford fast-moving spares. This irritated me, for my parts man was the only member of staff with a very great deal to do in the way of binning and storing, yet was having to sit around on his bum all day because someone at Vauxhall Motors had his finger well and truly stuck in. I decided to borrow from a telegram sent to Fighter Command during the war by - as he was then - Squadron-Leader Douglas Bader, and sent this off to a General Motors big-wig: 'Bedford Way Motors now operational regarding vehicles, staff, tools and equipment. But non-operational, repeat non-operational in respect of promised spare parts and accessories.'

That worked. Within 48 hours a huge Bedford 32-tonner arrived laden to the gills with spare parts. As long as I live I shall never forget that really hot April day when, stripped to the waist, we started to unload that truck. The very first 'fast-moving' item we unloaded was 50 gallons of anti-freeze!

Without doubt my worst problem was service management; my new salesman was a bit odd, but quite successful as long as he was supervised, and between us we managed to start moving some new Vauxhalls and to buy and sell some used cars. But I had three service managers within nine months, all of whom upset clients and staff alike. After a great deal of thought I decided to run the workshop myself – if nothing else it would be an interesting management exercise – and to advertise for a sales manager. Everyone who knew me said that it was a mistake as until then selling had been my life and they all said that I would never in a thousand years be able to delegate this responsibility to someone else. I had to agree, but I reasoned that with my own very simple, but highly efficient sales systems I could keep an eye on the sales side from a distance. I would then be free to see if I could manage a service department in a proper and profitable manner; and surely, even the efficient running of any department involves a degree of selling, if only a service. The problem was to find the right man for sales.

My advertisement for a sales manager produced, among others, an extraordinary character by the name of Terry Eales. It must be a truism that opposites attract for it has to be said that Terry, having been accepted on the basis of his obvious experience and devastating personal charm, demonstrated from day one that he represented the complete antithesis of everything I stood for. He was casual in both his appearance and his dealings, he was one of the most untidy persons I have ever met, punctuality he had never heard of, and his demeanour when dealing with clients, particularly lady clients, was to say the very least, astonishing to a person of my conservative outlook. Yet after the initial shock had subsided to some extent I was to discover that Terry, with all his apparent faults, was undoubtedly the man for the job and for the moment. There was soon to dawn a whole new method of selling cars to the masses; art of selling was about to be replaced by something we call marketing in this new consumer age. Had I but known, Terry and I were in just the right situation at just the right time.

The Hamblin Group were forward-looking and some of their directors were quite outstanding. One of the first things I discovered, with considerable surprise, was that all Hamblin's new-car dealerships went into the marketplace and actively traded in used cars. This was at a time when virtually every main dealer in the country spent a great deal of time and energy simply getting rid of those used cars they had been obliged to accept in part-exchange. Nowadays, of course, they are all at it, but it took them a very long time to discover that buying and selling used cars can produce as much, if not more, profit per capital invested than new-car sales. A new dealership for any make of car has to be built up over a period of time, and while this happens profitability has to be achieved, particularly when you work for David Hamblin. We obviously expected to lose money during the formative months, but it was expected of me that I should to show a return on capital at the earliest opportunity, and preferably sooner!

With my four years' experience with Vauxhall Bedford at Stockwood Motors at least I knew the ropes and I was well placed to go to the various car auctions and purchase used-car stock for resale. When we started on April 1, 1970 I was just 26 days short of my 40th birthday The Series 2 HB Vauxhall Viva, which in my opinion was one of the prettiest small family saloons ever produced for the mass market, was due to be phased-out and replaced by the more expensive, some thought over-expensive, HC model. The all-new 'Transcontinental' Victor range was due in 1971, together with a brand new mid-range van; all in all it was no bad time to start. Within a short time Heath won the election, taking over from Wislon (with apologies to *Private Eye*) and there followed the so-called Heath/Barber boom. By August we had shown our first monthly profit, and from that day we never looked back. By year's end the company showed a nett loss, mainly through setting-up costs, of around £9,000, but this was very soon to be written-off.

Meanwhile, my excursion into service management was proving to be interesting. My lady from the original company had taken over the records and most of the costing, and by this time I had four fitters. I had some custom from existing local Vauxhall owners who had no desire to travel all the way to Wellingborough for routine service or maintenance, but I lacked both corporate enthusiasm from staff and a full workshop diary each day. This in turn meant that we lacked sufficient profitability and the large throughput of clients which can be expected to generate sales in the long-term. To encourage enthusiasm and to retain the very best mechanics I increased both income and profitability by the introduction of a simple bonus system. I then set about marketing our service facilities. Few garages in the early Seventies owned sophisticated electronic engine tuning equipment, and those that did lacked the staff capable of using it for diagnostic purposes. In this respect I was lucky in that I had a young fitter who had recently moved to the area and had applied for a job. At his interview he told me he was a specialist in the use of Crypton engine test and diagnostic equipment and held certificates for advanced courses. That was good enough for me; I went out and purchased the latest and best model available, put Mick 'Smithy' in a white overall, and constructed a special bay in a prominent corner of the workshop.

Electronic plug-in equipment, doing everything by telling the fitter in print-out form precisely what needs to be replaced, reset or adjusted, is old hat these days. It is largely a substitute for applied workshop know-how and an indispensable means of servicing the high-tech engineering and computer systems that have become commonplace in all but the cheaper family saloons. This was not the case in the early Seventies, when good Crypton and Sun Tune operators were few and far between, and Smithy was outstandingly good. I started by offering a free Crypton test with a written report on any make of car. Clients who flocked in were not obliged to have the recommended rectification carried out by us, but most did, and in this way we built up a list of regular clients. They were encouraged to watch Smithy carry out the check and to ask questions. This way a close relationship was built up and many a minor, no-charge, rectification helped to build up customer confidence and goodwill. We also challenged the locals to build in a fault, offering a cash prize if we were unable to trace it on the machine. Some of the faults were quite ingenious, but Smithy found them all with no trouble. By year's end the service department was both busy and reasonably profitable when I was fortunate enough to be approached by a much-needed professional service manager; he was able to provide clients with the right type of technical experience and he arrived at just the right time. The Heath/Barber boom was about to take off in spectacular manner and the motor trade was poised to move into this brand new era of marketing.

During these times my wife and I had been out and about socializing and had got to know one or two of the local gentry. We attended and provided the odd dinner party and as a result I was invited to apply for membership of the then very exclusive Rushden Skew Bridge Ski Club. On being accepted I found that a previous application from a Mr David Hamblin had been blackballed. I heard that the local establishment, many of whom bought their BMWs and Jaguars on the 'never', thought that David was rather *nouveau riche*. Some little time later, however, David became a full-time member. He bought the club!

The Hamblin Group were expanding at this time by diversifying into leisure and entertainment. Two large cinemas had been purchased and converted into successful bingo halls, while the loss-making *Corby Bowl* had been acquired, renamed *The Star Dust Bowl* and become a nightclub. Their astute manager once booked a virtually unknown band some six weeks in advance, and by the time they appeared they had reached a phenomenal number one and packed the *Corby Bowl* to bursting. The band? Gary Glitter, no less, who honoured his agreement to the letter, notwithstanding that he was by then appearing for little more than petty cash. By contrast, in the Eighties I booked a very well known Liverpool group for a large charity Rotary function in Ipswich. In between, they had a number one revival of a Sixties football ballad; on the actual day of the function their agent cancelled as the leader had 'gone sick', and later we found he had made a healthy and doubtless lucrative appearance elsewhere. At the very last moment Joe Brown stepped in for us and the evening was a total success.

Terry, meanwhile, had been building up both new and used sales during my enforced absence in the service department. We had taken on two young car salesmen and a full-time truck and van salesman, who was canvassing the area with increasing success. I felt sufficiently secure to purchase a new home nearer the business in Wellingborough, and all in the garden of life seemed pretty good.

CHAPTER TEN

A NEW WAY OF MOVING THE METAL – 1971

The business had made a good start. Money lost in the first year had been recovered, the economy seemed to be in good shape, the new HC Viva had been accepted by the public after a slow start and Vauxhall were proceeding apace with the all-new Victor, VX 4/90 and Ventora range. Bedford Way Motors, as the newest acquisition in the Hamblin Group, was being watched keenly, but our monthly returns were encouraging and rising, mainly due to our continued interest in the used-car market. Each week Terry and I would attend the car auctions at Measham and at Frimley, in Surrey, seeking suitable, slightly off-beat rather than run-of-the-mill used cars. Jaguar XJ6s were a favourite of mine in those days; we always found them to be a quick-selling car, yet most dealers seemed reluctant to take a chance with them, fortunately for us. It was all so laid-back in those days; little did we know that we were fast approaching the end of an era. Valued customers had yet to become consumers. Major 'as seen on TV' Bircher had time for a laugh and a joke, and each car passing through his hands after 2pm in the No 1 saleroom was sold individually and in a seemingly leisurely fashion, yet with a great deal of effort and good-natured banter to encourage bids from 'Mr A' or 'Mr C' as the afternoon passed on; and no car was declared to be sold until he was quite certain the very last bid had been extracted.

One of David Hamblin's acquisitions around this time was an old-established motor dealership in Northampton which had got itself into severe financial difficulties. The greatest single problem had been the proprietor, who had inherited the business from his very successful father without, alas, also inheriting the necessary business acumen. One of my first official tasks when I joined Harry Frisby at Hamtune Motors had been to represent Harry at the father's funeral. The pedantic eldest son's main interest in life was the presidency of the local branch of the Motor Agents Association. I met him once – and once only – in his official capacity. Arriving late with a guest for an MAA function in Bedford, we both made a dive for the nearest bar to grab a quick snifter prior to dinner. We were about to receive our drinks when the barman was peremptorily informed by the president that he was not to hand them over; it seemed we had inadvertently strayed into the president's private bar! He had spent so much of his time telling others how to run their businesses that he had totally neglected his own, and progress had passed him by. He was a humourless, bumptious, officious and boring old snob, to whom common or garden motor traders like yours truly were beyond the pale. Hitherto he had never bothered with car auctions, which he regarded as the province of horse traders, but now, as a retained figurehead director of a Hamblin garage, he had no choice.

It happened that his first experience involved the enforced disposal of his company-owned Datsun 280 ZX sports car; David had no objection to directors running flash personal transport, providing they were contributing to group profitability. On the day, the usual cluster of Hamblin executives were in the hall when the car was driven in under the bright lights. This type of car would not attract a huge interest, being somewhat specialized, and those in the know could tell that latterly the Major had been conjuring bids from his mythical Messrs 'A', 'B' and 'D' to reach a respectable price of perhaps £2,500. Suddenly the red light went on, signifying that the reserve might have been reached. "Well", said the Major to no-one in particular, "he's going to be very disappointed with *this* price, I can tell you, but we're going to have a go. I'll take another fifty anywhere. Is the owner about please?" With that, the owner, who was standing within our group instead of behind the rostrum, where he should have been throughout, promptly raised his hand. Eagle-eyed Bircher missed nothing. "Two-five-fifty bid – thank you. Have you all done and finished?" CRASH! – down came the hammer and on went the blue light. The proud owner had bought his own car!

Our weekly trips to Frimley auctions, being a comparatively long journey, were regarded as a day out. Terry and I with one or two local motor traders would set off early, arriving in good time to sort through the huge entry for both auction halls prior to the start at 11am. At 2pm the upmarket, up to two or three-year-old, low-mileage (A) lot numbers would start to come on stream. It would be our intention to enjoy a leisurely lunch from midday until then, perhaps buying one or two of the slightly older cars preceding the main sale if good low-mileage examples were available. The bar was directly over the No 1 hall. The magnificent restaurant had glass windows overlooking the saleroom, and our permanently reserved table also overlooked the entrance, enabling us to slip down stairs between courses as our selected cars went through and complete a deal; not good for the digestion, but convenient! We took it in turns to pay the quite respectable bills each week, which in my case were met without question by Hamblins. Against that we averaged some three or four purchases per week, all of which were sold for substantial profits. Little did we know that these pleasant excursions were soon to come to an end because for almost three years the constant search for good used cars would no longer be necessary as our profits were to be generated from a totally new and quite unexpected direction.

Meantime I saw a great deal of Robert David Hamblin as head office was just around the corner in the Rushden one-way system and it was from there that we obtained our petrol. In those days he was approachable and working hard – doubtless subconsciously – at establishing his reputation as a 'character'. He liked to be known for never carrying either money or cigarettes. On the by now rare occasions when he visited Measham he would approach one of his executives during the morning and say: "Fancy a cup of coffee and a cake?", and on getting an affirmative reply: "Right, get them in, I'm just off to the lav."

He knew that I had contacts in the old-established heavy commercial vehicle firm of Seddon Diesel, for I had an old client in London who bought four or five a year from me. He wondered if I could arrange a meeting as the Hamblin Group were busy setting up a separate heavy commercial vehicle outlet and sought new franchises. Through John Verdellis, the director of sales, I had arranged an invitation to lunch with Mr Seddon, the elderly chairman. On the day, David and I set off for Oldham, in Lancs, in his new Rolls-Royce, complete with chauffeur, where we were met by John Verdellis. After coffee we were taken on a tour of the factory where these fine trucks were all hand-built. At lunchtime we were entertained in the directors' private dining room with a very great deal of old-world courtesy. David sat on the chairman's right and I sat on his left. Outside, clearly visible, sat the Rolls with the chauffeur eating his sandwiches. With some ceremony Mr Seddon personally carved the joint. After a first-class meal coffee was served and David turned to Mr Seddon: "You haven't got a fag by any chance?" A box was promptly provided by the waiter!

Some four times a year we would have a full-scale directors' meeting in David's first-floor office on the corner of the Hamblin building in Rectory Road. At this time David, while acknowledged as Group chairman, was still responsible for the day-to-day running of this particular garage. One hot afternoon we senior directors all sat as usual in a semi-circle round David's desk, which backed onto windows overlooking the main road. Invariably, after a general discussion of the various activities and progress in the main garage units then comprising the Hamblin Group, David would be off on his favourite 'high horse' – new car overstocking. We all had a great deal of experience, and none of us were bloody fools, but David always had this bee in his bonnet because he preferred to see money in the bank rather than in vehicle stocks. "You're all the same", he would thunder, "you let these car manufacturers dictate to you and run your businesses to their own advantage!", none of this harangue being either true or indeed fair. The assembled directors, two of whom were David's brothers, chose to say nothing and wait for him to wind down. It soon became apparent that this afternoon's wait was to be longer than usual. David had just got himself nicely warmed up when, visible to us all, five brand new Chrysler cars appeared framed in the window behind him on the top of a huge vehicle transporter. There were, of course, more on the lower decks. Still David held forth in total ignorance while brother John Hamblin looked at me and winked. That did it; I collapsed into uncontrollable giggles while the other directors began to laugh out loud. David looked at us as if we had all gone quite mad, and finally spun round in his chair to see what all the mirth was about. "I think those cars are all yours, chap", said John with masterly understatement.

My wife was an avid reader of the *Daily Mirror*, and perusing its pages one morning over breakfast I chanced upon an advertisement by a motor dealer somewhere in the North of England: '£25 AND YOUR OLD CAR IN ANY CONDITION AND SEVEN POUNDS WEEKLY BUYS THIS NEW VAUXHALL VIVA!!!'

Now even in those days you couldn't hire a Viva for seven quid a week, let alone own one, so this was eye-catching material. Polishing off the bacon and eggs, I set off for Rushden and dropped in on Terry for his opinion. He was in my office within half an hour with the answer. In simple terms the deal was based on the relatively cheap Vauxhall Viva two-door L and a four-year hire purchase agreement at the maximum rate of interest. This provided the enterprising dealer with two profits on the transaction, that on the car, together with a commission from the finance company on the four-year transaction. As it happened these two sums were virtually the same. All government restrictions on hire purchase terms having recently been abandoned by Chancellor Barber, anxious to provide a boost to the economy, it was quite in order to give away one profit by over-allowance on an all but worthless trade-in, thereby providing the client with a down payment on his new car.

Clearly this needed careful consideration; I didn't see that we could ignore this national advertising and pretend that it didn't exist. The *Mirror* was a mass-circulation newspaper, and in any case the advert was to appear in other newspapers in due course. It seemed to me that providing the deal was legal and the clients proved credit-worthy and acceptable to our hire purchase contacts, we should get in on the act, the main difference being that we hoped to sell this proposition locally rather than nationally, which meant that we could at the same time be choosey and flexible. The last thing I wanted was to attract bad business, which in the long term would cause problems with our contacts in the finance world. I firmly believed that this proposition would have an appeal to local hard-working families on sound, rather than good incomes, but with children sufficiently grown up to enable both husband and wife to provide. From personal experience I knew that most families of this kind, for which I am sure advertisers have a group code, were owning and driving cars at the time that were little better than 'bangers', with regular annual MoT problems.

Of one aspect I was quite certain – if we asked for £25, then £25 was all we would get. But I had to make the deal attractive because I wanted to reach the widest possible audience. So, I wondered, how could we ask for more? After considerable thought I decided to try a completely different approach. Because of the relaxing of the credit regulations some firms had been offering a 'no deposit' scheme for new and used-car purchase, with low repayments based on a second mortgage. To benefit, of course, the client had to be a house owner. But in the early Seventies house owners in this social bracket were few and far between, and in any case, most house owners then could well afford to buy a new car without having to resort to a second mortgage. So, basing my advertising on a corruption of the company name, I formulated the Bedway Plan, and below a suitable line block of a Vauxhall Viva saloon, we offered: 'BUY THIS NEW VAUXHALL VIVA TODAY. NO DEPOSIT. £5.00 PER WEEK.'

While it contained an element of truth in that the deal was certainly there – providing you owned a house – we did not mention this small fact of life. Terry and I formulated the plan between us, arranged the first tentative pilot advert in the *Bedfordshire Times* and briefed the sales staff. The car advertised was the cheapest available base-model Viva, which alternatively we could provide on a £25-and-your-old-car basis for £7 per week to tenants who might have seen the national advert. In this manner we were, if nothing else, competitive. It was not our intention to market the base Viva. The immediate result of our first advertisement was astonishing. The paper appeared on Friday morning, the phone continued to ring all day and we all went home late that evening. On Saturday afternoon and Sunday morning we were overwhelmed. That following Monday, from a total annual new-car sales target (all models) of some 150 units, I placed a firm order for 50 extra Vauxhall Viva cars for that one month. That was just for starters.

In practice the Bedway Plan worked as follows: In the showroom sat, in pride of place, the bog-standard Viva – very basic, very cheap and predominantly aimed at the fleet market – bearing the legend '£5.00 per week!'. All round the premises were scattered more desirable De Luxe and SL models in a variety of colours. After a suitable interval the clients, almost always man and wife, together with kids and dogs as applicable, would be approached. The age, model and general condition of the vehicle they had arrived in would already have been carefully noted. We knew they had come hot-foot as a direct result of the advert. "Of course, sir, nice of you to come, there indeed is the car. Other models available within the same scheme? Certainly, sir; of course you are a house owner?" The disappointment registered by the family at this point was almost tangible. There was no need to await the answer. "Not to worry, sir, we can offer an almost identical scheme which, by the way, is considerably less expensive in the long run (it was). The repayments are almost the same, all we would need is a small deposit and your present car." Now the deposit in the old days of tight government controls had always been the problem in preventing just this kind of family from buying a good car. This family would have been conditioned to expect to pay a deposit of around £330, representing about a third of the purchase price. That kind of money was every bit as hard to find then in a lump sum as a third of the price of today's new car. Their existing car in real terms was probably worth £50 to £100, or even less

Now two things had changed; one, the deposit required was negotiable around 15 to 20 per cent of the total price, and two, we were able to provide most of this from our extra commission on a four-year hire purchase agreement. The question we were now waiting for would be: "How much deposit?" The salesman's job then would be to ascertain how much the family could afford. With experience we were usually able to arrive pretty accurately at an acceptable figure between the minimum of £25 and a maximum £100. It was really a question of negotiation as with any deal. Once this was settled it was simply a question of choosing the car. The repayments seldom being a problem, the tendency was to buy an upmarket model for the weekly payments only rose by units of a pound or so through the two-door/four-door De Luxe, SL range and on to the estate cars. I don't think we ever did sell a basic Viva. Some clients even moved up into the Victor range! One aspect common to almost all transactions was that the lady of the household provided the weekly/monthly repayments from her income.

From that first day we took off and never looked back for nearly three years. Not only were we selling the cars, but having a relatively small annual sales contract relative to our area we were selling far in excess of this and winning top prizes in every dealer incentive scheme that Vauxhall were able to devise. I went to New York for a whole week and first-class on the QE2 Mediterranean cruise at the entire expense of Vauxhall Motors, and more to the point I was able to corner Bob Hamblin at a director's dinner and remind him of his promise of that 'good drink' made prior to our opening. Bob bought me a pint at the bar! Coming from him that was not a problem; he had genuinely forgotten the conversation. The business was such that we were able to play off one finance house against others with impunity. At least 95 per cent of the transactions were with respectable families who, having bought a new car, honoured their HP agreements to the letter. Indeed I can only recall one repossession! Inevitably we got our share of slightly dodgy clients, who nevertheless were usually accepted by a finance company frightened of losing our considerable patronage.

By far the worst was a large middle-aged lady with several scruffy kids and a pair of large dogs. Not altogether surprisingly, she wished to make use of the Bedway Plan to purchase a new Viva SL estate car. On offering the transaction to our usual friendly hire purchase broker the business was firmly declined on the basis that the lady had no less than 14 prior County Court judgments recorded for debt. The following day Terry telephoned a rival finance house, which had been chasing our trade for some time. He offered them three perfectly sound transactions, which we all knew would be entirely acceptable, then threw in Mrs CCJ at the end for good measure. As he had correctly surmised, the company were so keen to get in on our act they accepted all four off the cuff without carrying out the usual checks. Mrs CCJ was quite taken aback when we told her she had been accepted, and in due course off she drove, kids, dogs and all, in the bright new Viva estate car. Within the week I had an official letter from the Department of Social Security asking for full details as to how Mrs .... had managed to purchase from us a new car!

Several clients arrived from rival dealers' territories, one couple indeed arriving on the bus from our own garage in Corby, wishing to buy a new Vauxhall, but being unable to approach alternative dealers with an old car because they did not possess one. Terry got over that small problem by selling them one of our existing bangers for a nominal pound note, then accepting it, with some cash, as deposit on a new car!

Was this a fair and reasonable way of conducting business – if you like, overcharging for hire purchase loans in order to provide a down-payment? The Motor Agents Association went on record as denouncing the scheme. Their view was that dealers promoting this scheme – for we were certainly not alone – were encouraging people to buy cars on low deposits which would be worthless after a year or two and the client would be left owing more on the vehicle than it was worth. My view was that even if true this was balanced out by the fact that more and more families were enjoying ownership of new cars and making repayments that they were well able to afford. This in turn got them out of old bangers, which for the most part were unreliable, only just roadworthy and costing large sums of money to keep on the road. Worthless, anyway, at the end of the day. In truth, although I agree this was a fortuitous accident, the Heath/Barber boom brought forth such inflation that after two to three years, assuming reasonable care, the cars purchased were in fact worth a great deal of money and the owners were able to part-exchange for newer cars without any difficulty at all.

Meanwhile, I was having a little fun of my own. As we moved into profit it was understood that I had a reasonable choice of personal transport, new or used. The company had demonstration cars – Victor models for service and sales management, Vivas for the sales staff – so I opted for used, keeping my eyes open on trips to Measham for something appropriate and reasonably priced. At the time I had a yen to drive behind a three-pointed star, and in due course I bought a Mercedes from Measham, later to discover from people who knew that while I loved the car, it was the wrong model, the wrong colour, the wrong everything. In due course the novelty wore off and the car was duly advertised for sale, with no takers; Geoffrey had bought a lemon! Now it was not unknown in those far-off days for motor dealers wishing to unload something to endeavour to part-exchange it for a new vehicle at a main dealership. In this way, if you were lucky enough to catch a half-sharp salesman – and there were plenty around – the price you might obtain relative to its true cash-out value could be rather better than a *bona fide* trade discount on the new car in question. Thus one damp Saturday afternoon, when I knew that the sales manager would be away, I dispatched my wife to Bedfordshire in the Mercedes, which was registered in my name, to inquire about the possibility of a new Vauxhall Ventora in red with a black vinyl roof, with the Merc in part-chop. The young sales person checked his *Glass's Guide,* which I suspect he misread, and made a substantial offer, stating that we might have to wait awhile as the factory were on holiday, but that he would try to locate the spec required at another dealer. My wife twisted his arm for a free radio without difficulty, signed a contract, paid a large deposit by cheque and came back to Rushden. The part-exchange allowance shortfall, relative to what I had paid for the Mercedes, would not totally cover my discount on the red Ventora with black roof that stood in my showroom. But I had had my money's worth out of the car, so a nominal loss was quite acceptable.

On the Monday, Terry telephoned the company in Bedfordshire: we required two new Vauxhall Vivas for clients from weekend sales and with the factory shut for holidays these would not be easy to locate. Fortunately this company had both, but in view of the temporary shortage they would naturally require other new cars in exchange. "What", they asked, "had we to offer?" Terry was crafty. "We have a Victor estate car." "No, sorry, don't want that." "We have some HA and CF vans." "No, certainly don't want those." "We have a Ventora!" "What colour?" "Just hang on a moment while I check." Terry read the leading article in the *Mail,* then picked up the phone. "It's red with a black roof." "Coo, can we have it?" "Well, you can for the two Vivas," said Terry, and as an afterthought: "providing you bring them over, we're short-staffed today!"

On Monday afternoon the Ventora left for Bedfordshire, on Friday afternoon Jennifer went off in the Mercedes with a cheque and brought it back, complete with radio. We then set off for a week's holiday in Scotland. On my return there were messages requesting that I should telephone a certain sales manager in Bedford. I did, only to be called just about every derogatory name that he could bring to mind. When at last he calmed down I pointed out, not unreasonably, that his company through its employees had conducted what they obviously considered at the time to be a proper transaction. The fact that the car in question should subsequently prove to have belonged to a Hamblin garage or Joe Soap really had nothing to do with the matter. It was, after all, the same car. "I know that", he said. "What pissed me off is that we collected the bloody Vauxhall from you on Monday, and you come and drag it back on Friday and screw us for two new cars and a radio!"

Financially these were the best years of my life. I was able to achieve a lifetime's ambition and buy a 30ft motor cruiser on which I spent many happy hours while the boom lasted. My private life, unfortunately, had not latterly been so happy due to a disastrous second marriage, and I was to learn the bitter lesson that money is certainly not everything in life. As a company, 'mine' became one of the most successful in the Group, and success brings enemies. When the boom came to its abrupt end in 1976 and hire purchase restrictions were yet again restored, our profits took a nosedive. But by quickly changing course and reverting back to the used-car trade they were nonetheless respectable compared with certain others in the Group, whose profits had not risen so spectacularly during these boom years and in consequence had not fallen so much. Certain senior directors in the Group got together and convinced David Hamblin, who should have known better, that profits at Bedford Way had dropped off because Geoff Owen was spending too much time on his boat, which was certainly not true, and that both Geoff Owen and Terry were spending time together, using gallons of company petrol in flash expensive motor cars, with their wives on the Norfolk Broads.

The truth of the matter was that I had been away on my boat on a *bona fide* two weeks' holiday. A local hotelier had admired the 'flash' American car that I had been running with David Hamblin's full knowledge for at least a year. As a result a new one was placed on order with me for his wife. He had also expressed interest in a secondhand Rolls-Royce, and Terry had managed to locate and borrow one from a friend in the trade, which he brought up to the hotel during the fortnight that I was away and sold (we did not even meet). In appreciation, I invited Terry and his wife for the final weekend of our holiday. The new 'flash' car was delivered by myself the following weekend, which I again spent on my boat, returning in one of the three part-exchange cars we had taken in against the two supplied, all of which provided a substantial profit! David Hamblin refused to listen because he didn't want to listen and thereby alienate one of his most senior executives, who had been with him for many years longer than I. Therefore I had to suffer the ignominy of being treated like some naughty schoolboy.

At this point it is worth noting that at the end of the company's first financial year in April 1971 the excess of *liabilities* over assets stood at £7,219. During my tenure as managing director I had constructed new office accommodation behind the old circle, I had built and fully fitted out a paint booth to the required very high and therefore expensive standards, I had built a used-car preparation area, I had resurfaced the whole of the huge rear car park and obtained outline planning consent for further buildings as might be required. Also, I had had to invest considerably in new tools and equipment as needed. At year ending April 1975, the published total of assets over liabilities stood at £72,599. Not bad, one would have thought, for four years' trading. This was my first experience of boardroom politics, but worse was to follow.

David had bought yet another garage premises in Bedford, again completely empty, in spite of the fact that he had also by now acquired two or three motor businesses in the North of England which were proving to be both unprofitable and an embarrassment. At one stage it had even been suggested that I might care to move house and home again to sort these out, but this suggestion was firmly declined. This new business in Bedford was hawked around his board of directors, but there were no takers. Eventually, because I genuinely liked David behind his back, as well as to his face – unlike some of his directors – I agreed to take it on as yet another challenge. Once again I had a vacant building, this time with no franchise and once again no staff, with strict instructions that I was to find my own and not to poach or rob from within the Group.

I moved in on April 1, 1977 with nothing. After a month or so I received a telephone call telling me that Bedford Way Motors had caught fire. I drove down to Rushden to find David Hamblin filming the conflagration; most of the vehicles were undamaged due to someone's quick thinking and fortunately none were destroyed. The old prewar wooden stage was burning fiercely, as were the vast quantities of wood above in the old curtain and scenery mechanism, but the fire service managed to save the shell – just. A sad end to an era indeed.

However, by year's end I had reconstituted the Bedford building, obtained, set up and opened a fully staffed Peugeot dealership and traded successfully in new and used cars, with the result that every month profits climbed ever nearer to the month's operating costs and break-even. My marriage broke up in the November, but I threw myself into my work to provide a sense of proportion and to keep me sane. I had found collectively a first-class body and paint shop operative, a top-quality parts manager and a workshop foreman/manager, all good friends who were known throughout as the three musketeers. I also found Bruce Willey, or rather Bruce found me. He called in one day looking for a job as he had had a run of misfortune. Bruce proved to be the best thing that happened to me during the short time that I was in charge. He knew absolutely everyone worth knowing in Bedford and, as will be seen, this was to prove invaluable when it came to our getting established. We had taken on Peugeot for the simple reason that theirs was the only franchise available to us. Furthermore, having recently lost their representation in Bedford they badly wanted another. In the event it proved to be a good franchise with a powerful following of very satisfied owners who were soon knocking on our door for service, spares and replacement cars.

We all worked bloody hard during those first few months. Again I had to acquire tools and workshop equipment from my friends in the oil company, and the whole place had to be decorated inside and out, for Peugeot insisted on our following their corporate image to the letter, something that David did not, or did not wish to understand. I cut corners by buying the greater part of our spares requirements from the late dealer in Bedford, together with all of his bins, for next to nothing. Firemen painted the workshop and stores for cash on their off-days. Peugeot painted the outside and provided the corporate signing. I personally got down on my knees and repolished the whole showroom floor, which would display up to 10 cars. I also helped to remove the collected grime from the huge showroom windows and cleaned and refurbished most of the toilets on the premises. All this between buying and selling cars and setting up a brand new dealership from jump street. As I said, we all worked bloody hard.

I had been to the official opening of the Hamblin Nissan dealership in Kings Lynn. It was a food and hard liquor freebee, with a local pop group and a host of gate-crashers. It cost a packet and I doubt whether it was particularly worthwhile relative to either sales or goodwill. I decided on something more restrained and cost-effective. My interest was really good publicity, together with a guest list calculated to provide custom and recommendation. I decided that our opening should support a worthy cause and I opted for the RNLI, where I had friends and contacts. The event was planned in three parts, with as many people as possible to be attracted to the premises during the working day, with lots of free tea, coffee and biscuits. This does not cost a great deal. It was to be followed in the evening by a strictly invitational French wine and cheese function in the showrooms, for which I had a generous allowance of cheese and good French wine from Peugeot. New Peugeot cars, of course, were on display. To round off the day's events, those who attended were then to be invited to a buffet and disco function in the newly decorated workshop area, for which a nominal payment per head had to be made, all proceeds to be donated to the lifeboat. As we had sliding doors centrally at the rear of the showroom allowing access direct to the workshop, movement control was quite simple; nobody could gate-crash through the showroom side entrance and if it rained nobody would get wet.

That was the broad plan. Bruce was put in sole charge of invitations and saw to it that everybody worth inviting in Bedford received an invitation; virtually all accepted graciously as the RNLI is such a popular charity. I had obtained the loan of an Atlantic 21 inshore lifeboat and the services of most of the crews of Southwold and Wells next the Sea lifeboats, all of them good friends. A display was constructed in the workshop, hard by the doors, where the money was to be collected by crew members. A hoist was turned into a stage for the disco, a long table was provided for the buffet, and chairs and tables for every guest were scattered around the dance area. There was free wine for the ladies and beer for the men. During the morning and afternoon we had arranged for a lion cub from Longleat to be on the premises, which we promptly christened Purr Joe! This brought the kids and their parents in droves, particularly as we had a photographer on hand. By late afternoon everything was ready, the showroom had been blacked out, the cars gleamed under the lights and the staff were ready. The workshop, lit by a local specialist (Bruce again), looked a picture with a magnificent display of food from an upmarket caterer, the glittering disco equipment and the lifeboat display in orange and grey with the crew in their distinctive jerseys. Meanwhile, Purr Joe, who had been cuddled and stroked by half the kids in Bedfordshire and been the subject of endless photographs, was having a well-deserved nap under the showroom stairs.

David and Betty Hamblin arrived early for a critical look round, Betty captivating the crew members with her obvious charm and being assisted aboard to have her picture taken at the controls. After a while they were both escorted to my office upstairs where I had arranged a small private VIP bar. By this time the little lion was wide awake and ready for mischief; he had crept up the stairs and was quietly padding along behind my party down the corridor. Without warning, Purr Joe, who had behaved impeccably with the kids all day, promptly wrapped his front paws round the Group chairman's foot and playfully bit his leg! For me that was the high spot of the whole evening, but poor David was visibly shaken, although totally unharmed.

The guests began to arrive and very soon the excellent French wine was flowing freely as the showroom reverberated to laughter and small talk while the guests mingled and found friends and acquaintances around the cars on display in the showroom area. Around 8.30pm one of the sliding doors to the workshop was opened and many were the audible sounds of appreciation at the scene behind. The evening was a resounding success. I noted that in lieu of the nominal entrance fee most of my guests were handing over crisp fivers to Coxswain David Cox, of the Wells lifeboat, proudly wearing his Silver Medal. The mood and the quality of the disco were such that the party simply went on and on until the small hours. I have no idea what time it all ended and the last guest departed. *Pro rata* the numbers attending it had not cost a great deal, and in any case the following Friday's *Bedfordshire Times* provided many more times the cost in free publicity; Hamblins of Bedford was well and truly launched.

By end of November the month's figures were significantly close to break-even, but of course we had December to come, which is notoriously quiet for vehicle sales. Nonetheless I was confident that come the New Year we would move into profit and recover some of the deficit caused by the usual setting-up costs. During that December I had received a surprise visit from Alan Kerr, a fellow board member, who spent most of the morning prowling about on his own as I was engaged with a client. Now Alan was a Hamblin Group director whom I had regarded as a friend from my first years with the Group in Corby. I had visited his home on several occasions, he had been entertained on my boat and had often had the use of my home to entertain his numerous married lady friends during the dying years of his first marriage to Morag. When Alan was within an inch of being ignominiously slung out by Hamblins for gross incompetence, his wretched skin was only just saved by the personal intervention of Bob Hamblin and Geoff Owen. For a year or so he had been obliged to languish in the wings until David eventually gave him a second chance. Like all of the directors he had been given the offer of the business from the start, but had turned it down out of hand. Now that the initial donkeywork had been completed, Mr Kerr had obviously decided that the business had distinct possibilities for, unknown to me at the time, he had then presented himself to Mr David Hamblin and made an offer. He undertook to take the North Country garages off David's hands provided he could gain control of Hamblins of Bedford.

That he was prepared to even consider the North Country problems speaks volumes for what I had managed to achieve in such a short space of time. At the start of the year he could have just walked in and taken over without any strings whatsoever! The only obstacle now, of course, was Geoff Owen, so a little plot had been hatched whereby I was to be told that I could, of course, retain my present position at Bedford, but that henceforth I should be responsible to Alan Kerr. He chose to telephone me on New Year's Eve, my immediate thought being that he had intended to invite me to his home for a party as he was well aware that since my wife Jenny had departed I was on my own. On coldly being told the real reason for the call, my reaction was as instantaneous as it was predictable. I told Alan to get stuffed, arranged to visit David Hamblin in Rushden on the first working day of the New Year and told him flatly what he could do with this situation. I refused to resign, so was promptly fired on the spot. By the time I got back to Bedford to collect my things, my successor, appointed by Mr Kerr, had already arrived from Market Harborough and was in my chair!

I took a month or so off during which I was fortunate enough to meet Christine, my present wife. David implied that all was forgiven and sent me off with the company auditors to investigate several businesses which, it was stated, were to be purchased for my benefit. None of the propositions, however, were to bear fruit. John Hamblin then offered me a temporary situation which served to provide some income and to give me time to take stock. Peter Hamblin then gave me another situation at a back-street garage in Oakham where, fed up to the back teeth, I prepared for my future while I quietly took a little revenge and prepared my case for an Industrial Tribunal. I should have read the small print!

CHAPTER ELEVEN

A NEW BEGINNING – 1979

With Christine I now had a home and I still had the boat. One lovely late summer's day we were sunning ourselves somewhere on the Norfolk Broads after a good lunch when, without warning, she dropped the bombshell. "If you are going to have problems then you might as well have problems of your own making." At first I didn't see what she was driving at so I said nothing. "Sell the boat and start your own business, simple as that." I was horrified; that boat was the fulfilment of a lifetime's ambition and the thought of parting with it was almost unbearable. Well almost, but not quite, and by the end of the afternoon she had convinced me and provided some much-needed fire and a new ambition in life.

I decided to seek suitable premises in the Bedford rather than the Northampton side of Rushden, which was thick with motor dealers. Accordingly we placed an order for the *Bedfordshire Times*. The very first weekly copy to drop through our letterbox carried a once-only advertisement with a blurred photograph of a garage with pumps in the village of Sandy, which looked promising. It was clearly old and dilapidated, but it seemed to be surrounded by useful open space for the display of used cars, so we decided to view. Sandy is completely bypassed by the A1. I had not been into the town for many years, but had driven past several times over the only set of traffic lights on the A1 north of London, these latterly replaced by a roundabout. It was therefore with considerable interest that on a cold and wet night we crossed these lights into the town proper. We had been told by the agent to make for the Market Square, and on drawing to a halt it took us a moment or two to realize that we had stopped right outside the premises. The photograph was deceptive; certainly there was lots of space around, but not unfortunately for the display of used cars. The building, in fact, sat on an island, which it shared with an optician in the centre of the Market Square, although the latter in reality could more accurately be described as a triangle, comprising a public car park surrounded by several shops, three banks and a couple of pubs.

It was a typically dark and cold November night and it was pouring with rain. The premises were filthy dirty and rundown, with three tatty fuel pumps feeding an overhead supply above the pavement area. I almost did a U-turn to head for home, but we were hungry, and on the opposite side we spotted a handy fish-and-chip shop. The building took on a totally different aspect from across the main road. After all it was dead centre of the town's main car park and surrounded by a very great deal of commercial activity. The building had been described as comprising some 2,000sq ft and overall it was not unattractive. Perhaps, I wondered, it could be made into a showroom with picture windows, and furthermore it seemed possible for three or four cars to be displayed at one side without causing any obstruction.

We finished our meal and walked back across the road. There was not much light, but from what I could see through the filthy windows it certainly seemed that the interior walls were non-supporting. The front aspect of the building was divided by quite an attractive exterior chimney, which would certainly lend itself to picture windows being installed either side. I drove home in a better frame of mind and decided to take a day off and use Mr Hamblin's car and petrol again to see what could be done. In daylight the place looked a good deal better. The retiring owner, who had toiled there man and boy with his father before him, showed me around. Basically what was on offer was a square area at the front, which was original, with a slightly larger rectangle behind, which had been built on at some time. The rectangle had wood sliding doors at one side to the Market Square and contained a small toilet area and a pit. The square area, which also had a pit, was half taken up by two tiny offices, one of which again provided access from the Market Square and the petrol pumps. All walls that mattered, I noted with relief, were certainly not supporting. As a small bonus, next to the opticians there was an additional area of perhaps 24ft by 12ft hitherto used as a parts store, which would suffice as an office.

While wandering around I had been observing the frail and elderly Mr Smith with a permanent fag on, serving his petrol from the overhead supply across the pavement along which the mums were innocently pushing prams and shepherding kids! Within half an hour I had made up my mind that I could convert the rear half of the rectangle to workshop space by building a dividing wall with a hinged panel. This would provide vehicle access from the double doors into the showroom or the new service area. All that remained would be to put windows each side of the chimney, with glass sliding doors to the side in place of the offices, after demolishing the interior walls. Having then removed a considerable amount of rubbish to leave a clear floor we would be in business. I made a rough costing (later to prove almost spot-on) and decided there and then that, given a bit of luck, we could put it all together and get ourselves a business.

It was to take nearly five months to overcome the purchase and contract problems before we could even complete the transaction, let alone start the business. The first requirement was planning. Biggleswade Borough Council, in the shape of their Mr Peter Ashley, were charming and helpful on the telephone. I wanted, I said, to convert the Sandy Market Square garage into a car showroom. There was a pause. "You must understand, Mr Owen, that this is a listed town-centre site; we do not quite see it with banners, posters and this week's special offer." "Fair enough, Mr Ashley, that is not how I see it either; in any event it would be difficult to make it look worse than it is at the present time." "OK", was the reply, "point taken; send me some scale drawings and I'll see what I can do." I did my drawings with a great deal of care on graph paper, and within a week I had a provisional acceptance – subject, of course, to a planning meeting and building regulations. With my auditor we approached the Midland Bank, which turned out to be a good move as Midland were the last of the three available banks to move to Sandy and needed the business. It took time and persuasion, but in the end we got the cash I felt we needed, helped by a substantial loan from the old man and a contribution from Christine, who had a few quid under the carpet.

Having got the money and the planning permission, the next and by far the biggest problems were the negotiations to buy, with both sets of solicitors seemingly hell-bent on delaying everything, even when Mr Smith and I were in agreement, which wasn't often. I made a sensible offer based on a professional valuation, which was turned down flat. I was terrified that some other smart-arsed motor dealer would see the possibilities and I then offered as much as I could reasonably afford. Then Mr Smith advised me that he had someone willing to pay the full asking price, who also had planning permission for his requirements. At this point I had no choice but to withdraw, for there was no more cash available. Only Christine was convinced that we would get it in the end and never lost faith. Meanwhile I felt it prudent to seek alternative premises. Some weeks later Mr Smith phoned and asked if I had reconsidered as his buyer was having a small difficulty with his proposal which, while no problem, was taking time to resolve. I told him that I would think about it as by now I was evaluating other premises. I tried to telephone him the following day as I had a small query, but he was not available. I therefore telephoned his solicitor, who obviously had been misinformed as to who was on the line. Before I could say as much as "Good morning", he said: "Now look here, Mr Smith, I think we have taken Mr Owen further than we should; nobody else has expressed any further interest so you really ought to take his money while it is still on the table." I quietly replaced the receiver. I then telephoned my own solicitor. By the afternoon we had won an interest-free delay on part of the final payment and bought ourselves a premises.

That very same morning I had been asked by Peter Hamblin to call in at Uppingham on the way home. I presented myself to Peter in high spirits, having no idea why my presence was required. I bloody soon found out. He had the grace to look embarrassed: "I don't know if David has anything for you, but we are closing down Oakham and I have to terminate your employment there." For some time just I looked at Peter – with whom I had had no quarrel at all – wondering what to say, then I opted to be earthy and to the point: "Peter, I couldn't care less; I have just bought my own business. I shall accept a month's notice, which is the very least of my entitlement, and I propose to retain my car for the month." He looked positively relieved as I strode out, stopping only to fill the petrol tank, and drove off home. I had bought my business in Hamblin's time, with Hamblin's telephone and in Hamblin's car, using Hamblin's petrol throughout. I have no regrets whatsoever on this score. My father would have been appalled had he ever found out, but to this day I have a totally clear conscience and consider it small compensation for the manner in which I had been treated at Bedford.

There was worse to come. I was advised by ACAS that my claim at Bedford was now out of time – it seemed that I had been retained specifically for this reason. When the case eventually came up at the Bedford tribunal David Hamblin appeared with his two brothers plus a team of three from accountants Thornton Baker Co, of Leicester. I was not represented and felt a touch lonely. I was advised that what ACAS had told me was perfectly true, but the chairman was sympathetic and advised me to claim for improper dismissal from Oakham. This advice I accepted and won a unanimous decision, but alas a paltry award. Then matters took a childish turn. The award was not forthcoming, so I was later obliged to put my claim in the hands of the bailiff in order to get paid!

On Monday, April 2, 1979 G C Owen Ltd, Market Square, Sandy, Bedfordshire, opened its doors. We had three used cars for sale, plus one for our own use, and we had Dennis Wilson, our amiable West Indian mechanic, whom I had pinched from Bedford. We also had on the temporary staff Christine's elderly but tough stepfather, who was immediately christened by Dennis 'Lump Hammer Harry'. Mr Smith had asked to stay on so that he might sell the remainder of his petrol, which was fine by me as we were to clear the pumps and fill the tanks with concrete. I had two immediate priorities: one, to knock down the office walls, and two, to clear the astonishing pile of accumulated rubbish so as to leave a clear area throughout as a showroom. While I organized the hire of a 3-tonner for the rubbish, Dennis and Harry attacked the brick walls with lump hammer and pick-axe, using the rubble to fill the unwanted pits. Mr Smith stood by his till between customers, permanent Woodbine curling smoke from his lower lip as he morosely watched his life's work being demolished before his very eyes; I really did feel for him. At one stage he became quite agitated as I dumped boxes of long obsolete spares on the truck. "You're not going to throw those away?" I shrugged my shoulders: "You can have them if you want them." There was no reply. Suddenly, from somewhere deep in the rubble, a telephone rang. I found it with some difficulty and the call was for Mr Smith. After a little while he put the dusty receiver back with a shaking hand. There was clearly something amiss for his face was ashen and even his fag had gone out. By now the office area looked like a battle scene from a war movie. "Mr Owen, that was my solicitor, your cheque has not gone through!" It was no more than a technical error, quickly settled with a phone call and a signature on yet another legal document, but it nearly finished the old boy off.

By the end of the week the place was clear, the junk had gone and Mr Smith, having sold the last of his petrol, had departed. Meanwhile we had sold our first car to a local lady schoolteacher. My office at the back boasted a desk and a telephone, Dennis had moved his tools into the workshop area and was busy servicing those sales cars we had managed to obtain. Now it was the turn of the professional builders to move in, cutting holes and reinforcing the outside walls ready for doors and windows. My planning permission expressly stated that on no account were goods to be displayed outside, but with the builders working inside all day we really had no choice. Each morning I would arrive early to clear the stock for the builders and line it up at the side of the garage, all priced and ready for sale. One morning, to my dismay, I saw Peter Ashley prowling round the cars with an older man. Blimey, I thought, now I'm for it. Approaching Peter with a guilty smile I was greeted with a cheery "Hi, Geoff, I have just brought father-in-law to look at a few cars, I know that you'll look after him." I did, I sold him one straight off the forecourt! Having sold father-in-law a car, I thought that I should at least broach the subject of the outside display. "Don't give it a thought", said Peter, "unless anyone complains no-one from the council will ever bother you." No-one ever did.

It was a revelation building up a service and car sales business in that quaint old town where everyone knew just about everyone. Being in the centre of the Market Square we were the centre of the action, as it were, and anyone with a problem came to us. Dennis mended wheels on kids' toys, cars and bikes, and ladies' pushchairs, and our air line blew up endless blow-up toys. He was even known in the trade locally as The Toy Town Mechanic. Inevitably ladies were forever locking themselves out of their cars in the car park, so Dennis became quite an accomplished burglar. One car, though, did defeat him, with the lady's child locked in and fast asleep. We were all becoming a bit concerned when she had an idea: "I have a spare door and ignition key at home." "OK, Den, run the lady home and get the spare keys." Then her face fell. "My front door key is in the car!" In the end Dennis had to go with her and break into the house through a convenient window. Then one day a local old boy approached me: "Can you sell me a drop of oil for my lawn mower?" "I'll do better than that", I said, "you can have that for nothing", handing him some of Smithy's left-over old stock." "Well blast", he said, "if you don't treat me better than that little gal you got working for you." He meant Christine!

I was impatient for the first picture window to be fitted in the big hole next to the chimney so that I could display a car or two at night after we had gone home to Rushden. On the big day a huge Gibbs and Dandy van from Bedford arrived in the Square with a bloody great and expensive piece of glass tied to the outside. What followed was reminiscent of a scene from *Monty Python* as bods walked this huge window from the Square into the showroom on webbing straps while I stood at the front, cine camera at the ready. The glass was laid gently on the wood frame, the straps removed and on a signal from the foreman pushed upwards with a distinct click into a perfect fit. Well not quite; some idiot at Bedford had apparently confused feet and inches with metres and centimetres. There was a large gap down one side! In came the bods, on went the webbing straps and out went the glass window. It was a case of back to the drawing board. But by the end of September everything was in place including the workshop partition, all decorations completed, our name in lights on two sides and enough fluorescent to light up the whole Market Square at night. Indeed, we had been told by a grateful police sergeant that we had considerably reduced petty crime and vandalism on the Market Square!

In October 1979 the country was still in recession, nonetheless we had somehow managed to sell enough cars to pay our expenses and draw a meagre salary, even while the showroom was a mess of building materials. Christine still had her job in a local Rushden shoe factory, but while it paid well it was arduous, dirty work. My target was to generate enough income so that she could join me full-time, for it was obvious that she was becoming an appreciable asset to our business of selling cars. She had no experience and therefore no preconceived ideas as to how to deal with customers. Some of her methods were a revelation! One Sunday morning a customer walked across the builders' debris to view a cheapish Toyota that we had taken in part-exchange. He was cocky and aggressive, so I was quite happy to leave him to Christine to sort out. In due course I could hear her somewhat distinctive, slightly high-pitched voice rabbiting away as they went round the car. After a while the client suddenly got down on his haunches, took hold of one of the front wheels with both hands and shook it backwards and forwards with such resolve that he seemed to be trying to wrench it off. Christine looked on incredulously, having no previous experience of amateur mechanics. When he finished she simply said: "I hope you don't treat your wife like that!" I went back grinning into my office, not in the least surprised that she didn't make a sale. But the following day he was back, to drop a stack of readies on my desk: "For the Toyota, mate; I think that I upset your missus yesterday." I made no comment.

Her stock greeting to anybody who as much as put their head round the door never varied. Half a dozen times a day when she was on the premises minding the shop while I caught up with the paperwork I would hear that distinctive, squeaky voice: "You can open the doors and have a look if you like, they're all low-mileage." I told her once to make a tape recording so that all she had to do was press a button, but I have to admit it was a novel approach as an ice breaker; it never failed to work. Another rough-cut London gentleman she took for a test drive in a Ford Capri said halfway down the high street: "I know what you car sales people are like, so it's no good you trying to give me a load of bull." With perfect truth Christine told him that she had only been in the business for five minutes, so she was hardly in a position to give him any bull at all. "Put like that", said the customer, "I'll buy the bloody car." And he did!

With the showroom space at our disposal I had reckoned on sales of around 15 low-mileage used vehicles a month. The illicit outside display was certainly a great help, but it could never be totally relied upon as the planners could shut this off at any time. My biggest problem throughout had been to buy stock suitable for an as yet undefined market. However, we had no sooner got the showrooms organized than yet again, for the third time, Lady Luck was to play a considerable part in my destiny. Working six and a half days a week and presently living 23 miles from Sandy was causing us a few problems. We had decided to take the plunge and become self-sufficient, so Chris gave up her job to work with me full-time and we made the garage habitable for weekends so as to give us a break from travelling. We had a shower unit fitted by extending and tiling the loo, and we also fitted a small wardrobe and a large double studio couch in the office. We never looked back, and with breakfast provided by the *Lord Roberts* pub across the road, plenty of ale and a colour TV we were very cozy indeed, even in the winter months.

One of the drawbacks to travelling was that because we needed our best cars on display for sale, we tended to drive the older part-exchange cars for personal use, some of which were none too reliable. One day, while out on some errand in one of our better used cars, I came to an untimely halt on the dual-carriageway A1. On each side of the road were AA design-award upturned flower box emergency telephones, both vandalized and out of order. My only hope was to try to beg a lift for the 7 miles or so back to my business. Begging a lift on the A1 was no easy task, for obvious reasons, but after some futile attempts to attract the attention of at least a tough, self-reliant lorry driver, I was considerably surprised when an elderly couple halted their car to offer me help. On the way to Sandy while thanking them profusely I wondered why they had taken such a chance with a complete stranger. "Oh", said the husband, "it's just that we are boat owners on our way back from Buckden Marina, so when we spotted your RNLI tie we knew that you would be OK." I later wrote to the AA, criticizing their ridiculous telephones and stating that it would seem that the RNLI were able to offer a superior service on the A1 than an accredited motoring organization!

One Sunday afternoon after my siesta, following an excellent lunch and a pint in the pub, I made us a cup of tea. While having a browse through the motoring section of the local *Bedfordshire Times* I chanced upon a private advert offering a Lancia 1.6 Beta saloon. During my latter days at Hamblins, Lancia Beta Coupes had been all the rage amongst directors' wives and ladyfriends. When they tired of their cars I usually managed to obtain them for resale and had found them to be very saleable and very reliable cars. They were also a delight to drive. Also during this time I had managed to buy a virtually new Lancia from a Bedfordshire Council chief executive who had blotted his copybook and retired ignominiously. This had also proved to be a quick-moving vehicle, so I felt quite able to drive over and make an offer for this very low-mileage car, which was accepted. I drove the car to Rushden that night as we were sleeping at home, and on this twisty and narrow part of the A45 I was impressed at how well the car took the bends and how lively was the engine when mated to such a delightful five-speed gearbox. By the time we had arrived home I could well have kept the car for personal use, but alas in those early days I needed the money, so Monday found it on sale in the line-up. By Friday it was sold. As mentioned earlier, events always seem to come in twos and threes in our business, so I was not at all surprised to be offered another Lancia within days, this one a Coupe. That also sold, with the result that I was able to offer a local publican an attractive deal on his Lancia Coupe in exchange for a Jaguar XJ6 we had in stock. In two weeks we had sold three Lancia cars, all of the owners were delighted with their purchase, and I was casting my mind back to the old Armstrong Siddeley days.

With a small business like ours a successful specialist market could be a godsend, particularly if it were a marque that as a used vehicle was not as acceptable or sought after by the trade as, for instance, Fords or Vauxhalls. This is no reflection on the vehicle: Mercedes-Benz, BMW and Jaguar were hardly volume-sales cars, and only specialists, of which there were many, would normally accept such cars into stock. So quietly that October we began to describe ourselves as 'Lancia specialists' and made it known in the trade that we were cash buyers. By the end of March 1980, our first year's trading, we had sold 15 Lancia cars, including one new, and our advertising and notepaper, etc, had us heavily committed to the marque. On Wednesday, April 9, 1980 I had seven immaculate low-mileage Lancias in the showroom for sale and I was busy planning for our second year's trading. We had organized the beginnings of a Lancia spares department for the growing amount of service business we were creating, and Dennis was becoming more knowledgeable each day. These are the real advantages of specialization, everything is to hand. We had also taken a year's advertising space in *Glass's Guide* on the Lancia pages stating that we bought these cars for cash. Thus engrossed, I was somewhat startled when one of my latest Lancia customers stormed into my office, throwing a copy of the *Daily Mirror* newspaper on my desk and demanding: "What the hell is all this about then?"

I had known of course that Lancia, Fiat and Alfa Romeo had had their share of rust problems during the Seventies, but what motor manufacturer, British or foreign, hadn't? Vauxhall were still reeling from their reputation for corrosive bodywork in the mid-Sixties, Austin and Morris 1100 models and their derivatives had all been notorious for rotting rear subframes, while all of the early Japanese cars had suffered from severe rust problems. The problems were two-fold: the first – and more serious – was rusting from within the inner metal box sections and other structural members, while the second – and more obvious – was surface rust, something which had caused problems for most manufacturers over the years. Indeed, that is why by 1980 nearly all vehicle manufacturers had introduced anti-corrosion warranties of two years and upwards, based on new manufacturing processes such as zincrometalling of the sheet metal prior to pressing and substantial anti-rust treatment by wax injection after manufacture.

In January 1980, Lancia UK had introduced a six-year anti-corrosion warranty on all of its cars. After shipping to Britain from Italy they were given a comprehensive wax-injection rustproofing before being offered for sale. The fact that Lancia felt the necessity to do this in addition to the new zinc plating process introduced in their Italian factory around 1978 underlines the major preoccupation with corrosion at that time, and this was not just at Lancia. As far as I was aware, the problems for Lancia had been confined to Series 1 production Beta models and were expressed as corrosion to body panel surfaces above and, particularly, beneath the vehicle, the root cause of this deterioration being the prodigious amount of salt with which we were covering our main roads at the first sign of bad weather. While the Series 2 Betas introduced in August 1975 were far superior in design and production, one problem still persisted. On some cars the narrow top underside of the front wings would collect and retain road muck with salt contamination over the years. In due course telltale pinholes would appear in the paintwork, and from that moment the front wings were doomed. This was overcome on the later six-year warranty models by fitting heavy plastic covers below the wings, a feature now used by all car makers. As we were not dealing in five-year-old cars and I was very careful to examine front wings closely prior to purchase, I had absolutely no reason to believe we would have problems regarding our choice of specialist manufacturer, particularly as we had already discovered that the mechanical components were such that we could offer, with every confidence, a 12-month comprehensive personal guarantee with every car sold.

The newspaper on my desk was not encouraging. The headline, in typical Mirror fashion, occupied 25 per cent of the front page and announced:

EXCLUSIVE LUXURY CARS IN RUST RIDDLE

This had every appearance of becoming 'one of those days', the luxury cars being Lancias. The story seemed to suggest that front engine mountings on Lancia cars were subject to metal deterioration, causing a complete collapse of the vital engine subframe. Having not previously seen the paper I was at a considerable disadvantage. On the other hand, this gentleman had only recently taken delivery of a brand new Lancia Beta 1.6 saloon, so I pointed out that whatever the truth or otherwise of this story, it simply couldn't apply to his Lancia, on which he held a six-year anti-corrosion warranty. Not unreasonably, he pointed out that news of this kind would not do a great deal for his car's resale value. I could do nothing more until I was able to obtain some information, and on this rather unsatisfactory note he departed. At this point the telephone started to ring as up to 15 irate clients were demanding information in respect of their Lancia cars. When the initial flap had died down a bit I sat Christine down and broke the bad news that I think she had already surmised. This little lot had finished us for good and all. Pointing in the general direction of the seven Lancia cars gleaming in our little showroom, for which we had worked so hard, I had to face facts. "Sorry, love, but it looks as if we shall go to the wall long before we can possibly sell that lot."

Firstly I telephoned Fiat/Lancia at the Great West Road head office. They were, of course, up to their ears in media reaction and unable to provide much information other than to say that the story had been grossly exaggerated and distorted out of all proportion. They were, however, able to state categorically that Lancia engineers had been aware of the problem affecting some Series 1 Lancia cars for several years. No less an authority than the Automobile Association's chief engineer, Mr Marcus Jacobson, had agreed that it didn't constitute a safety hazard, therefore the cars were not to be the subject of a mandatory recall. Further, the problem described most certainly did not apply to any of the current Series 2 Beta models, redesigned and constructed long after this problem had first been the subject of Lancia's and the AA's thorough investigations.

The substance of the front-page *Mirror* story, which appeared under a sub-heading:

CAR GIANT LANCIA ARE BUYING BACK THEIR
OWN LUXURY MODELS TO SCRAP THEM

was that Lancia had discovered a serious rust defect in their Beta range. Lancia dealers had been quietly instructed to look out for rust-damaged models (this at least confirming that not all cars were affected) *which were to be bought back at over-the-odds prices* (my italics). The front page concluded by stating that the problem concerned the mountings at the rear of the front subframe. Readers were then directed to a 'News Inquiry' on page 11, where the whole page was devoted to what the *Mirror* had headlined:

MIRROR PROBES RUST SCANDAL OF A MOTOR GIANT

The paper had carried out a thorough investigation, it printed photos of Lancia saloon cars being taken to a West Country car park on a transporter, one clearly showing an N-registration suffix, which established that it was a Series 1 car then six years old. The *Mirror* insisted throughout that R-registration, ie Series 2, cars were also being scrapped, but interestingly, although it stated that *Mirror* reporters had watched Lancia Betas being driven to the scrapyard, with all their resources the paper had been unable to provide a picture of an R or later-registered vehicle. They interviewed a Lancia spokesman, who categorically denied that Series 2 cars were being scrapped.

The *Mirror* had traced the late owner of the N-registration car and two others. The first said that he had bought this car secondhand for about £2,000 in 1977 from a Lancia dealer. He had sold it back to the same dealer "last October" (1979) for £950 in exchange for a newer Lancia and was "perfectly happy with the transaction." The next owner interviewed, a car mechanic, liked his Lancia, which he considered to be "in perfect condition", but he had taken it back to his Lancia dealer as the insurance was more than he could afford. He was "surprised", he said, to get £200 more than he expected in part-exchange.

Not, one would have thought, a lot there to get excited about. The third owner was at least disgruntled. The *Mirror* said he was a 38-year-old plumber who had bought a five-year-old Lancia "last August" for £1,100 and it had failed its MoT test in November. "The Lancia engineer offered £800, which I accepted." It could reasonably be said that anyone daft enough to pay £1,100 for *any* car with only a three-month MoT could consider himself lucky to get anything back.

I then managed to get most of the true facts from a Mr Ray Lenton, managing director of a Lancia dealership near Kettering, with whom I was on friendly terms. He confirmed that for some time severe corrosion had become apparent on the front engine mountings of some early-production Lancia Beta models. It was believed that this was a direct result of corrosive elements being able to collect in a box-type structure produced from a batch of poor-quality material. Lancia had advised their dealer network that, while this was obviously not desirable, extensive tests at high speeds with fractured subframes had established that it did not constitute a safety hazard and that both braking and steering integrity would be maintained in the event of failure.

Now at this point Lancia could well have chosen to do nothing; which is exactly what British Leyland did in the Seventies when they were all too well aware that their over-five-year-old 1100-series cars were needing to have rotten rear subframes – which carry the rear suspension and rear wheels – replaced at an alarming rate at their present owner's expense. Had Lancia done nothing the *Mirror* might well have been deprived of a story, and without the attendant publicity the problem would doubtless have quietly gone away. Because the replacement of a front subframe carrying the engine, gearbox, transmission and front suspension would be expensive, and therefore not practical to second, third and subsequent owners of cars exceeding five years of age, even if cost-effective, Lancia, unwisely as it turned out, embarked on a huge buy-back scheme. Their instructions to the dealer network were to quietly check subframes and mountings on as many Lancia cars they could get their hands on. If the deterioration existed – and by no means were all Series 1 cars affected – the car was to be taken from the owner at all costs, either in part-exchange for a new or used car, in which case an 'over the odds' allowance would be subsidized by Lancia, or the car had to be purchased outright for the lowest possible acceptable price. Contrary to the *Mirror's* representations, there was originally no obligation to buy a new Lancia, or even a used one for that matter, but as a matter of good sound commercial sense the sum allowed in either of these cases would obviously be appreciably higher.

Having sorted out at least some information to pass on to my selection of clients, it was quite late. Not surprisingly I was mentally tired out, so we decided on a good stiff drink or three with dinner in the pub across the road and an early night, sleeping on the studio couch ready for whatever the morning might bring. While Christine had her shower I watched the TV news, and there was the Lancia story again being flashed all over the screen, together with all of the *Mirror* irregularities and exaggerations being repeated as matters of fact. It had not been a good day.

There was a glimmer of hope when the facts of the rust problems which had beset all motor manufacturers were broadly confirmed the following day, April 10, by the *Financial Times*. They also confirmed the opinion of the chief engineer of the Automobile Association, Marcus Jacobson, in regard to the safety aspect. The Department of Transport were stated to be investigating the matter. As nothing further was heard we can assume that eventually they came to the same conclusion, no mandatory recall ever being requested. My purchase of the *Mirror* confirmed my suspicion that they had no intention of letting up, having got their teeth into what was obviously regarded as a good story. Re-reading the articles, which appeared with front-page banner headlines over three consecutive days, it is difficult to avoid the conclusion, in retrospect, that the paper was motivated purely by spite. How any newspaper could accuse Lancia of acting in a scandalous manner by repurchasing faulty cars of five years old or more for acceptable prices from first, second, third and in some recorded cases fifth and even sixth owners, is beyond me. It was quite obvious that this was going to be another memorable day for G C Owen Ltd.

The day started with follow-up stories in the other newspapers and by more TV coverage including Miss Esther Rantzen (surprise, surprise), who made a complete fool of herself by indicating with immaculate index finger the wrong area of the car where the fault was to be found. Christine went to the pub at lunchtime for sandwiches, somebody made a snide remark, and they promptly had a flaming and very public row. Oddly, most of the pub sided with Chris when she said that the person should read a 'proper' newspaper, such as the *Financial Times* or the *Telegraph*, before shooting off his mouth. Meantime I was telephoning my more persistent clients trying to put their minds at rest, but without a great deal of success, when in the middle of all this horrendous hassle, Stan Enright strode into the showroom.

Now Stan was a local civil servant executive officer; he had been one of our very first customers after walking in one day and buying a little car that had caught his eye, though as he repeated on several subsequent occasions, "I had only come out to buy a stamp!". Sitting in the front window was a two-year-old Lancia Beta 1.6 Coupe in a lovely Apple Green with, of all things, orange trim! On the Lancia it looked quite lovely. Without any preamble Stanley said: "I never believe anything I read in the papers other than the price, the title and the date. I am buying that car." I could have hugged Stanley that day! We arranged delivery for the weekend as I wanted to leave it on show with a large 'SOLD' label on the windscreen. When Stan had departed I sat in my office with the door firmly shut eating my sandwich and reading the latest *Mirror* story. But this time the paper had overplayed its hand. What I was reading was pure unadulterated nonsense trying to pass as a serious news item. Unbeknown to me, by taking the first steps to rubbish their own story they were saving me from Carey Street and, indeed, putting us on the road to a highly successful and profitable six-years trading pattern.

On April 10, 1980, the sub-heading of the story in the Mirror read:

FURY AT LANCIA

Quote: "John Day, of Wingletye Lane, Hornchurch, Essex, told us: Two months after I bought a 1974 Beta 1800 for £1,500 the engine dropped through the floor. I left it parked one day. When I came back the engine was on the ground. I could have been driving the car at 70mph when it happened."

Quote: "Eric Stafford, 56, of Hollingworth Lake, Greater Manchester, said that the engine of his N- registered Beta fell out when he was on a busy main road."

Now this really was something out of James Thurber. Even the most naive of Mirror readers would be aware that no matter how long neglected and derelict old cars have been left to rot in barn or field, when finally shifted the engines are *in situ*; engines simply do not 'drop out' of any make of car, particularly a front-wheel-driven car.

That day I put pen to paper. I challenged the *Mirror*, under supervision, to cause an engine on one of the scrap Beta cars to drop out while the wheels were on the floor by any method they cared to use, be it hacksaw, blow torch or box of spanners. In the event that they could reproduce this phenomenon I would gladly pay up front the sum of £1,000 to any charity they cared to nominate. In the event that they were not successful, I would require from them a like sum for the credit of the RNLI. One would have thought that the *Mirror* would have been highly delighted to take up this offer, thereby providing continuity to their story with the bonus of a not insubstantial charity contribution and further confirmation of their public-spirited attitude. The *Mirror*, however, were strangely silent. The following Monday I telephoned, only to be told that the reporter responsible was "on holiday". I repeated my offer on several further occasions, but it was never taken up. On Friday, April 11, the *Mirror* printed their last Lancia scare story. Meanwhile I had written to all of my owners and the local press, confirming that Lancia would be pleased to examine their cars through the local dealer free of charge and to provide a certificate of fitness. I also publicized my offer to the *Mirror* and the negative result.

Jumping ahead a dozen years to July 1992, there was an interesting sequel to all this when *Auto Express* magazine found a 14-year-old Lancia Beta languishing in a scrapyard. They arranged as a publicity stunt to have it destroyed by a replica of the Trebuchet 14th Century giant siege catapult. This hurled the vehicle 100ft, through a 50ft arc at up to 20g, they chortled. The result, and I quote: "The Lancia exploded with frightening force on impact with the ground. Windows blew out, the chassis split in half and the body was squashed to half its original height. Parts were scattered over a 40ft area." The engine, I later ascertained, stayed firmly in position!

Meanwhile, back to 1980. At that stage we had six of the used Lancia Beta saloons and Coupes left in the showroom, plus a Princess 1.8 taken in exchange for the new Lancia from the gentleman who had been making the most noise for the least reason. Incredibly, by the following Friday we had sold every Lancia car on the premises – but we still owned the Princess!

We had the notepaper and we had the advertising; could we, I pondered, remain Lancia specialists? For interest, I put a two-line advert in the *Sunday Times* motoring pages stating that we wished to purchase late, low-mileage Lancia cars. That following Sunday afternoon I had to disconnect the telephone. It seemed as if every Lancia owner in the country wanted to unload his car and would be grateful for almost any offer. I decided to be selective and to buy only those that had covered well below average mileage. As with the Armstrong Siddeleys, I would always ask if the owners were thinking of purchasing another new vehicle, and in this manner sold several new cars of alternative manufacture. Apparently few others in the trade would touch the cars at any price, so I was able to buy and sell at sensible prices and still make a better than average profit. Furthermore, I had no difficulty at all in asking the owners to bring the cars to me; they were only too pleased.

We were also receiving countless calls from the motor trade regarding our regular advertisement in *Glass's Guide*. Buying from this source we knew would never be a problem. The motor trade always over-react to situations of this kind. Some of the prices I was paying for superb low-mileage cars, delivered to my door, from so-called professional motor dealers were quite unbelievable. Even the local Lancia main dealer in Bedford was refusing the cars in part-exchange for new ones and sending the business to us! So what about selling? Well, I like to think I am a good salesman, and certainly we both had to work hard, but at the end of the day selling is about sincerity, together with enthusiasm and knowledge of the product. The product was – and still is – superb Italian engineering at its very best. To this very day I own and drive three Lancia cars: a lovely Lancia Dedra 2.0 *ie* Turbo, a 21-year-old 1.6 Lancia Beta saloon, which manages to get through its MoT each year without any difficulty with its engine firmly in place, and my 23-year-old pride and joy, a 1.3 Series 3 Lancia Fulvia Coupe, which I have owned for the last 20 years. For the sheer joy of driving, particularly on a wet and twisty road, in comfort and with magic ambience, I suggest there is absolutely nothing to touch a Lancia car. Ask anyone who has ever owned one, even a rusty one! We actually had clients who, having got their compensation for their written-off Series 1 Beta from the Bedford main dealer, came straight to us and purchased a used Series 2 model. How's that for dedication! This, then, is what we had to sell, coupled with the fact that the car on offer at its now depleted price was cheaper than a comparable secondhand Cortina.

I devised a test route of some 8 miles, covering all conditions including a blast up the A1. The first part I would drive myself. By judging my client's reactions I would drive hard if appropriate, demonstrating the astonishing sure-footedness of the cars under any conditions, and the consummate ease with which fast changes could be made, providing the gearbox was properly handled. I would then let the client drive and encourage him to make full use of the acceleration by utilizing the high revving capacity of the engine. In short, we made the effort and more often than not we sold the car. Where reliability was concerned, we put our money where our mouth was by offering, on every Lancia car purchased, an unequivocal personal guarantee on parts and labour costs for 12 covering everything. As I used to tell my clients, tongue in cheek, down to the air in the tyres! The only exceptions were tyres, exhausts and batteries, which we covered for three months. In six years I had one major claim, which cost us £1,000 for a replacement automatic gearbox. I wonder how many dealers of any make would care to match that commitment today on any used car entirely from their own resources?

One particular client from Bedford bought a year-old Lancia HPE from me. In three years he covered 87,000 miles, during the course of which he was obliged to purchase, apart from normal service items, one handbrake cable and two front wheel bearings. He therefore purchased from me another Lancia, a 2.0 Trevi, on reliability. We then sold his well-used Lancia HPE at an appropriate price to a local gentleman, who required an AA inspection in order to obtain a loan from his employer. The car passed with flying colours; I have to say even I was surprised! Lancias were to prove the most reliable cars I have owned, sold or driven in my lifetime. They were also, without any doubt, the cars most enjoyed by any single group of valued customers. When I sold a Lancia, I acquired not only a good customer, I made a friend. Stan Enright was to buy no less than six up to his retirement, when he finished with a new Lancia Delta. Many clients bought two or more while we owned the business. Inevitably we became known to the parent company Fiat/Lancia in London, where we would obtain spare parts and used cars. On one such visit my wife and I were invited to the managing director's office, where Mr Tony Hemelik introduced us to his service director and we had coffee. He wished to know if there was any way they could assist us, for they had heard that we were selling Lancia cars, unlike most of the dealer network. Never one to look a gift horse in the mouth, I requested point-of-sale advertising material, particularly illuminated 'LANCIA' signs for my showroom windows and walls. These were duly promised within two weeks. Was there perhaps anything else needed?

By this time we could afford to run a decent car, so I asked that in the event that the factory should have a Lancia 2.5 Gamma Coupe demonstration or press car, I would appreciate first refusal. Tony Hemelik promised to see what he could do, bade us a courteous farewell and wished us continued success. Ten days later I had my illuminated signs delivered, totally free of charge, together with a large selection of self-adhesive Lancia shield signs for the walls and windows and a host of publicity material. The local Lancia dealer was not pleased! The 2.5 Gamma Coupe was arguably one of the best-looking cars Lancia produced, furthermore there were not too many about, which was why I wanted one. In 1981 its list price was £10,000, which was more than I could afford at the time, hence my interest in a good used example. Within a week after delivery of our signs I had a telephone call asking that Christine and I should again visit Mr Hemelik at Fiat/Lancia. We were courteously received, as previously, and during coffee Tony casually told us that there were one or two brand new Gamma Coupes around, and if I cared to pay £3,000 I could have one of those. I was so taken aback it must have showed. "Mr Owen", he said, "if our dealer network were to show one half of the enthusiasm generated by yourself and your wife, we would not be in the trouble that we are today." One week later the lovely new car arrived on a transporter, complete with radio/cassette, one year's licence and a full tank of petrol.

Which magazine published their annual report on cars, and predictably Lancia were slated for their rust problems, but they were also criticized for being mechanically unreliable! Accordingly, I wrote a polite and detailed letter to the editor, noting my own experiences of the marque, together with those of my many clients and offering gratis access to my service records. I had a formal acknowledgement, no more. The following year they went further; not only, said *Which*, were the cars unreliable, they were expensive to maintain and unstable, "*particularly in the wet*" (my italics). This was too much, and I wrote to Miss Sue Leggate at length, again pointing out that they had been offered service records, now a year older and in consequence more comprehensive, that I had by now also sold two used Lancia cars to local trading standards officers for their own personal use (later three), and on the question of roadholding, if Miss Leggate would care to be driven by myself, in any Lancia model of her choosing, on a wet twisty road, I would guarantee her totally safe return from an 'interesting' ride. I did, however, recommend she bring a change of underwear! *Which* are never interested in being proved wrong; but then, most discriminating people seldom find the need for guidance from a magazine which seems to me to be devoted so wholeheartedly to self-promotion.

We built our reputation on hard work, repeat business and recommendation from satisfied clients. I know for a fact that we lost one particular Saturday sale due to the weekend *That's Life* programme, but we resold the car within hours to an alternative client, and 12 months later the first one came back full of apologies and bought a Lancia car anyway! But nothing lasts forever. One day we woke up to find our Market Square was to be redesigned and our little showroom was surrounded by yellow lines. Trade was still brisk so, perhaps unwisely as it turned out, we tried to compensate for our loss of outside display facilities by expanding our showroom and moving our workshop to another site. We had failed to appreciate that while Lancia continued to win world-class rallies with monotonous regularity, and new and further improved models were introduced, the whole scene would alter. Dealers who had been pleased to unload their part-exchange cars now found that they were able to sell them, with the result that within the year we were hard put to acquire sufficient stock to maintain turnover. Depression set in as I realized that specialization in our beloved marque was rapidly coming to an end and that we might have to consider retailing bread-and-butter family used cars to keep the business solvent.

Salvation, when it arrived, came in an odd manner. I had slipped out for a few moments to buy a few odds and ends for our forthcoming Christmas holiday in the sun, and on my return two gentlemen were waiting in the showroom. To my polite: "How can I help you?" they did not mince words.Some three months back the local supermarket had moved into brand new, purpose-built premises just across the road from me. Part of their existing premises had been turned into a temporary retail shoe store, and it was from here that the gentlemen had arrived. They represented a national company and they said they had been testing the market with a view to opening in Sandy. They wondered if I would like to lease my property long-term. I thanked them for their offer, but I didn't really wish to retire at that time, so my initial reaction was "No thank you". They suggested that I might give it some thought, and departed. Within the week we were in Tenerife on three weeks' holiday over Christmas and the New Year, during which, while relaxing in the sun, I had time to put my thoughts together and a vision of early retirement began to take shape. A great deal, of course, would depend on the terms and the available rental. These could well be advantageous, for we were in the midst of the Thatcher boom years, and I well knew that my property was not only ideal, but the only property available in Sandy at the present time apart from the old supermarket, which was obviously far too large. I decided on my return to research property rentals and perhaps contact the gentlemen later in January. I didn't have the chance; they were waiting for me on my return. They were proposing a 25-year full-repairing lease with rent reviews every five years. They wanted to be *in situ* by March 1 and they were most certainly not messing about. By March 1 they were in and I had a starting rental that was more than satisfactory. After 40 years of commercial life I was unemployed.

Retirement, while sitting reading a good book on a sun-drenched balcony in the Canary Islands in December, had seemed like a jolly good idea. I felt that I had earned it and that having a pad somewhere near the sea and another boat would provide the makings of a good way to spend my future years. Accordingly, in the autumn of 1987 we decided to move to Suffolk and found a new three-bedroom detached house at Shotley, where construction had started on a brand new marina.

During our years at Sandy my 50th birthday had arrived, and with it a custom-made card from my father. A good friend who was a talented commercial artist had produced it to his specification. The front of the card read as follows:

TODAY WE ARE
50
BUT LET'S FACE IT
WE DON'T LOOK IT DO WE?

Then inside was a lightweight shaving mirror with the legend under:

UGH!!!
WE BLOODY WELL DO!
HAPPY BIRTHDAY

Apart from the fact that I never thought the old man had such a black sense of humour, an idea took shape. David Hamblin's 50th was due later that year and I knew full well that he was a bit of a hypochondriac. I had a de luxe one specially made and dispatched on the appropriate day, which after some discussion with Christine we decided should be sent anonymously.

From an old friend, once an executive in the Group, who was friendly with David's secretary, I later found out that on the big day it was duly opened, examined and then promptly hurled across the room into the fireplace, to be retrieved some time later and left on the mantleshelf in the hope that someone might eventually say: "See you got Geoff's card then!" No-one ever did.

CHAPTER TWELVE

BACK TO WORK AGAIN! – 1988

Shotley sits on the estuary where the River Orwell meets the Stour. The new house was fine and from our back bedroom, which I used as an office, I had a fine view of Harwich and the Parkstone quay where the huge ferries made daily trips to and from Europe. In no time we had settled in – well, more or less. Having got up at my usual 6am, walked my dogs, had my breakfast, read the paper and done a few odd jobs, which got harder to find as the weeks went by, I was bored to tears. When you spend a whole life in a six and a half day business you don't have a great deal of time for other pursuits like golf, or even boating. I was obviously becoming a bit of a pain, for when I tentatively told Christine that I might try and find a job she handed me the car keys and simply said: "Thank God." I took this as a sign of approval.

I replied to a couple of interesting advertisements in the trade papers, one being a company called TKM, importers at the time of the Italian Alfa Romeo cars. Their ad stated that they required 'SIX OF THE BEST' experienced personnel to revitalize their dealer network. As directed in the advertisement I presented myself at the hotel near Heathrow on the appointed day for an interview. The suite was quite deserted apart from an attractive secretary, myself and the consultancy interviewer who, having read my CV and assured me that my experience and professional competence were beyond doubt, stated that the company principals would consider me to be beyond their age requirements. Not one to take no for an answer, I then wrote to the principals direct, pointing out, not unreasonably, that experience usually comes with age and that in any event I genuinely felt that the situation advertised was tailormade for me. Having received a patronizing letter, pointing out in no uncertain terms that I was considered to be far too old for a situation of this kind, I could not resist the temptation to reply, wondering "would it be considered tactless for me to point out that I was presently the same age precisely as Field Marshal Bernard Law Montgomery had been when he won the Battle of Alamein?" I did not hear further!

In the meantime I was scanning the local 'sits vac' and touring Ipswich calling on various dealers, all of whom were polite but not interested. I did secure one job, short-term, with a very large national organization, but I would not wish to embarrass the local motor trade manager, a Mr Woodard, by relating how we parted acrimoniously.

Driving back into town one afternoon I chanced by Airport Garage. On an impulse I drove into this huge site and went to the office to present my credentials. A rather sparse elderly gentleman with a balding head and an engaging grin rose from a huge chair to greet me. I was about to meet Paul Nowosad, probably one of the best-known and loved of the many characters residing in Ipswich. Paul had a thick Polish accent, which occasionally was hard to follow, but his meaning was always clear. I explained my situation and he listened with some care. At the conclusion he explained that these days his son Michael ran the business and was currently on holiday. He gave me the impression that some help could well be appreciated to cope with this busy site. Paul had founded the business shortly after returning from the war and resettling in Ipswich. He had acquired premises in Elliot Street, off the London Road, where he was in fact still trading and spent a great deal of his time buying used cars for both companies.

Paul knew London's Warren Street better than I did, and we had an engaging hour or so swapping stories of the old days. At the conclusion I left a photo album-cum-scrapbook and promised to call back when Michael returned. While having a general look round it became clear that the speciality of Airport Garage was high rather than low mileage, but at least some of the machinery on offer was way out of my recent class and quite expensive. On first meeting the proprietor it was clear that he was not intending to change his trading methods to suit anyone, and why should he, but some competent assistance to help run the business would be appreciated. I was not unduly put out for I have always considered myself to be adaptable, but it was something of a disappointment to hear that if accepted I was to take no part in the buying of stock, other than in part-exchange.

However, we eventually agreed terms and I found myself in a totally new environment. I managed to reorganize the layout of the stock, improve the advertising and generally tidy the place up. Michael's passion was his golf, at which he was virtually up to professional standard, so we eventually enjoyed an understanding that he was free to enjoy his golf at any time knowing the business was in safe hands. In some respects it was very much like my experience in the Ilford High Road. Michael had a good reputation, everybody liked Paul, but the first requirement was that to sell a car you had firstly to give the potential client confidence by selling yourself. High-mileage cars, of course, are sold mainly on price, relative to history and condition. We had the advantage of huge council estates in the immediate area for the bread-and-butter cars, and Michael also stocked BMW, Porsche, Mercedes-Benz, Rolls-Royce, Bentley, Jaguar and other expensive machinery, for which there always seemed to be a ready market during Mrs Thatcher's finest hours.

One day I had a telephone call from David Hamblin's secretary. It seemed that his 60th birthday was nigh and a huge celebration had been organized to which Christine and I had been invited. That she had taken the trouble on David's instructions to locate us was flattering enough, and of course we were delighted to attend and said so. It was to be held in the Corby Civic Centre, and I very much looked forward to being re-acquainted with a great many old friends and colleagues. On arrival, all guests were welcomed personally by David and his new wife, who had organized the entire night. Much to my surprise, when our turn came he hugged me with both arms and said how very pleased he was to see us – and he meant it. During pre-dinner drinks I met colleagues I had not seen for 13 years or more and the sheer warmth of the greetings was a fitting start to a memorable evening. Christine and I were just enjoying a reunion with my old sales manager, Terry Eales, and his lovely wife Mary when I chanced to catch the eye of Alan Kerr. Wisely he chose not to come over!

Later we all sat down at round tables in the great hall, where dinner was served. I sat with good friends and present and past directors from my Hamblin days and many were the tales circulating from the old days. I was very touched when one of my late colleagues from the Hamblin board expressed the entirely unsolicited view that when Geoff Owen joined the Group he brought professionalism. It is nice indeed to be appreciated by one's peers. Later still, after the inevitable speeches and having obtained Charlie Chester's autograph for the second time on a menu after some 30-odd years, I approached John Hamblin at the top table, whom I had not seen for some years. Before I could as much as offer a word John announced to his two brothers and all and sundry at the table that the one abiding memory he had of me was that "when Geoff was in charge all of the used cars had to be lined up like guardsmen, accurate to the millimetre". All in all a very satisfactory night out. At the conclusion we had a video of the event, which I treasure.

For two years my situation was reasonably successful, the business in Ipswich was going well, I had made a mark by substantially increasing profitability, even though I had no influence on buying policy, which must have been something of an achievement. Michael was happy to let me get on with it and pleased to be able to enjoy his golf, during which his handicap dropped even further. My problem, however, was that I was under-employed. The situation was hardly a challenge and I couldn't help but feel as the days went by and my 60th birthday drew near that somehow this was not the way I wished to finish an eventful career.

My last year at Airport Garage was not a good one; house prices had collapsed and it was all too clear that the country was heading for recession and the economy was going to get worse before it got better. With this in mind, as the year neared its end I evaluated the vehicle stock, as I had for the past two years, with a view to reducing retail asking prices prior to the cars being numerically one year older on

January 1, 1991. Having revalued some 90 per cent of the stock I set about reducing the screen prices, which to date had been my entire responsibility and hitherto had provided the profitability, in a manner I considered to be prudent in view of the very obvious storm clouds on the horizon. Naturally, I had amended our advertised prices accordingly for the following weekend.

With close on 100 vehicles this was no small undertaking, and revamping the screen prices alone took up most of a very long day. The next being Thursday, my day off, I spent at home, but on my return the following morning I was confronted by Michael, who informed me without preamble that he had put all the prices up again! With the best will in the world I couldn't take kindly to this; I felt it was my brief to look after his interests, as I had done for over two years, and all I wanted to do was recover dead cash and reinvest in new stock at today's much lower prices. However, he would have none of it and I was overruled; it was after all his business and his money that was at stake. Having lost his confidence I became frustrated and lost interest; it was no longer a pleasure to come to work, and work to me has always been a recreation. Accordingly I decided to try to find a new interest.

For a start I chose to offer my considerable experience in the field of used-car marketing on a consultancy basis. With the help of the Institute of the Motor Industry, of which I was member, I circularized in considerable detail my background and intentions in a personal and confidential presentation to some 150 fellow members who held the top positions in motor vehicle manufacturing and/or distribution; most manufacturers own or control at least some of their retail outlets. Of those who took the trouble to reply – around 70 per cent – most very obviously had not bothered to even glance at my covering letter, let alone examine my presentation, and had designated a secretary to sign and dispatch a standard letter thanking me for my 'application for employment', with regrets! One such letter in fact was a reply, in confidence, to another applicant for such a situation, who presumably in his turn received my confidential reply, this from a 'caring' dealer! For the rest, I had two or three expressing some interest, which came to nought, one positive reply from Peugeot UK and one courteous and highly complimentary reply, wishing me every success, from Mr Nick Lancaster, chief executive of the Malaya Group, then dealing in Mercedes-Benz and other makes in Suffolk. Nonetheless it proved to be an interesting exercise, particularly in relation to future events. Of all the letters I had dispatched, only one recipient chose to be offensive. The chief executive of a very large Ford main dealership, a public company, wrote a rude letter telling me in no uncertain terms that his organization was perfect in every way, that all of his sales staff were proficient, that he had absolutely no used-car problems and that he had no use for anyone who thought that they might tell him how to run his business. The letter was so offensive and uncalled for that I could not resist a reply, if only a brief one. I wrote: Dear Mr Brown, So was the Titanic! Yours sincerely . . .

As the country drifted further into recession, not a few of those companies, including that particular one, were subjected to severe financial difficulties and their quoted share prices nosedived.

Just prior to the year's end I had a telephone call one evening from a very good friend and business associate of some 20 years' standing. I first met Robin Pentelow shortly after I had started Bedford Way Motors for Hamblins. He had been having some dealings with my sales manager, Terry Eales, and as a result we had purchased a few used cars from him. From what I had been able to gather Robin was a sales representative for a national confectionery company, but had been buying and selling used cars through motor dealers in his spare time. Those that we purchased were always of a high quality, but I could not help noticing that we always seemed to pay top price, perhaps justifiably. It just happened that one day I found that one of our cars had gone out on loan to Robin, had been sold, and that he had then expected to purchase it from us for rather less than what I considered to be its true value. In consequence we started off by having a flaming row, yet from this inauspicious beginning grew a friendship that has already lasted 30 years.

Robin proved over these years to be something of an enigma. In my humble opinion he has done absolutely everything wrong (on the face of it) while building up a successful business and making a very great deal of money buying and selling hundreds, nay thousands of cars, from premises which have to be seen to be appreciated, in Raunds of all places – a large village in the wilds of Northamptonshire which owes absolutely nothing at all to passing trade. Gells of Raunds Ltd, the company he purchased in 1970, is the complete antithesis of everything present-day new and used-car distributors strive to attain, spending thousands of pounds and not achieving a very great deal in the process. It is firstly a three-pump, one-way petrol outlet with a minuscule office built, quite literally, into a steep grass bank. Atop this bank, some 30 to 40ft above on level ground sits, from left to right, a small paint shop, a workshop, an MoT bay and two toilets, the whole being reached from the main road by a steep climb up the bank from the left-hand entrance to the petrol area, between the latter and some empty derelict buildings, above which are two general offices. Alternatively one may ascend a flight of steps in the centre.

It has often been said that first impressions count. Any potential customer arriving to inspect the fine selection of superb low-mileage cars advertised extensively every week will firstly see just a row of front-end undersides with accompanying wheels, tyres and radiator grilles, always providing he can first find space to park on a through road which is reasonably congested on most working days and

Saturday afternoons. Having climbed the bank or ascended the stairway to inspect the vehicles at eyesight level, the client and his lady will be encouraged to proceed up yet another relatively steep road to the very top area, where they will discover an Aladdin's cave of perhaps another 50 or so used cars jam-packed in three rows. The provision of a given vehicle for a test drive is possible, just, because long experience has ensured that just the correct amount of space has been provided for the choreography required to extricate the required car. Because of the sheer volume of vehicles on display, few are free of at least a layer of dust, and all bear little information on the windscreen other than the asking price. I have known Robin for years and I can state unequivocally that from these inauspicious surroundings he regularly sells in excess of 75 vehicles a month – profitably.

How does he do it? I know only part of the answer. He carries the right stock at the right price, which is fundamental of course, but he talks to his clients in such a seemingly casual manner and in so doing discovers broadly what they require and how much they can afford to pay, in addition to the probable value of their present car. From this he usually manages to fit a car to the client with devastating logical argument and much good humour, for he is astonishingly witty and has a quick answer for absolutely any occasion. I recall one instance when someone asked why two cars, at first sight almost identical, were priced at different levels. Quick as lightning came the laconic answer: "Twice the doors and half the mileage!"

Some years back he treated himself to a brand new, top-of-the-range 'Princess Di' Mercedes-Benz SL sports coupe with all the trimmings. He had to join the queue, but eventually he obtained delivery in June of that year and, not unreasonably, collected the car on trade-plates so that he could postpone registration until August 1, with the new registration letter. Meantime, Christine and I were invited to view this magnificent automobile in his garage, doubtless as many others had done previously, and a demonstration was provided by the immensely proud owner of the workings of the electric foldaway hood, windows, door locks, computerized seats and God knows what else that went with this luxurious car. Eventually, the big day – August 1 – arrived . . . and the car refused to start; Robin had flattened the battery!

Now, in my darkest hour, Robin was on the telephone with an out of the blue, totally unsolicited offer that I might care to work with him. It happens that we share the same auditor, also a longstanding friend. Roger had been saying for years: "You two should get together", so could this be the moment? He said he had been offered an all but bankrupt garage in Chatteris, in the Fen country, which he felt had potential. It had a good, albeit short, lease with a guaranteed option to renew long-term if required. Robin's view was that the short-term would all but see us out, whereupon we could sell the business with the renewed lease as an ongoing and profitable concern. He said he would conclude the purchase providing I would agree to run it on his behalf. From his description of the premises I felt confident on that score, and it was arranged that we should meet there the following week. Christine and I had arrived early to have a quick look round the town. It was obvious from the various upmarket older properties and the more recent estates that there was a bob or two in the area; March, Huntingdon, Wisbech and even Peterborough were not that far away, and I could only find one car dealer at the far end of town on a rather tatty site offering even more tatty used cars. The high street, it must be said, was not imposing.

The garage, however, was everything Robin had said it would be, and the potential was obvious for the kind of upmarket cars he handled. The question of remuneration did not arise at this stage, neither did it need to. I had already been told that when the time came for us all to retire and the premises to be sold, I would be entitled to one-third of the proceeds as a bonus. Christine and I were shortly off for our winter pilgrimage to Tenerife, so it was agreed that we would meet Roger in the New Year while Robin was finalizing the transaction. While we were away the Gulf War started, but we had no problems with our return flight in spite of all the false tales being spread by new arrivals from the UK. What did upset me, however, was the behaviour of some British airline staff at check-in, spreading gross rumours that hundreds of missiles had been falling on Israel with 'mega' casualties.

On my return to Airport Garage Mike was in a funny mood. Profits, he said, were well down for the year, which was self-evident due to the recession taking an ever increasing grip on the economy. What he failed to say was that in spite of the downturn, plus the fact that I had no influence on stock choice or purchase, profits were rather higher than they had been at any time prior to my arrival. He also made it clear that while I was away he had sold loads of cars, with clear implications, so I elected to say nothing. Later, while chatting with Paul, whom I liked immensely and knew that my feelings were reciprocated, he expressed some concern about the deterioration in our relationship. But there was not a great deal to be said; things had gone too far, so I simply left.

In due course we had our meeting with Roger, who handed me a business plan which we discussed at length. I had a very satisfactory statement of my terms and conditions, which were accepted on sight, and we were all in business when Murphy's Law struck home. I had arranged to rent a small cottage in Chatteris until such time as we could find suitable accommodation. The new premises were empty, so we stored the majority of our belongings in a secure building on the site and I moved in to make provisional arrangements while Robin harried the solicitors for completion sometime in February/March. I had enough to do to keep me occupied, and meantime had sold our first car to my landlord. That car was soon to become unique, being the only vehicle ever to have a rear window sticker and number-plates stating that it had been supplied by Gells of Chatteris Ltd. In February we were advised by our solicitor that there was a slight problem with the second part of our lease. By mid-March the slight problem proved insoluble due to a hitherto undisclosed multiple ownership over a right of way to the premises, and we were advised that ownership of the second half of our lease simply could not be guaranteed.

Having arranged absolutely everything needed to commence trading, including me, Robin had no choice but to write the entire project off and swallow a hefty bill for absolutely no return. In an effort to retrieve something he asked me to research another garage and used-vehicle site, which we had found was up for sale, only to discover that it had already been purchased at auction by the owners of the tatty used-car site at the far end of the high street. Christine and I were stranded, literally. We had leased our house at Shotley and were now resident in a small cottage with two dogs and three cats. I realized that I had become an embarrassment to Robin, who was still paying my salary, so in some desperation I approached the tatty garage.

The premises were run by a Mr Keith Maynard and his director, a Mr David Cook. I later found that Mr Cook and Keith's wife were the only directors as father and son were not deemed to be eligible. It was David I was to meet firstly, discovering to our mutual surprise that he was acquainted with my old employer Cyril Chidley in Tottenham. He felt that the owners could be interested as he admitted that the used-car site had not been a great success and the new one down the road was not only considerably larger, but on the opposite side of the road to the main building, which would make it difficult to control. The only problem was that neither Keith nor his father would be keen to pay a salary to invest in a further venture that so far had been non-productive. As we were discussing the pros and cons Keith arrived. David gave him an outline of my experience in the motor trade and I offered to work for nothing on a commission-only basis. At this point in the proceedings I was to hear for the first time words that seemed to be repeated about six and a quarter of a million times over the next 18 months, namely the family's standard opening answer to positively every question put to them on any conceivable subject: "Well, Geoff, now I'm going to be quite honest."

Keith spoke in a high-pitched voice out of the left side of his mouth; I gathered that he thought that – "to be quite honest" – Dad could well be interested in an arrangement of this kind. The following day Mr Ronnie "call me Ron" Maynard, all the way from Barking, Essex, arrived on my doorstep together with Keith to hear what I had to say. While Christine provided tea I told them how I came to be in Chatteris, outlined my experience to date and provided Robin's name as an incontrovertible reference. My personal computer was on the table – rare in those days – and I offered to provide a detailed business plan inclusive of forecast sales, profitability and, of course, my projected income. Ronnie was impressed and immediately declared his intention that he was "going to be quite honest!" and would like to see the plan on Friday next.

I got the impression that while a rough diamond, which he most certainly was, he had a bob or two. I had no intention of dealing in the kind of machinery presently on display, so stated clearly that those were all down to Keith and David Cook to dispose of. I drew up a strategy for a stock of 15 to 20 low-mileage cars, with the financial outlay required, an advertising budget, together with a forecast for monthly sales and profitability. In this respect I had Roger's figures for Gells, which were a great assistance to me. This in turn enabled me to formulate my own income, and I calculated a commission on a percentage basis. All that remained were the disciplines in respect of the use of a company car, Christine's wages to assist in car valeting, the usual odds and ends and, finally, my absolute insistence that I had sole discretion concerning both the purchase and the sale of the vehicle stock. In short, I had to protect my own interests in as fair a manner as possible to us both.

The following Friday Ron sat down at my table with Keith and the computer was switched on in case of queries. While drinking his tea Ron studied the document with some considerable care. Eventually he looked up. "Well, Geoff", he began. I held by breath. "Now I'm going to be quite honest – you are talking figures we have never heard of." I took that as acquiescence and a deal was concluded on the spot. Ron was, he said, "to be quite honest, not interested in putting things in writing", his word being his bond. Nonetheless, I took the trouble to write to him and confirm the arrangement. For the first year all went well insofar as I purchased good low-mileage cars, Christine and I valeted them and we sold them. We earned an acceptable income, always paid on request, and from my point of view the sales department at least made a profit. However, from a distance I could see that under Keith's direction the workshop, parts and limited petrol sales were a complete dog's breakfast. Ronnie was away for most of the time, living in London. Keith had a house in the Fens and the garage was, or should have been, his entire responsibility.

On an average day David Cook, who had to travel all the way from Bishops Stortford, around 40 miles, would arrive at 8.30am, open up, organize the day's work for the fitters and get things moving. Keith, who had to travel all of 12 miles, would arrive between 9.30 and 10am, breeze into the workshop and usually change all the schedules, being as ever "quite honest" in the process. At around

5.30pm everyone would depart, leaving the petrol pumps, the shop, the stores and the whole building apart from my used-car site and office, which was self-contained, in the hands of a lazy teenaged girl whose happy band of yobs would arrive as soon as I departed and have the free run of the building. What that lot must have salted away on a nightly basis beggars belief.

Meanwhile, Christine and I were beginning to see the ebullient Ron in a new light. It soon became all too apparent that he was a likeable rogue with a dubious history. He was undoubtedly a man with great personal wealth; he owned a villa somewhere on the Continent, he had a pilot's licence and his own aircraft and he had a substantial boat. The money that went into the business was flown in at regular intervals from Ireland in a suitcase, £50,000 at a time in cash! We saw this with our own eyes because I often had to wait for Ronnie to fly in with the readies so that I could purchase extra stock. He was a man who used foul language totally without realizing it. On one occasion, while Christine and I were cleaning a car, Ron regaled us with some yarn or other, interspersed at regular intervals with effing this and effing that, when along came Keith to tell him that the gent was back yet again with the effing Cavalier with the same effing problem. Ron spun round on Keith in horror: "Watch yourself, Keith, there's a lady present!"

One day, with much humour, he told me a little of his life story. It seemed that he had a factory in the Lea Valley area of North London making furniture. Things were a bit quiet when a friend called and asked if he could produce from a sample some ladies' wooden heels, which were all the rage at the time. Ron could and did, on a cash-in-hand basis. Word got round the various back-street shoe manufacturers to the market trade and in no time orders were flooding in to such an extent that the Inland Revenue inevitably took an interest. Ron told me that eventually they landed in court after a Revenue man, on searching his factory, found incriminating documents in a sand-filled fire bucket. Further evidence was provided by pin-sharp pictures of Keith departing from back-street shoe factories with carrier bags full of readies. Inevitably they had suffered a hefty fine for tax evasion, both were banned from becoming company directors, and they found another interest.

When he got his first-year accounts it seemed that he had lost money, which hardly surprised me. I had been told by the locals in the Rotary Club that the workshop they were trying to run with just three fitters had once been a Vauxhall dealership which had totally failed to make money with six in the good times. The premises were simply badly sited and too large, therefore the costs of heating and the ratable value were quite beyond the scope of turnover, this with professional management; with Keith in charge it was a recipe for disaster. Ronnie, of course, couldn't accept that his son and heir was at fault. Inevitably he looked for cuts in other directions and tried to interfere with my advertising and even Christine's meagre part-time salary. I had to resist, for I could not allow him to restrict my profitable side of the business at the expense of my income. Things went from bad to worse until one day he became so offensive that we simply walked out and left them to it. The following year the company went into liquidation and closed down.

Determined to remain self-employed and retain independence, I approached the lease owner of the now deserted premises which Robin had had to abandon on the the off chance that he might wish to engage me to reconstitute the site on similar terms. Tim Graven must have been having problems himself with that lease for he declined the offer, but he provided an alternative at his self-service petrol station just up the road where he said he had a motor business that had been losing money for some time. He could have fooled me. I had noted in passing three or four cars parked on his frontage from time to time and assumed that they were a part of his well-known self-drive company; there was never any indication that they might have been for sale. However, he visited my home and we came to an amicable arrangement, so once again I was in business with an assortment of rather disreputable used cars, and once again I was starting from scratch.

The situation was not ideal, being primarily a large petrol forecourt with limited and often inconvenient used-car display facilities. However, it stood on a junction of two major roads. The first cross that I had to bear was the likeable salesman-cum-director of the company, one Harry Johnson, two years my junior, who had been with Tim for donkey's years. Harry, as I was to discover, had been with Tim when Gravens Motors had been a leading Ford dealership and tractor agency. The original company, founded in Ely by Tim's father, had been slowly depleted to the point where all that now remained was a car hire-cum-head office in Ely, the petrol station in Chatteris and the original tractor showroom, part of a huge decrepit mansion in the town centre, now adjoining an Indian restaurant, and of course the deserted garage and showroom, still ignominiously carrying notices in the by now filthy windows announcing that Gells of Chatteris were to open soon!

Once again there were loss-making cars to dispose of and fresh stock to purchase before I could earn my keep. With room on the forecourt for around 15 cars, including a few part-exchanges, it was a bit limited, and as there were no facilities for car valeting we had to lease a small garage some 10 minutes' walk away, which was not ideal as it meant I was away from the sales area most of the week and therefore had to retrain Harry Johnson to my way of thinking. Colloquially this might be known as teaching an old dog new tricks, but in this instance the sheer effort and frustration was more akin to flogging a dead horse. To say that Harry, whose proud boast was that he never read a newspaper, was set in his ways would guarantee first prize for the understatement of the year. Eventually, however, we achieved a minor miracle, helped in no small measure by a tangible increase in Harry's commission as the company gradually became profitable.

I had been with Tim Graven just six months when, unknown to me, he decided to get his accountants to carry out a half-year audit to review progress. During the two financial years prior to my joining, Gravens Motors Ltd under the patronage of Harry Johnson had lost an appreciable amount of money. This clearly could not go on and Mr Graven, not unreasonably, expected me to stem the inevitable drain on his capital. Of this particular half of the financial year I had been with the company for just five months, the first month my tenure having been engaged in clearing out the existing stock and reconstructing the business in such a way as to make it profitable. I was not a little astonished, therefore, to be summoned to head office at Ely shortly after to be told that Mr Graven was "surprised" to note that we had as yet failed to move into profit! Worse was to follow when, at the conclusion of the following full year, I received through the post a copy of the year's accounts, together with a derogatory letter. Mr Graven, it would appear, was far from satisfied with the results.

I really didn't know whether to laugh or to cry. I sent a copy of the letter and the accounts to Roger, my long-time accountant, and kept out of Tim's way by taking a week off. On my return I was able to reply to Tim enclosing a copy of Roger's professional and splendidly restrained reply (*extract below*) while pointing out that, given the relatively short time available, I could achieve the impossible, but that miracles would inevitably take a little longer. I heard no more! Roger commented as follows:

Dear Mr Owen

Thank you for your letter of 22nd June 1994 enclosing copies of the above company's draft Profit and Loss Account for the year ended 31st March 1994 and Mr. Graven's letter of 21st June 1994.

I would make the following comments:

Appendix 1: Suggests the business was not achieving its objectives before your involvement. Between 1992 and 1994 you have increased gross profit by £28,850, which is a percentage increase of 282%. As a result of which losses have been eliminated and a profit of £10,340 has been achieved.

Appendix 2: Shows you have achieved a higher level car sales and total gross profit than budgeted. However your budget does not mention overheads and therefore I can not comment whether net profit is higher or lower than expected.

In conclusion it would appear that a return on capital of approximately 25% is being achieved, which would appear an adequate return although I can appreciate why Mr Graven wishes to improve and maximize this.

Yours sincerely,

I was the first to see the interim six months results and the above, almost before the ink was dry. Conversely, as the yearly results became appreciably better I was the last to see them, even well after Harry Johnson, the reason being given that Harry was a director. This did not bother me to any great extent because I kept my own records on computer. Also, not a few car-sales expenses were mixed up with those of the petrol and forecourt shop sales and hard to quantify. When Tim opened his huge new Esso petrol station not a quarter of a mile away, with the very latest equipment (but no car-sales facilities) and 24-hour service, turnover inevitably nosedived on the site where I operated. I could not help but notice that as the petrol turnover diminished car-sales overheads climbed through the roof. This did not bother me in the slightest as it did not affect my income, and Tim of course was fully entitled to distribute his own cashflow as he pleased.

But these years were to herald for me yet again a new opportunity in used-car dealing. I have mentioned previously that in the used-car trade it can be advantageous to specialize, thereby becoming noticed for marketing a particular product which is attractive to a significant section of the buying public. Specialization had been profitable for me with Armstrong Siddeley and Lancia, both long since finished, but not a great deal had been on offer since. But it slowly became apparent that significantly more very low-mileage used cars were becoming available from a rapidly growing and seemingly bottomless source: Motability Finance Ltd.

This period marked the beginning of a totally new and now all too apparent phenomenon in the so-called dependency – something for nothing – society conceived from old Labour's cradle-to-the-grave welfare state. I mention this not simply as a political comment, but because politics affects all our lives and political fallout can often breed extraordinary situations. Motability existed to provide those souls entitled to disability benefit with leased transport over a three-year renewable period. A basic car would be provided to those of slender means, but for the more affluent who were able to pay a larger deposit a rather more upmarket vehicle might be obtained from any dealer operating the scheme. As these cars were leased, their maintenance and running costs, other than the fuel consumed, were met in full. Motability retained title and very strict rules had to be observed. Regular servicing as per the maker's schedule had to be observed in order to protect the warranty, and in all cases there were excess-mileage penalties.

When I started trading at Maynards in 1991 I would visit the Peterborough auctions on a weekly basis seeking low-mileage, late-registration company fleet cars. There were a large selection at the time because all the major manufacturers were providing cars to the huge fleet buyers at such huge discounts that most could return a profit by moving them on for replacements after just a few months. There was a joke circulating at the time that the National Westminster Bank made more money from car dealing than it did through banking! Some time during these weekly auctions there would be a little flurry of excitement when it would be announced by my old colleague from Bedford, Bruce Willey, now chief auctioneer and director, that the following cars offered would be "direct from Motability". Most cars in this very small group would have a guaranteed very low mileage and full service history and be in appropriately superb condition. Not a few of them would have been leased to the elderly or infirm, who sadly had passed on before having the chance to enjoy their new acquisition, and some of the mileages were so low as to be almost unbelievable had there not been a proper service history to corroborate the figures.

Of course, a few of these cars found their way to other auctions, and some even had complicated technology applied to them to enable their owners to get about without the full use of arms or legs; often we had to dismantle this equipment and discard it. Today, however, the situation has changed beyond belief. Now there are at least eight fortnightly auctions nationwide from which I can choose from as many as 70 ex-Motability cars at any one sale, and I cannot recall when I last bought one that had modifications. I understand that there are now more worthy citizens claiming disability benefit than there are claiming unemployment! This within a nation which is living longer and more healthily than at any time in its history. As I said earlier, this is not intended as a political comment.

By mid-1993 at Gravens the dribs and drabs being offered at Peterborough had ceased entirely and Motability sales had been transferred on a weekly basis to British Car Auctions at Measham, now part of the ADT group. At midday this particular selection of around 30 to 40 cars would be offered for sale by BCA's embryo high-speed, high-tech replacement for the now departed Major 'as seen on TV' Pip Bircher. William Sowbury is equally a character, with many a merry quip within the limitations of high-speed auctioneering and endless patter while disposing of a car a minute. Indeed, on finally bringing down the hammer at the conclusion of each transaction, it becomes clear that William has inherited the original descendants and close relatives of the Major's Messrs 'A', 'B' and 'C', right through to Robin's 'G' euphemism.

With the limited space available I decided to specialize in these somewhat unique used cars, concentrating almost wholly on those that had completed only minimal mileage. It was by no means unusual to buy one to two-year-old vehicles which had covered less than 1,000 miles, complete with stamped-up records of service carried out on a time rather than a mileage basis. As was my habit, I didn't skimp on advertising, setting out to describe the cars in considerable detail with a view to selling my wares to potential clients prior to actual inspection. In most cases the actual sale was more or less a formality, depending only on reasonable valuation of a part-exchange. Even this was seldom a problem for most clients were people who had been enticed by very attractive prices, would normally have purchased new, and were therefore in their turn offering comparatively low-mileage one-owner cars.

In most of my life, the best breaks have come almost by accident, and one afternoon I chanced to be on the forecourt when an elderly couple drove in. They said they had come to view the very low-mileage automatic Ford Fiesta advertised that week. I had to tell them that the car had in fact been sold. They were visibly disappointed, particularly as the gentleman informed me "we could have got over earlier if your advertisement had carried your address or telephone number; we had a job to find you". This I found impossible to believe and said so. With that the old boy produced a copy of the '*Swaffam Bugle*', or some such obscure publication that I had never heard of, and sure enough there was our ad on the motor pages, minus address or telephone number. For the moment this would have to wait. It so happened that I had purchased another automatic Fiesta the day before which, as we spoke, was on its way with other vehicles on the transporter from Measham. I gave the couple a brief description, including the specification, colour and quoted low mileage and price, at the conclusion of which the gentleman informed me that he would "have that one, thank you very much", paid his deposit after I had valued their car, and they went on their way.

With that I telephoned Judy, the local manager of our newspaper group. She confirmed that the paper was one of their group and, doubtless being short of copy that week, had run our ad for free! I pointed out that it would have been helpful to print our address and telephone number, so with that she agreed to run a complete version again the following week. This brought more inquiries and at least one further sale, so I signed up at once on a fortnightly basis. It was a free publication, circulating in North Norfolk under a series of localized names, none of which of course were '*Bugle*', but from then on this is what we always called it, and we never looked back. It became the least expensive and most cost-effective advertising I have ever used.

One sunny afternoon I had a telephone call out of the blue from Michael. I had seen him on the occasions we visited Suffolk to see old friends. I would always call in to have a chat with Paul, who would welcome Christine and I with a huge grin and a hefty handshake."When you come back?" was his standard greeting with his pronounced Polish accent, while Michael and I warily exchanged greetings in a civilized manner. On the telephone he had news: he said he had purchased a new garage in Ipswich, so perhaps I would like to have a look next time I was in the area. I wished him well and more or less forgot about it; I was doing perfectly well where I was, Harry was more or less house-trained and we had a lovely new home.

In December 1995 we were off once again to Tenerife, and on the very day we departed Tim handed me a huge envelope containing a list of changes he intended to implement in the workings of the sales department, with the suggestion that I might care to study them while on holiday! Not on your life, I thought, having given them a quick run through prior to packing the suitcases ready to depart the following day. Nonetheless , while it didn't ruin our vacation it most certainly didn't contribute to my enjoyment of a well-earned rest. After all I was 65 years of age and by now probably unemployable. The money I earned from Gravens was part of my target fund for eventual retirement which really I didn't want to lose; in a word I was vulnerable, and I think he sensed it. When I came back and studied his proposals in more detail it became clear that his intention was more paperwork and less income for me; not a great deal in gratitude from a man who had lost money for years and was now, thanks to me, earning a profit.

On my first day off in February it chanced to be dull. I was a touch fed up as Tim's new paperwork was causing problems, and I felt that in all the circumstances it was both petty and unnecessary. I decided on impulse to visit Ipswich and our property at Shotley. We walked the dogs along the River Orwell and after a meal at our old local, the *Bristol Arms*, we were feeling quite homesick. We set off to Airport Garage on the way home for a chat with the old man. "When you come back?", was once again his inevitable greeting. Mike came out of his office all smiles and suggested that I should go with his son, Andrew, to have a look at the new garage. We did, but it was closed.

I had been told that Michael's brother Peter was latterly running the new premises together with Andrew. Out of the blue Peter had had an offer he felt unable to refuse from the local Honda dealer and had departed. Andrew lacked the experience to manage and develop a venture of this size, for large it most certainly was. The premises comprised a good-sized showroom with room for eight cars and a sales office, a self-contained cleaning bay at the rear of the showroom for two cars, an outside display the full length of the showroom for at least a dozen cars, and across the rear of these premises a workshop to hold four cars together with a large carport for a further six or seven under cover. Clients were thus able to drive up one side of the premises, round the back and out the other side, but if they wished to stay and browse further, by driving past the carport and straight on they moved into a huge customer car park and further display area. There was, however, one drawback – there always is. The premises, while on a major main road junction and roundabout on the old Felixstowe Road, had no main frontage as it stood four-square behind a Texaco petrol station.

I rely entirely on my descriptive advertising, and yes of course it's nice to have a selection of cars on a main-road site, but then with perhaps 15 cars on display the chance of a person driving past on a given day and seeing exactly the car of his dreams is, when you really think about it, pretty remote. In any event, how can he know that this might be the car of his dreams? All he sees is a metal box on four wheels that may have completed 2,000 or 200,000 miles; hardly worth the bother of stopping to investigate. As I have said, at Robin's premises in Raund all one would see were two wheels. On the debit side I would miss the regular petrol throughput and Harry Johnson. Harry's strength was that he either went to school with, or was related too, virtually everybody in Chatteris. Christine knew what was in my mind at once; I was confronted with a challenge and she was all too well aware that that was something I can rarely resist. Setting up and establishing a new business is hard work and brings lots of problems, but I love it still, even when well past retiring age.

On our return to Airport Garage I said nothing, and Michael, ever careful not to reveal his true feelings or intentions, simply said: "If you think any more about it give me a ring." I thought a very great deal about it all the way home and all the next day. Having put my thoughts together I wrote, saying that I was impressed with what I had seen and that, subject to mutual agreement, I could be interested providing I was allowed to trade as I had been trading over the past six years or so as a self-employed 'consultant', running the business on his behalf, with very low-mileage Motability used cars. If he cared to telephone I would be pleased to hear from him. He telephoned within days and we made an appointment to meet again.

With great care I drew up a profit-and-loss business plan with a forecast for the coming 12 months and the precise terms and conditions I would require in order to achieve these ends. At the conclusion I told Christine that Michael would never accept it in a hundred years, but if we were to up sticks and move 100 miles or so I simply couldn't risk leaping from the frying pan into the fire. We met at the new garage and I presented my brief. Michael studied it for some time, eventually saying that he was quite unable to accept the terms. This did not surprise me, but I simply had to have a commitment to give up our home and move into God knows what rented accommodation in Ipswich, with two large dogs and now four cats. I said that I was sorry, but that was the only deal on offer as I was the one taking all the risks if it all went wrong, which was true enough. With that he said "OK", shook my hand, and we were in business.

As usual Lady Luck played her part and we rented an idyllic cottage with a lovely garden and a long lease in the pretty Suffolk village of Hasketon. No shops, one church and the *Turks Head* just yards down the road; undoubtedly the best pub in the whole of East Anglia! I moved into the new business on May 1, 1997 and lost no time in advising my connections in Motability of the new situation, attending the sales and obtaining an initial stock. Apart from this most basic requirement I spent the first month in reorganization. This really is the hardest part of any new business, which I was determined to stamp very firmly with my own trademark. Most of the visitors were existing clients of the parent company, looking for comparatively high-mileage four-wheel-drive vehicles, BMWs, Volvos, large diesel estate cars and other exotica, or conversely, comparatively inexpensive cars, all of which had firmly established the Airport Garage's reputation for a good deal over the years. There would have been no point in my trying to establish an identical business just a quarter of a mile away. As the premises had a drive-in, drive-out one-way system around the showroom, most did just that. Some, however, took the trouble to visit the car park *en route* and wandered up to the showroom and forecourt, now bursting with very low-mileage one to three-year-old vehicles, looking they said "for the bargain basement". On June 1 I started my first full trading month and sold 13 used vehicles out of a monthly target of 15, and in July I added a further 19, helped it must be said by building society windfalls.

Way back in 1959, during my Armstrong Siddeley days in Northampton, I had provided a demonstration drive for a client in my Star Sapphire. He liked the car very much, but before finally making up his mind he asked if I could provide a similar drive in the equivalent Jaguar of the time. On contacting Mr Blackwell at John Grose Ltd, the old-established Jaguar and Rolls-Royce dealership in the town, I was told that they were unable to provide the right car at that time, but that he could arrange for me to take my client to the factory. This seemed to me a pleasant way of spending a day out, and my client was in full agreement, so one fine day we set off for Browns Lane, Coventry, where we were met by a Mr Alan Currie, Jaguar Cars' home sales manager. After the usual pleasantries we were then provided with a drive in Jaguar chairman Bill Lyons' personal car. As a young 29-year-old provincial sales manager I was considerably impressed with all this high-level attention, and I was in no doubt that my client was equally impressed. However, to my delight he chose to buy a new Sapphire!

Some 40 years later, in one of my locals, the *Kings Head* in Woodbridge, I made the acquaintance of a distinguished looking gentleman who, like me, had spent a lifetime in the motor trade. Alan had latterly been a director of the same John Grose Ltd, which had since expanded to East Anglia as a Ford main dealership. He was interested in my proposed book and asked if he might review a draft copy. I was only too pleased, for by this stage I needed all the help and criticism I could obtain, especially from a complete stranger. In due course he returned it with surprisingly flattering comments, which were gratefully received, and in his turn he lent me an old 1970 copy of *Who's Who in the Motor Industry*. Within these pages I found the names of many old friends and acquaintances, including John Verdellis of Seddon Trucks, Mr Hemelik of Lancia, even Mr C A Holditch of Wolseley Motors and, of course, Mr A Currie of Jaguar Cars. When borrowing his book I asked Alan if I might have his full name. "You already have it on the inside cover; it's Currie – Alan Currie."

As the late Arthur Maynard would have put it: "Well, stone me!"

EPILOGUE

2000 AND BEYOND . . .

Now, after more than two years the business has settled down into a fairly constant routine governed only by the state of the economy and the vagaries of the buying public. In the years after the war the motor trade had enjoyed reasonable stability subject only to government alterations in purchase tax and hire purchase regulations. Properly managed companies made either a reasonable, pretty good, or exceptional profit month by month, which usually evened out at the end of the year to a satisfactory average. In the Heath/Barber boom years the motor trade, like property, went through the roof, and then most motor dealers survived the inevitable recession that followed. Indeed, I started my own business during the tail end of this period, one year prior to Margaret Thatcher becoming Prime Minister. The following boom years of the Eighties came to an untimely end with the demise of Mrs Thatcher and the Gulf War, but still the motor trade in general managed a respectable existence. In April 1992 Prime Minister John Major was re-elected and one month later the motor trade, and just about everything else, died the death. May 1992 marked the end of the first and only year in my whole commercial life when I just failed to cover my expenses. As a self-employed commission-only consultant I finished the month owing Maynard money, which "to be quite honest" he was pleased to defray until the month following! It took until September for business to pick up sufficiently to once again earn a reasonable living, by which time I had left and joined Tim Graven.

These days there is no such thing as a good or a bad time of the year for used-car sales; you just never know. From long experience I have found that when my business is quiet, virtually every other motor sales business is likewise quiet, based on information coming from fellow dealers, hire purchase representatives and newspaper advertising managers. The mystery that none of us are able to solve is what it is that motivates the entire used-car buying public to rush out to buy *en masse* at just about any time of the year – including those months that used to be notoriously poor – and conversely to back off at almost any time of the year, entirely without warning – even during the months we used to rely upon to be the most profitable of the year. As a self-employed person I work on a monthly basis, and reviewing my invoices over the past seven years I find that I have enjoyed outstandingly good and spectacularly bad returns during virtually every month in the calendar. Fortunately, the annual results average out pretty evenly, but it does make stock forecasting difficult.

So, what of the motor trade today . . . and tomorrow? Well, I would certainly not wish to start all over again as a young man in the business in the climate now prevailing. For a start, any successful business is about profit, or at least a reasonable return on capital invested. When I established my own business back in 1979 I had no wish to get involved with new cars because there was simply no longer worthwhile profit in relation to either the capital or the effort involved. The situation today is even worse, and in some cases almost farcical. In June 1994 the highly respected weekly trade journal *Motor Trader* published a detailed and comprehensive review of the financial performance of the top 200 motor dealer groups (that is, dealers with new-vehicle franchises) for 1992/93, based on turnover relative to number of outlets. The review, compiled by Sewells International Ltd and sponsored by Forward Motor Finance, covered some seven pages of data and detailed analysis in which the groups were subdivided into the top 10 in various categories. Under the heading 'Return on Sales', one short sentence said it all:

"A return on sales figure in excess of *2 per cent* guaranteed a top placing, which once again shows the terribly low margins in the motor trade compared with the majority of other business sectors."

And not a great deal has changed since. The same review in May 1999, this time sponsored by Grant Thornton and Capital Bank Motor, contained the following analysis:

"It was not long ago that the benchmark for return on sales was 3 per cent, irrespective of the mix of franchises held. Following the recession of the early Nineties, any sort of return over 1 per cent seemed reasonable, but in the last few years a return to that 3 per cent benchmark has again been the target, with prestige retailers tending to hold the advantage.

"While there are some success stories around, only 13 of the top 20 managed to achieve a return of 3 per cent or better, and the return of the number 20-ranked retailer has dropped from 2.71 per cent to 2.44 per cent in a year. While the top 20 consists of a mixture of company sizes, it is a worrying trend to see lower returns on sales being achieved on average. Was 1998 that tough a year for the motor retailer?"

It never ceases to astound me that businessmen still seem happy to invest considerable sums of money in hugely expensive, corporate-image premises, largely designed to the manufacturers' exclusive requirements. They then further invest in (meaning purchase) expensive stocks of vehicles, plus parts and accessories, not to mention modern high-tech equipment, simply for the retailing, leasing and servicing of motor vehicles, almost entirely for the benefit of the major manufacturers, who in their turn undercut these same dealers in the fleet market. Nearly all are now working on gross margins reduced from 17.5 to 10 per cent of the maker's basic price, or even in some cases to no more than a handling charge on specific vehicles. Because customers have been conditioned over the years to expect comparatively high prices relative to the true value of their part-exchange vehicles, dealers are still obliged to make broadly similar allowances for cars offered in part-exchange on reduced margins.

This might well appear at first to be to the advantage of the consumer, but I wonder. Many of these same dealers have begun to realize that even when they write-off the whole of their greatly reduced margin from the allowance price of the used vehicle taken in, they finish up owning a two or three-year-old used car at a price in excess of that for which an identical car can be bought at auction on the open market without any of the hassle of supplying an over-priced new car. The effect of this means that these same dealers, having invested their money in expensive premises and equipment at the specific behest of whatever friendly manufacturer they happen to be beholden to at the time, are selling their cars in large numbers for little more than honour and glory. Even at present-day low interest rates, for a return of only 2.4 to 3 per cent most would be better off leaving their cash in a building society.

An ever increasing number of main dealers have discovered what people who have made a living exclusively in used-car retailing have known for some time: that a respectable sum of money can be made from the marketing of one to three-year-old used cars at well under new-cost price. Furthermore, their clients will not expect quite such a high valuation on their part-exchange cars, where in many cases further respectable profits may be made. So now each week will find main dealer representatives at the car auctions with their mobile phones, snapping up the Fords, Nissans, Rovers, Vauxhalls, etc that are generally there in abundance. But where, you might ask, do these late, low-mileage cars all come from? The vast majority come from major fleet users such as car leasing companies and the major clearing banks and, of course, Motability Finance. These vehicles are being supplied direct by the motor manufacturers at prices far below those available to their own main dealers, unless, of course, these dealers incorporate large leasing fleets, as a few do. Further vehicles come from the manufacturers' own fleets, where cars are regularly registered at the end of each month to boost retail(?) sales figures.

New 'M' registrations for August 1994 were so far below expectations that Ford were obliged to register some 14,000 'sales' in the last two days in the month compared with a daily average of 2,000 to 2,500. Rover registered nearly 2,900 cars on the last day compared with 1,000 to 1,500 on most other days, while Vauxhall, Toyota, Nissan, Renault and Hyundai all managed to register a disproportionate number of 'sales' in the last two days of the month.

The car makers still insist that, in real terms, UK consumers are not being overcharged compared with their European neighbours!

Now the trend in the retail motor industry is growth and expansion of huge corporations by takeover. The problem with huge groups of companies cornering the greater part of the market at the expense of the smaller family motor agent is that they become impersonal. For all that these groups spend on national advertising, with the soft music and voice-overs telling us such as "above all they are Rover dealers" (so what?), or that "Henlys care" (doesn't almost everyone?), or that "we care more" (more than whom?), or that "we are nice people to do business with" (meaning the others are a bunch of nasties?), countless surveys by specialists on behalf of clients have shown that the reality, as far as the consumers are concerned, tends to fall far short of the expectations.

Years ago, when we wanted a bit for a car, we would phone the main agent:

"Good morning, Bloggs Motors." "Parts, please." "Hang on." After a reasonable wait a disembodied voice would say: "Parts." We would describe and order the bit.

Today, when we want a bit for a car, we phone the main agent:

"Good morning, thank you for calling J W Bloggs Motors plc, this is Sharon speaking, how may we help you?" "Parts, please." "Certainly, sir, may we ask who is calling?" (one day I ask why?). "Oh sir, so that our parts person may welcome you by name." "Geoff Owen." "Thank you, Mr Owen, I will try to connect you." Cue very irritating and quite unwanted music, interspersed at intervals with a message that says, notwithstanding the fact I am being kept waiting, "we would like you to know that your custom is important to us", then eventually it stops abruptly and a disembodied voice says: "Parts." We still get the wrong bit from time to time!

One presumes that this futile, irritating, time-wasting exercise is intended to demonstrate that we are "above all – caring – caring more – or nice people to do business with". Many a long year ago we dealt on a fairly regular basis with a company called Miecox Electrical Ltd. Without fail the same bright young lady would always answer the telephone: "Good morning, Miecox Electrical", to which the sardonic answer would almost always be: "Cor, wish mine was!" But then, we had more fun in those days.

I care, but I don't shout about it or advertise the fact. I care very much, for instance, that whatever company is using my expertise as a used-vehicle consultant earns a very good profit, month by month, not least because my income depends on it. That they do so on a regular basis is because I am proficient at what I do, while the company in their turn also care that their valued customers become satisfied customers. Having bought on their behalf very low-mileage cars with a history, which I can then offer at acceptable prices, my wife and I take the trouble to turn them out to a very high standard of cleanliness and detail finish. We do not need to boast that we indulge ourselves in 114 mechanical checks because genuine low-mileage cars should not be in need of more than a proper road test, an oil and filter change and a superficial interim or – if due – a maker's recommended service. Over-preparation in a modern workshop is by nature expensive. If the service manager is short of work, given a free hand he will very soon find it. This quite unnecessary expense then has to be recovered either in the asking price, or worse, from the end profit.

This in my view is really the core of present-day motor trade problems, where far too many dealers, particularly new-car dealers, are trying to attract more and more business by endeavouring to provide a Rolls-Royce service in return for 'Mickey Mouse' profits, which quite simply is not possible. To further substantiate my trading methods I encourage my employers to offer a personal, entirely self-financing parts and labour warranty covering virtually everything for at least six months. This is infinitely preferable to any of the long-term bought-out mechanical breakdown insurance policies, which for the most part cover absolutely nothing other than those components most unlikely to break down on a modern car.

The long-term profitability of such companies who have retained my services as a consultant depends entirely on goodwill, good products and a good reputation. A good reputation may not be purchased or acquired by advertising, it has to earned. In consequence it follows that somewhere along the line there must be a degree of care for the customer and by our being "nice people to do business with". Which there is, and we are; we simply do not advertise it, and deep down nobody would really believe us if we did! But at the end of the day we succeed because we are able to provide a top-class service, albeit in a low-profile manner, because we are profitable and successful. And that really sums it all up.

What, then, of the future? It seems to me that the 'wind of change' is currently blowing at something like Gale Force 8; so much is happening or quite obviously about to happen. One thing for sure is that new-car prices in the UK will come into line with those in Europe one way or the other. However, it will have to be appreciated by the customers that used-car values will inevitably fall *pro rata*. The extent of the nett gain to the consumer will, as always, depend on the state of the market and the economy. I personally believe it improbable that the internet or the supermarkets will seriously predominate in the market for precisely the reasons that one of the latter caught a cold when they tried it. Sure they were offering cars at a huge discount, but – and this was the big but – part-exchange allowances were only available on computer from one of the car auctions. When the happy shoppers discovered the *true* value of their pride and joy in part-chop, even in exchange for a heavily discounted product, they simply walked away. To sell new cars in numbers you need to have the proper facilities and the skills to sell the used cars that arrive in part-exchange, and for which the clients have been educated for years to expect top price, together with the undeniable convenience of a relatively quick hassle-free transaction.

The Daewoo company initially learnt this lesson the hard way. While they were at least initially allowing competitive prices and moving the metal, the time very quickly arrived when they had a king-sized used-car problem because, having decided not to use the UK established distribution network they failed to provide the facilities to move them on other than at the car auctions, where values tend to be realistic. As time went on the bottleneck spread to their own products as these, in their turn, re-entered the market as used vehicles, which few wanted other than Daewoo, whereupon residual values fell through the floor.

For a while the huge used-car supermarkets seemed to be all the rage, and expanding as if there was no tomorrow, some even with the active help of the major motor vehicle manufacturers desperate to move more metal. But to sell cheap there is a requirement that first you must be able to buy cheap. If the supermarkets continue to grow, the supply of cheap stock will gradually diminish and prices will inevitably rise. Mrs Thatcher would describe the phenomenon as market forces, and then the more selective, thoroughly professional used-car traders and successful main dealers will once again come into their own.

For myself, I have always been one of those people fortunate enough to enjoy their chosen means of earning a crust. As long as this happy situation continues, so doubtless shall I, but only in the field of good-quality used-car retailing, which if it is to be successful is still a complex and highly professional operation. It has nothing whatever to do with 'Arthur Daley', supermarkets or bomb-site trading. It has everything to do with presentation, preparation and skilled advertising of good-quality, low-mileage cars and, of course, having that instinct for identifying which cars, and at what price, a discriminating public is prepared to invest their hard-earned money in at any given time.

Nearing the end of a thoroughly interesting and, on the whole, satisfying business life, I shall view the next decade or so with more than a passing interest. I have witnessed many changes and been presented with a whole range of opportunities. I'm very grateful for these, for they formed the foundation of a career that has turned out to be more varied and more rewarding in the fullest sense than I could ever have imagined possible.

APPENDIX A

An extract from *Glass's Guide* dated July 1950 listing popular new cars then available from volume manufacturers and a comparison between their new and secondhand valuations. New-car prices quoted are ex-works including purchase tax.

PRICE NEW	MAKE AND MODEL	CC	BODY STYLE	USED RETAIL
£329	FORD ANGLIA	933	2 DOOR SALOON	£545
£383	MORRIS MINOR	918	2 DOOR TOURER	£570
£397	FORD PREFECT	1172	4 DOOR SALOON	£675
£480	VAUXHALL WYVERN	1442	4 DOOR SALOON	£825
£502	AUSTIN A40 DEVON	1200	4 DOOR SALOON	£865
£505	HILLMAN MINX	1265	4 DOOR SUN SALOON	£735
£546	MORRIS OXFORD	1476	4 DOOR SALOON	£915
£550	VAUXHALL VELOX	2275	4 DOOR SALOON	£875
£569	AUSTIN A40 COUNTRYMAN	1200	2 DOOR ESTATE	£715
£569	MG TD	1250	2 DOOR ROADSTER	£690
£595	HILLMAN MINX	1265	6 DOOR ESTATE	£700
£601	HILLMAN MINX	1265	2 DOOR DROPHEAD	£815
£659	AUSTIN A70 HAMPSHIRE	2199	4 DOOR SUN SALOON	£1025
£659	STANDARD VANGUARD	2088	4 DOOR SALOON	£1010
£672	MG MODEL Y	1250	4 DOOR SUN SALOON	£950
£672	MORRIS SIX	2215	4 DOOR SALOON	£975
£704	WOLSELEY 4/50	1476	4 DOOR SALOON	£1010
£735	STANDARD VANGUARD	2088	6 DOOR ESTATE	£835
£761	AUSTIN A70 COUNTRYMAN	2199	4 DOOR ESTATE	£929
£761	JOWETT JAVELIN	1486	4 DOOR SALOON	£950
£767	WOLSELEY 6/80	2215	4 DOOR SALOON	£1025
£780	FORD V8 PILOT	3622	4 DOOR SALOON	£990
£799	HUMBER HAWK	1944	4 DOOR SUN SALOON	£1150
£885	AUSTIN A90 ATLANTIC	2660	2 DOOR DROPHEAD	£1210
£889	SUNBEAM-TALBOT 80	1185	4 DOOR SUN SALOON	£1075

£991	SUNBEAM-TALBOT 90	1944	4 DOOR SUN SALOON	£1150
£991	TRIUMPH 2000	2088	4 DOOR SALOON	£1125
£1100	ROVER 75	2103	4 DOOR SALOON	£1525
£1144	HUMBER SUPER SNIPE	4086	4 DOOR SALOON	£1310
£1225	RILEY 2.5	2443	4 DOOR SALOON	£1400

From this point in time retail used car prices began to equate with new, an indication that the supply situation was beginning to ease. Indeed, from prices around £1,300 upwards some used car valuations were actually slightly below the equivalent new car prices. Nonetheless, it was not until 1952 that the volume-selling new family cars became anything like 'off the peg' and used car prices started to reflect a degree of wear and tear.

Notes:
* Estate cars of the time were based on van bodies with twin rear doors, hence up to six in all.
* Sun saloons were, of course, cars in which a sunroof was fitted as standard.
* At this time my earnings were £5.00 per week plus commission, which meant an average of around £17.50 per week.

APPENDIX B

Reproduction of the letter I sent to all customers to whom I had supplied Lancia Beta cars.

1st May 1980

Dear Mr

I have today been in touch with a Lancia main dealer and confirmed that your Lancia Beta, in common with all Beta's, should be returned to ANY LANCIA DEALER for an inspection. I must emphasize that this is purely a precautionary, and in my view sensible, request in the light of somewhat sensational reports as published in the "Daily Mirror". I take this opportunity of enclosing for your interest a rational and rather more accurate account from a proper newspaper* and am pleased to advise you that no problems are anticipated with Series 2 Beta's produced after May 1976.** I am advised that the inspection takes 10 minutes but has, of course, to be done by appointment.

I shall be pleased to take your car if required, in which case I shall require it for half a day to arrange for collection and delivery.

A very great deal of trouble has been caused by the totally irresponsible and generally inaccurate content of the "Mirror" report. For instance, it was stated as a matter of fact that two engines had "fallen out" of Lancia cars in the edition dated 10th April. On that day I telephoned an Assistant Editor and made the following offer:

THAT I WOULD DONATE ONE THOUSAND POUNDS TO ANY CHARITY OF THE MIRROR'S CHOICE IF THEY WERE ABLE TO CUT THROUGH A LANCIA BETA SUBFRAME – WITH HACKSAW OR BLOW TORCH – AND MAKE THE ENGINE TO FALL OUT IN SITU – PROVIDING THAT IF THEY WERE TO FAIL TO REPRODUCE THIS PHENOMENON UNDER THE APPROPRIATE SUPERVISION THEY IN TURN WOULD DONATE THE SAME SUM TO THE RNLI.

Their reply, and I quote, was that "the reporter who wrote that report is away – until the end of next week". I have heard no more. The same reporters' name appeared on a follow-up report the following day, 11th April!

Yours sincerely

Geoffrey Owen

Notes:
* The Financial Times
** None of the cars supplied by me were found to have problems